Literature and the Contemporary

CW00496046

Longman Studies in Twentieth-Century Literature

Series Editor:
Stan Smith, Research Professor in Literary Studies, Nottingham Trent
  University

Literature and the Contemporary:
Fictions and Theories of the Present

Edited by

Roger Luckhurst and Peter Marks

LONGMAN

Pearson Education Limited
Edinburgh Gate
Harlow
Essex CM20 2JE
United Kingdom
and Associated Companies throughout the world.

Published in the United States of America
by Pearson Education Inc., New York

First published 1999

ISBN 0-582-31204-3 Ppr
ISBN 0-582-31203-5 Csd

Visit our world wide web site at http://www.awl-he.com

British Library Cataloguing-in-Publication Data

A catalogue record for this book is available from the British Library

Library of Congress Cataloging-in-Publication Data

Literature and the contemporary/edited by Roger Luckhurst and Peter
Marks.
    p. cm. — (Studies in twentieth-century literature)
  Includes bibliographical references and index.
  ISBN 0-582-31204-3 (ppr). — ISBN 0-582-31203-5 (csd)
  1. Literature, Modern—20th century—History and criticism.
I. Luckhurst, Roger. II. Marks, Peter, 1958– . III. Series:
Studies in twentieth-century literature (Longman (Firm))
PN771.L565 1999
809′.04—dc21   98–37102
                                              CIP

Set by 35 in 10/12pt Bembo
Produced by Addison Wesley Longman Singapore (Pte) Ltd.,
Printed and bound by CPI Antony Rowe, Eastbourne

Contents

Contents

Acknowledgements

Five of the essays included in this collection originated from a conference on contemporary literature held at Hull University in 1994. We thank these contributors for their patience as this project underwent successive transformations.

We dedicate this book to the other members of the Spring Bank verbal-visual project – Steve, Julie and Sally (but not Mark, obviously).

The publishers are grateful to the following for permission to reproduce copyright material:

Boosey & Hawkes Music Publishers Ltd for various extracts from introduction & libretto of *Der Rosenkavalier* trans. by Hofmannstahl © 1954, revised 1969 & 1984., publ. Decca Records © Copyright 1910, 1911 by Adolph Furstner. U.S. Copyright renewed. Copyright assigned 1943 to Hawkes & son (London) Ltd (A Boosey & Hawkes Company) for the world excluding Germany, Italy, Portugal and the former territories of the USSR (excluding Estonia, Latvia and Lithuania)/Schott Musik International GmbH for various extracts from introduction & libretto of *Der Rosenkavalier* trans. by Hofmannstahl © 1910, 1916 Adolph Furstner, Berlin © 1987 publishers Furstner, Mainz for Germany, Italy, Portugal & the former USSR countries; Faber & Faber Ltd for extracts from *The Sacred Wood: Essays on Poetry and Criticism* by T.S. Eliot; Radical Philosophy Ltd for a slightly revised version of the article 'The Politics of Time' by Peter Osborne in *Radical Philosophy* 68, Autumn, 1994; the author, Jeanette Winterson for extracts from her *Sexing the Cherry* Bloomsbury Publishing 1989, *The Passion* Bloomsbury Publishing 1987 & *Written on the Body*, Jonathan Cape 1992.

Notes on Contributors

Bill Ashcroft teaches literature at the University of New South Wales. He is co-author of *The Empire Writes Back* and co-editor of *The Post-Colonial Studies Reader* and *Key Concepts in Post-Colonial Theory*.

Steven Connor is Professor of Modern Literature and Theory at Birkbeck College, University of London. He is the author of many books, including *Samuel Beckett, James Joyce, Postmodernist Culture* and *The English Novel in History 1950–95*. His *Cultural History of Ventriloquism* is forthcoming from Oxford University Press in 1999.

Thomas Docherty is Professor in the Department of English, University of Kent at Canterbury and Director of the Kent Institute for Advanced Studies in the Humanities. He is the author of many books, including *On Modern Authority, John Donne Undone* and, most recently, *Alterities* and *Criticism and Modernity*.

Andrew Gibson is Reader in the Department of English, Royal Holloway College, University of London. He is a James Joyce scholar, and the author of a number of books, including *Reading Narrative Discourse* and *Towards A Postmodern Theory of Narrative*. His *Postmodernity, Ethics and the Novel* will be published in 1999.

Nicola King lectures in literature at the University of the West of England. Her book *Remembering the Self* is forthcoming from Edinburgh University Press.

Roger Luckhurst lectures in literature at Birkbeck College, University of London. He is the author of a book on J.G. Ballard and of articles on contemporary literature and culture.

Peter Marks lectures in literature at the University of Sydney, where he teaches twentieth-century British literature. He has published on Orwell and the politics and literature of the 1930s.

Mandy Merck lectures in Media Studies at the University of Sussex. She has been editor of the journal *Screen*, and produced several lesbian and gay series for British television. She is the author of *Perversions: Deviant Readings*, co-editor of *Coming Out of Feminism?* and editor of *After Diana*.

Mpalive Msiska lectures in Humanities at Birkbeck College, University of London. He has published widely on post-colonial theory, and his most recent publications include a book on Wole Soyinka and the co-edited *Writing and Africa*.

Peter Osborne is Professor in Modern European Philosophy at Middlesex University and a member of the editorial collective of the journal *Radical Philosophy*. He is the author of *The Politics of Time: Modernity and the Avant-Garde*, and has co-edited the collections *Thinking Art* and *Walter Benjamin's Philosophy*.

Caroline Rooney lectures in post-colonial literature at the University of Kent at Canterbury. She is the author of numerous articles on the intersection of gender and race, most recently in *Writing and Africa* and *Oxford Literary Review*.

Carol Watts lectures in literature at Birkbeck College, University of London. She is the author of *Dorothy Richardson*, and numerous articles on contemporary literature and film. She is currently at work on a study of the legacy of Laurence Sterne.

Wendy Wheeler is Reader in English at the University of North London. She writes widely on contemporary literature and politics, and her book *A New Modernity* is to be published by Lawrence and Wishart in 1999.

CHAPTER ONE

Hurry up please it's time: introducing the contemporary

Roger Luckhurst and Peter Marks

I

> Contemporary adj., from *con-*, together + *tempus*, *tempor-*, time, *temporarius*,
> of or belonging to time.
> 1. Belonging to the same time, age, or period; living, existing, or
> occurring together in time.
> 2. Having existed or lived from the same date, equal in age, co-eval.
> 3. Occurring at the same moment of time, or during the same period;
> occupying the same definite period; contemporaneous, simultaneous.

It is only the 1972 Supplement to the *Oxford English Dictionary* that adds:

> 4. Modern; of or characteristic of the present period; esp. up-to-date,
> ultra-modern, spec. designating art of a markedly avant-garde quality.

For an adjective commonly used to designate the cutting edge, the up-to-the-minute, the now, this last meaning of the contemporary arrives tardily, limping into the *OED* supplement as a distinctly post-Second World War connotation. It is this meaning that this book wishes to treat; the *contemporary* contemporary, as it were. The awkward title of this collection aims to break open the phrase 'contemporary literature', to force the adjective out of hiding, the better to isolate the complex meanings and effects that attend the contemporary. But isn't this also rather too late? Students of literary and cultural history have already done with the literature of modernism, of *modernus*, of 'today'. What's left of the day that we might call 'contemporary'?

Since Charles Baudelaire's essay, *The Painter of Modern Life*, most definitions of 'modernity' have contained his sense of 'the ephemeral, the fugitive, the contingent . . . whose metamorphoses are so rapid' as to risk escaping capture.[1] Baudelaire's rhetoric has since been consistently surpassed, with many cultural critics arguing that modernity is forever accelerating, speeding

1

us ever faster through rapid mutations, each moment more breathless, more extraordinary than the last. In 1895 one cultural commentator expressed unease about the speed of modern life, such that 'even the little shocks of railway travelling, not perceived by consciousness, the perpetual noises, and the various sights in the streets of a large town, or suspense pending the sequel of progressive events, the constant expectation of the newspaper, of the postman, of visitors, cost our brains wear and tear'.[2] More recently, the speed of circulating capital, cultural fashion and technological advance can render criticism even more hyperbolic. Jean Baudrillard has suggested that the acceleration of modernity has reached escape velocity from the gravitational pull of any grounding in reality or history such that we are left floating in weightless, directionless space.[3] Jacques Le Goff has proposed that 'the acceleration of history' is the principle historians must now address, a speed of transformation that, in his view, 'has made the official definition of contemporary history untenable'.[4] Elsewhere, technological advances are held to proceed so fast in their imbrication with the body as to inaugurate the 'post-human'.[5] For Lorenzo Simpson, increasingly technologised 'life-worlds' are bent on the 'annihilation of time'; for Paul Virilio, 'computer time . . . helps construct a permanent present, an unbounded, timeless intensity'.[6] We read pronouncements of the end of history, the end of the subject, the end, even, of the end.[7] As we arrive latterly at a contemporary definition of the contemporary, it is only to discover that time, in its hurry, appears to have accelerated *out* of time altogether.

Such, at least, has been the position of a certain strand of cultural criticism that sought to define the state of the contemporary world and contemporary culture under a single definitional umbrella: postmodernity. Essential to the formulation of the condition of postmodernity was a sense in which the temporal had been displaced into spatial categories: architecture cannibalised all past styles and displayed them together as spatially adjacent; television channel hopping made the pictorial archives of history instantly and randomly juxtaposed, fatally dislocating the continuity of historical narrative. The remnants of disappearing history could only be energised by movement in space, as in the 'travels in hyperreality' undertaken by Jean Baudrillard and Umberto Eco through America.[8] The exemplary postmodern object became in many ways the city, whether in its architectural jumble of spatialised times or in the vertiginous speed of transformations of the urban fabric. 'It all comes together in Los Angeles', Edward Soja pronounced, in a book subtitled 'The Reassertion of Space'.[9] The urgency yet impossibility of mapping new contemporary cultural spaces became the purpose of much criticism: the metaphor of the map appeared everywhere.[10] Cultural critics seemed to spend an inordinate amount of time getting lost in the foyer of the Bonaventure Hotel in Los Angeles, even if Hollywood films obligingly provided spectacularly simple escape routes in plummets from the Hotel's towers.[11] Uncircumventable here was Fredric Jameson's seminal essay, 'Postmodernism, or the Cultural Logic of Late Capitalism', first published in 1984. If, as he stated, 'we are condemned to seek History by way of our own pop images and simulacra of . . . history, which itself remains forever out of reach', this was because time had been flattened and spatialised by the remorseless advance of multinational capitalism in its global reach and space–time compressions.[12] Jameson, on one level, was writing the new guidebook for the spatial mutations suffered by those living in the time after Time.

II

None of the contributors to this collection resort to these arguments, tinged as they tend to be with apocalyptic sentiments. Rather, the contemporary is thought in other ways. The anxiety that attends the now, the up-to-the-minute, might indeed intensify as modernity is seen to accelerate. As Thomas Docherty explains in the opening to his essay, however, the paradox of the now has *always* been a problem of representation, for to present it is necessarily to *re*-present it, thus introducing a crucial delay, a splitting of temporality. The instant of the 'now' always eludes the grasp, can never be self-identical: it is either no longer or not yet present. This effect can be marked as a loss, as the impossibility of seizing the present time. It can be transposed to the definition of an era, one given epochal coherence by rendering 'lost' temporality in spatial forms as displays of nostalgia or pastiche. Or else the difference at the heart of the 'now' can be seen as a *constitutive* and *productive* heterogeneity, a circulation of multiple times within the single instant. We might take this to be what the 'contemporary', *con-temporarius*, literally suggests: 'joined times' or 'times together'. This is to say that the capitalised and technologised accelerations of modernity do not *abolish* time so much as confront us with an urgent need to recognise a number of temporalities in various relations, never simply reducible to 'annihilation'. Ursula Heise may be correct in considering that 'the culture of time in the late twentieth century has evolved faster than the theoretical reasoning which has accompanied it',[13] but this should not result in the abandonment of the category of time. It should, rather, be the impetus to think time and temporality again, which may in turn allow new ways of approaching the literature of the contemporary. As Steven Connor suggests, if the contemporary is thought as the con-temporal, conjoined yet incommensurate 'times together', this can provide productive openings into the plural cultures of time beyond the panic narratives that have recently beset literary and cultural theory.

Looking through this collection, it is striking how diversely the problematic of 'time today' can be approached by different theoretical orientations; striking, too, how many cultural and literary forms can be read as confronting or displaying these effects of contemporality. We have organised this collection to accentuate different ways of considering the contemporary, inviting our authors to write on specific thematics or from specific theoretical perspectives. We have coupled essays together as a way of structuring responses, although we hope that the ways in which the essays speak across, echo or argue with our notional divides will activate the reader to discern their own routes through the book.

The first section, 'Time Today', is headed with essays by Steven Connor and Peter Osborne, both of whom confront the predominant view that time and history have entered into crisis in the late twentieth century. Connor's extremely lucid and wide-ranging survey pursues the frequently contradictory fates pronounced for time (hurrying up, slowing down, too little, too much time), and also investigates the proposals that have begun to emerge for conceiving of *counter-times* that resist the logic of temporal desuetude, before elaborating his own conception of con-temporality. The essay ends with a capsule reading of Salman Rushdie's *The Satanic Verses*. The multiplicity of times that circulate in *The Satanic Verses* (and the simplistic reduction of them in the catastrophic division of Eastern 'primitive' time and Western 'civilised' time in the debates that have surrounded the text) is the occasion for summing up how the notion of con-temporalities can problematise monolithic pronouncements on the fate of time in the contemporary.

Peter Osborne approaches the perceived 'crisis' of temporality from a rigorous philosophical standpoint, providing a helpful contextualisation from the philosophy of history for current articulations of the 'impossibility' of conceiving a 'total' history of the contemporary moment. Osborne usefully glosses the different orders of time that have been distinguished in philosophy (cosmological, phenomenological and socio-historical time), arguing that pronouncements of the 'end of history' are products of a fundamental *embarrassment* with the project of unifying these times. Why embarrassment? Because unifying temporal orders is a product of the nineteenth century: Greenwich Mean Time, establishing a global standard measure, is a gesture of imperialism and an act of enforcing conformity on other cultures and other temporalities. A totalising or unifying philosophy of history, such as that so influentially propounded by Hegel, is now inevitably seen as implicated in that colonial project, the idealism of an endlessly progressive history of Spirit mocked by the barbarities of nineteenth- and twentieth-century capitalist expropriation and imperialist violence. It is this which gives the impetus to such contemporary pronouncements as Jean-François Lyotard's injunction to 'wage a war on totality',[14] and this which explains the suspicion of modernity so central to definitions of postmodernism. Osborne, while sympathetic to these critiques, argues that the abandonment of 'total history' by critical theory only leaves it open to contemporary versions like Francis Fukuyama's *The End of History*, a vacuous mock-Hegelian epic which contends that the conflicts and struggles which drive history have come to end because American capitalist democracy has 'won' the war. Osborne proposes re-considering temporality as *experience* and therefore as the basis for a new politics of time, one which may allow for different, oppositional or competing articulations of history and experience and thus, as he suggests, allowing for 'the simple possibility that things might proceed otherwise'.

These two important critiques provide ways of re-vitalising the temporal aspect of the contemporary that are pursued by subsequent contributors. Both Thomas Docherty and Wendy Wheeler, although in very different ways, refuse the equation of the postmodern with the absence of time and history, and argue that the postmodern may be regarded as a *renewed engagement* with temporality. For Docherty, this takes the form of contending that the homogenisation of time by modernity is performed under the aegis of a 'universal history' in which the event is subsumed into a singular and expectant narrative – rather like the ways in which 'futures' are now packaged, unitised and traded in markets that seek to manage and neutralise risk, aiming to make any future event calculable and profitable. In contrast, literary texts that might be marked as displaying what Docherty terms 'postmodern contemporaneities' are those which display flashes of the ungraspability of the object and of the event, which communicate the incalculable heterogeneity of times circulating in the instant of the 'now'. The work of Seamus Heaney, Harold Brodkey and Ian McEwan provide the occasion for this suggestive glimpse of an aesthetics of the object and the event.

Wendy Wheeler considers that modernity, as rendered in the project of Enlightenment philosophy, is fundamentally *melancholic* – haunted, that is to say, by the losses induced by the commitment to the eradication of superstition and wholly materialist explanations of the world, yet denying the existence of any ghostly trace of prior beliefs. Modernity's aggressive self-positioning as severing itself from a 'pre-historic' world of superstition can only be done by disavowing the losses essential to its emergence. The time of 'development', of modern history, is a melancholic time. Through the contemporary novels of Graham Swift, however, Wheeler points to indications of a faltering emergence of an *acknowledgement* of loss, a recognition and thus a precipitation of a mourning for the melancholic compulsions which drove modernity. Swift's fictions are full of secret histories (*Waterland*) and debts to the dead (*Ever After*, *Last Orders*) which serve to show that the 'emptiness' of present time can only be rendered meaningful by an engagement with the traumas of the past. In this essay, we encounter our first ghost of the book, a spectre which, in different forms, flits through several contributions (there are disturbingly material ghosts in Msiska's essay, more ethereal ones in Rooney's), fully materialising only in the last piece by Mandy Merck. This is only logical, for what is the ghost but the irruption of one time into another, the (dis)embodiment of contemporary 'times together'? The ghost appears, 'the time is out of joint', disadjusting the glazed self-identity of the 'empty' present.[15] To turn, to face the ghost of the past, Wheeler suggests, is the beginning of the return to temporal existence.

The section on memory, containing essays by Roger Luckhurst and Nicola King, begins with a straightforward question: as we read pronouncements on the disappearance of history or the displacement of time into spatial categories, how is it that contemporary culture is saturated with endless displays of the politics of memory? Public memorials are ceaselessly contested by different interest groups with different commemorative agendas, histories are accused of their forgetfulness to remember, contemporary identities are built around a remembrance of forebears. The temporality of individual, collective and national memory is a central aspect of contemporary culture. Luckhurst notes that as cultural critics privileged the scrambled temporality of the schizophrenic as the model of contemporary subjectivity in the 1980s, psychiatry was simultaneously producing a new subject premised on the ability to recover lost memories with startling and pristine accuracy, a model of memory increasingly deployed by American and British fiction, from Jane Smiley to Kate Atkinson to Helen Dunmore. King's essay, too, on memory's limit-case of the Jewish Holocaust, reveals how contemporary fiction engages precisely with the problem of the communicability of memory in the second generation after the Holocaust, reading through Christopher Hope, Emily Prager and Anne Michaels. These are hardly indications of a loss of temporal awareness, but display that the injunction to remember is precisely the result of perceptions of the acceleration or erasure of history. To think the con-temporary, it is necessary to think remembering and forgetting *together*, rather than sliding into simple assertions of dystopian loss.

III

The second half of the book is conceived in a slightly different way. We have invited critics working with a specific theoretical framework to consider how that approach might engage with the notion of the contemporary. We use the term 'Intersections' to indicate how the interests of post-colonial theory, feminism and queer theory might assist – or productively interfere – with the general aim of rethinking the contemporary. What has proved interesting is the way in which nearly all of the contributors to this part of the book become engaged less in the immediacy of the contemporary moment than in an attempt to *excavate* the histories lying behind our current cultural forms and sense of 'crisis'. In this section, the abstract notion that the contemporary 'joins times', or is haunted by plural times, is enacted through a sequence of suggestive genealogies of the present. In order to investigate the forces that generate the contemporary, the essayists here move *back* in time – 1963 (Msiska), 1911 (Merck), 1853 (Rooney), 1739 (Watts) – precisely to move our interrogations of the contemporary *forward*. It is these ghosts of the past, or these spectral images flashed up, we might say, at the forgetful moment of contemporary danger,[16] that furthers the project of the book to re-instate the question of time and temporality in the study of contemporary literature and culture.

The theoretical approaches represented here are not arbitrarily chosen: each, in a crucial way, has brought those questions of temporality to the forefront. This is perhaps most obvious in post-colonial theory, given that the conditions of cultural production today remain thoroughly bound by the complex legacies of the colonial period. Both Steven Connor and Peter Osborne refer to the post-colonial critique of the 'imperial' temporality imposed on other cultures, and it has been the post-colonial theories of Homi Bhabha that have sought, in his words, to 'throw into relief the temporal, social differences that interrupt our collusive sense of cultural contemporaneity' by insisting that '[t]he present can no longer simply be envisaged as a break or a bonding with the past and future, no longer a synchronic presence: our proximate self-presence, our public image, comes to be revealed for its discontinuities, its inequalities, its minorities'.[17] It is this need to *interrupt* 'collusive contemporaneity' that is behind many of the interventions of our contributors.

Bill Ashcroft opens his essay by reminding us that the very notion of an English Literature is one key legacy of nineteenth-century imperialism, and one which continues to have effects on how different world literatures are conceived in relation to margins, centres and cultural identities. Ashcroft is concerned to find a model adequate to the wholly different experiences and temporalities of the post-colonial contemporary – the incommensurate colonial residues in, say, African states or the Indian subcontinent or Australasia. The figure of the 'rhizome', he suggests, allows for the proliferations of different temporal relations to be marked, and which avoids repeating monolithic conceptions of the West and its singular, post-colonial Other. Ashcroft's succinct yet broad sweep of such issues ought to concentrate contemporary minds on becoming aware of the rapid rise of international englishes and world literatures.

Mpalive Msiska takes the route of investigating a specific text for its peculiar – we might even say spooky – temporal effects. If Wole Soyinka has been known in the 1990s less for his Nobel laureateship than for his exile from Nigeria, then Msiska takes us back to the play Soyinka wrote for Nigeria's independence celebrations. A text published in 1963, Msiska suggests, encodes a certain anxiety over the post-colonial future in ways which uncannily anticipate the depressing cycles of reiterated colonial domination in post-independence Nigeria. That this oblique critique is partly done through ancestral ghosts begins to indicate the foldings of different times in the play. Msiska suggests that the play inscribes the inception of the 'post-colonial' as a plural moment, in which 'ancestral', colonial and post-indepence times inevitably circulate.

The ghosts in Soyinka's play transgress many boundaries – as any living-dead being would. A ghost slides through the wall dividing our sections on the post-colonial and feminism: Caroline Rooney is hunting for the ghostly echoes of an imperial past and its persistent imprint on the present in her chosen text, Ama Ata Aidoo's *Our Sister Killjoy*. Rooney develops a reading of the novel partly through analysing the (non-)place of Africa in Dickens's *Bleak House* from 1853. It is at this stage that intersections begin to generate more and more potential networks of temporal overlays in the critical study of literature in the contemporary. Here, the question of 'woman' and the question of 'race' and the question of the contemporary produce sparks of linkage – but also sparks of resistance, of friction. Race *collides* with gender in Rooney's essay, hinting in broader terms that the conceptions of the contemporary generated by the collection will not be straightforwardly additive or synthetic. Pointing to the existence of times together in the contemporary is exactly concerned with sustaining rather than resolving difference.

Julia Kristeva's essay 'Women's Time', written in 1979, is one of the most influential feminist texts on temporality. Its 'three generations' of feminism, although con-temporal, have often been rather inaccurately adopted to model putative feminist histories, or to mark the divide between Anglo-American and French feminism. Carol Watts revisits this essay from a specific late 1990s feminist perspective, noting that Kristeva's projections for women's time might locate our contemporary as Kristeva's imagined future. This is decidedly not the utopian place Kristeva in some ways projects, and Watts's reading demonstrates the shifting socio-political agendas that might be marked by the phrase 'women's time'. This is another place where there is an image 'flashed up at a moment of danger'. Watts's reading of women's labour-time – today the subject of political panics over women in the workplace, single mothers, neglected children and collapsing family life – is brought into focus by reading through Mary Collier's complaints in the poem 'The Woman's Labour' in 1739. This persuasively suggests that we need to ground our articulations about contemporary modernity in long historical perspectives.

The final two essays, in very different ways, traverse what has come to be known as queer theory. This last intersection is included not only because of the impact on conceptions of gender and sexuality achieved by queer theory in the 1990s, but also because it is a theory of *temporality*. Judith Butler's notion of gender performativity is one in which reiteration of the Same *through time* enforces the prohibitions of the heterosexual matrix. Different gender performances, other sexualities, subversions of the Same, rely on different temporalities in crucial ways. Eve Kosofsky Sedgwick, too, in her more literary-historical investigations, has attempted to expose and productively intensify the incoherences in the conception of homo- and hetero-sexualities. For Sedgwick, to see the contemporary as a 'moment of Queer' is about emphasising 'the open mesh of possibilities, gaps, overlaps, dissonances and resonances, lapses and exercises of meaning when the constituent elements . . . aren't made . . . to signify monolithically'.[18] A formulation such as this clearly intersects with our project here.

Andrew Gibson fuses the philosophy of Emmanuel Levinas with the work of Judith Butler and other queer theorists to generate a sustained reading of contemporary British literature's obsession with subversions of gender and sexuality. Gibson provides us with a provisional taxonomy of such moves – from the destabilisations of 'drag' in the fictions of Gordon Burn and Peter Ackroyd, to the tactics of 'gender shock' in Iain Banks, to the sardonic gender ironies of Martin Amis, before ending with close readings of Patricia Duncker's *Hallucinating Foucault* and Jeanette Winterson's *Written on the Body*. These texts, in Gibson's view, 'cross' contemporary sexual identities without finding a fixed terminus – and this becomes an identitarian version of the refusal to foreclose the contemporary.

That a collection entitled *Literature and the Contemporary* should end with an essay on an opera written in 1911 is decidedly perverse: this is perhaps as it should be. Mandy Merck's reading of the notoriously queer goings on in Richard Strauss's *Die Rosenkavalier* has, however, a genealogical purpose driven by a contemporary imperative. An image of the past flashed up before our forgetful contemporary eyes is again the strategy for shaking up any remaining idea that the contemporary is marked by empty, glazed self-presence. The ghosts that enter centre stage here are there, specifically, to disadjust historical trajectories of lesbian identity. The ghost, for Merck, is a decidedly 'queer' entity, a liminal and transgressive figure that cannot be fixed. In this way, contemporary sexual identities might be seen to be spectral, part and parcel of the *Zeitgeist*. In this way, and in another: we know by now that there can never be a 'timely ghost', and that if we are to investigate the cultural forms and meanings of the contemporary, then we must watch for the moments in which contemporalities intersect and diverge, in which one time transects another.

We began by tracking the way in which the experience of modernity has always been felt to speed away from our grasp. Too much recent criticism has fallen into the hyperbole of 'acceleration', however, a belief that the contemporary world is bereft of time or history. We hope that this collection will be an addition to that growing body of work evidencing a more thoughtful engagement with the *thickness* of time and temporality in the contemporary world.

NOTES

1. Charles Baudelaire, *The Painter of Modern Life and Other Essays*, trans. and ed. Jonathan Mayne (New York: Da Capo, 1964), p. 13.
2. Max Nordau, *Degeneration* [1895] (Lincoln: University of Nebraska Press, 1993), p. 39.
3. Jean Baudrillard, 'The Year 2000 Has Already Happened', trans. Nai-fei Ding and Kuan-Hsing Chen, in Arthur and Marilouise Kroker, eds, *Body Invaders: Sexuality and the Postmodern Condition* (London: Macmillan, 1988).
4. Jacques Le Goff, *History and Memory*, trans. Steven Rendall and Elizabeth Claman (New York: Columbia University Press, 1992), p. 19.
5. See, for instance, Scott Bukatman, *Terminal Identity: The Virtual Subject in Postmodern Science Fiction* (Durham: Duke University Press, 1993).
6. Lorenzo Simpson, *Technology, Time and the Conversations of Modernity* (London: Routledge, 1995); Paul Virilio, *The Lost Dimension*, trans. Daniel Moshenberg (New York: Semiotext(e), 1991), p. 15.
7. See, for instance, Francis Fukuyama, *The End of History and the Last Man* (Harmondsworth: Penguin, 1992); Jean Baudrillard, *The Illusion of the End*, trans. Chris Turner (Cambridge: Polity, 1994).
8. Umberto Eco, *Travels in Hyperreality*, trans. William Weaver (London: Picador, 1987); Jean Baudrillard, *America*, trans. Chris Turner (London: Verso, 1988).
9. Edward Soja, *Postmodern Geographies: The Reassertion of Space in Critical Social Theory* (London: Verso, 1989).

10. See, for example, Andreas Huyssen, 'Mapping the Postmodern', in *After the Great Divide: Modernism, Mass Culture and Postmodernism* (London: Macmillan, 1986); Jean Baudrillard's inversion of the map and the territory in *Simulacra and Simulation*, trans. Sheila Faria Glaser (Ann Arbor: University of Michigan Press, 1994); Iain Chambers, 'Some Metropolitan Tales', in *Border Dialogues: Journeys in Postmodernity* (London: Routledge, 1990). Centrally, Fredric Jameson's notion of 'cognitive mapping' influenced many attempts to conceive of contemporary culture cartographically. This was first elaborated in 'Postmodernism, or the Cultural Logic of Late Capitalism' (1984; in book form, London: Verso, 1991), pp. 51–4.

11. Jameson uses the Bonaventure in the culmination of the 'Postmodernism' essay. See, too, Soja, *Postmodern Geographies*, pp. 243–4, and Baudrillard, *America*, pp. 59–60. Films involving the Bonaventure Hotel include *In the Line of Fire* and Kathryn Bigelow's *Strange Days* whose final scene is set, suitably, in the closing seconds of the millennium, 31 December 1999.

12. Jameson, 'Postmodernism', p. 25.

13. Ursula Heise, *Chronoschisms: Time, Narrative and Postmodernism* (Cambridge: Cambridge University Press, 1997), p. 31.

14. Jean-François Lyotard, 'Answering the Question: What is Postmodernism?', in *The Postmodern Condition: A Report on Knowledge*, trans. Geoffrey Bennington and Brian Massumi (Manchester: Manchester University Press, 1984), p. 82.

15. See the opening chapter of Jacques Derrida, *Spectres of Marx: The State of the Debt, the Work of Mourning and the New International*, trans. Peggy Kamuf (London: Routledge, 1994), for a sustained treatment of the con-temporal meanings of Hamlet's announcement that 'the time is out of joint'.

16. This is an echo of the Walter Benjamin phrase from 'Theses on the Philosophy of History', 'To articulate the past historically . . . means to seize hold of a memory as it flashes up at a moment of danger', in Walter Benjamin, *Illuminations*, trans. Harry Zohn (London: Fontana, 1973), p. 247. This phrase will be re-encountered in the essay by Carol Watts, below.

17. Homi Bhabha, *The Location of Culture* (London: Routledge, 1994), p. 4.

18. Eve Kosofsky Sedgwick, *Tendencies* (London: Routledge, 1995), p. 8.

PART ONE: TIME TODAY

Temporality:
Chapters 2 and 3

Modernity, Postmodernity:
Chapters 4 and 5

Memory:
Chapters 6 and 7

CHAPTER TWO

The impossibility of the present: or, from the contemporary to the contemporal

Steven Connor

Here is the argument of what follows. The present has become impossible not because it has become more ungraspable or fugitive than ever before, but because it has become more than ever available to itself, just as it has proportionately made other times available to it. At the same time, the present is characterised by attempts to curtail the powers ranged on the side of what might be called Western time or the time of modernity, in particular its powers to control, quell and consume other times and time-scales in the dominative presentness of the temporality of progress or development. The first part of the essay reviews a number of perplexed or pessimistic accounts of the stalling of modern, progressive time. The second section considers some more optimistic recommendations of untimeliness. The essay concludes with the suggestion that the question of how we currently live in and reflect on the present, on 'our time', must always now dispose itself as a question of the problem of the 'contemporary', or in other words, of whose time our time is. Presentness, in other words, is always an effect both of present being and contemporary being: coming into one's own present, one is always coming into 'con-temporal' being, alongside others in time, and alongside the other times that abut on our presentness. 'Our time' is always a matter of the time we keep, and the company we keep, with others, and with their times.

I THE IMPOSSIBLE PRESENT

It has become customary to see the conditions of temporality in the present as a decisive mutation in the long unfolding of the temporality of the modern. Modern temporality, it is often suggested, begins with the replacement, during the late medieval period in Europe, of the cyclical, recurrent or sacred time of religion, with a form of linear, progressive and secular time centred not on God but on the State. This process was assisted by the invention of the mechanical clock in Europe in 1354 and symbolised by the appearance of public clocks, first on steeples and then on palaces and town halls, a transition which is read by Jacques Le Goff as part of the process whereby 'market time' comes to replace 'church time'.[1] The new linear time of the fourteenth and fifteenth centuries was increasingly also measurable time and time with a purpose. This process is usefully summarised in David Gross's 'Temporality and the Modern State'. Gross sees the beginnings of modern state time in the dissolution of a static notion of mythic or sacred time during the second millennium BC.

> The static notion of time was demythologized and historicized. Mythic atemporality gradually came to be replaced by a sense of continuous duration that never had to be confronted before. Moreover, this duration was experienced not as cyclical but as linear. Like a river that sweeps everything with it and lets nothing stand still, time began to be viewed as moving in only one direction: from a distant past to an unknown future with the present as a continuously vanishing moment in between.[2]

The rise and consolidation of early states brought about the need to centralise time, subordinating the various different local ways and rates of reckoning time to a single, legitimated and legitimating *longue durée*, in Fernand Braudel's phrase.[3] The calculable and purposive time that emerged in the late medieval period was to develop into the empty or homogeneous time whose instrumentality for capitalism Edward Thompson was among the first to analyse and which Benedict Anderson has called the 'time of the nation'.[4] By the beginning of the nineteenth century, Gross argues, the control of long-range social memory across most of Europe had been subordinated to and regulated through state institutions, legal, political, educational and scientific. Importantly, it is also during the nineteenth century that the time of the nation-state also began to consolidate itself in relation and distinction to the other, nonsynchronous times of the cultures it absorbed through colonialism, either by expelling those cultures from history, in the process analysed by Johannes Fabian in his *Time and the Other*,[5] or by historicising them in the complicated syncopation of assimilation-through-differentiation signalled by Peter Osborne when he writes that 'it is the idea of the *non-contemporaneousness of geographically diverse* but *chronologically simultaneous* times . . . that, in the context of colonial experience, becomes the basis for "universal histories with a cosmopolitan intent" '.[6]

However, in common with many other commentators, Gross recognises a certain decisive conflict within time brought about by the energies of global capitalism, which, at least since the beginnings of this century, have been cutting athwart the political and temporal powers of the nation-state. Where the state invests in temporal reach and continuity, through its mnemonic and predictive institutions such as universities and national banks, advanced capitalism is opposed to such long-term retention and protention.[7] David Harvey also acknowledges the distinction between the long-range histories of earlier capitalist models and the short-range turnover characteristic of late capitalism, with its effect of space–time compression, and substitution of evanescence and intensity for the planned periodicity of state and capital represented by institutions.[8] Though Harvey is at pains to demonstrate the unity of long-range temporality and short-turnover temporality, as distinct phases of the global development of capital, he too, like Gross and Fredric Jameson, cannot ignore what appears to be the epochal shift within the economies of time that seems to have taken place as a result of the intensification of capital.

Accounts of modernity have tended recently to swing between the two alternatives of the plenitude of the *longue durée* and the emaciated instantaneity of the present. Lyotard's much-publicised proposition that there has been a waning of the effectiveness of metanarratives, for example, seems to lead him to associate the performative pragmatics of archaic narrative practice and the contemporary self-legitimations of scientific research:

> The narratives' reference may seem to belong to the past, but in reality it is always contemporaneous with the act of recitation. It is the present act that on each of its occurrences marshals in the ephemeral temporality inhabiting the space between the 'I have heard' and the 'you will hear' . . . [W]hat is emphasized is the metrical beat of the narrative occurrences, not each performance's differences in accent. It is in this sense that the mode of temporality can be said to be simultaneously evanescent and immemorial.[9]

Lyotard here seems to point to a return of renewable time, the iterative but forgetful presentness of scientific performativity recalling the autolegitimating pragmatics of oral narrative in archaic cultures. The strangeness and surprise of this parallel derives partly from its compression of a traditional contrast between the sacred and the secular, the mythic and the historical, the instantaneous and the extended. But it is important also to try to grasp the ways in which these opposing forms of time are in fact already correlated even within the *longues durées* of Western time. Carol Greenhouse has shown how, at the very beginning of the process whereby the secular, instrumentalised time of law and the State erupts into the recurrent time of archaic or theocratic society, there is also a powerful sharing of purpose and form between the two temporalities. From the very beginning, the secular principle of linear extension is closely associated with the cyclicity, or thickening instantaneity, of the sacred. Linear and sacred time, for one thing, are both forms of 'ironic time', which sets possibility against experience. The linear time of late medieval Christianity, for example, was the time both of fall and of salvation. In it, writes Greenhouse, 'the instant was drenched in the poignancy of impossibility: the impossibility of refusing the struggle for perfection, and the impossibility of succeeding in it'.[10] Although Greenhouse agrees with the account that stresses the historical novelty of linear time, and its role in politically legitimating the bishops, monarchs and nation-states who evoked, deployed and synchronised themselves to it, she argues that 'linear time . . . cannot fulfill its own aims to redemptive completeness without borrowing from the other temporal idioms that express other, equally sacred meanings from other domains, for example, the idioms of cyclical time'.[11] Even the idea of the once and for all creation of the world, by God, the big bang, or whatever, and its single passage to its first and final annihilation, is itself perhaps only a certain kind of 'manipulation of the idea of cyclicity' to yield the paradoxical, but powerful idea of the unique cycle.[12] 'In effect,' Greenhouse concludes, 'the linearity of time reproduces both the cry for redemption and redemption's form in its fundamental proposition that the individual can find completion only by participating in a cosmic order – through social institutions that await the end of time.'[13]

It is the massive, uncircumventable work of Hegel that brings together in a characteristically modern form the secular time of linear succession and the sacred time of the telos. It is Hegel above all who enables historicity and ahistoricity to be thought together, in a dynamic synthesis in which each instant is at once an absolute emergence in or rupture of temporal continuity and the instancing of its own meaning in the long perspective of Spirit. This attempt to correlate the two temporal perspectives of the secularised instant and the sacred instance has been subjected over the last few decades to a philosophical assault amounting almost to a Blitzkrieg, notably, of course, in the Negative Dialectics of Theodor Adorno, which accuses Hegel of 'detemporalising' time,[14] and more recently in the work of Michel Foucault and Jean-François Lyotard. Michel Serres remarks that where Hegel derives the movement of time from contradiction, he gets things exactly the wrong way round; rather than contradiction precipitating time, it is time that 'makes contradiction possible'.[15]

Less often discussed, but a little more precisely to my current purpose, is the differently anti-Hegelian account of modern temporality given by

Emmanuel Levinas in a couple of essays from the 1980s, 'L'Ancien et le Nouveau' ('The Old and the New'), first published in 1982, and 'Diachronie et representation', first published in 1985. Levinas begins 'The Old and the New' with a distinction between the relative or purely formal oldness and newness conferred on events and experiences by their distance from the present, and the qualitative ordering of events brought about by the valorisation of the new in modernity, an ordering which opens up potential distinctions between the 'really new' and the merely recent. Levinas's reading stresses, in traditional manner, the affirmation of freedom from the past that inaugurates the modern:

> Everything is possible and everything is permitted, for nothing, absolutely speaking, precedes this freedom. It is a freedom that does not bow before any factual state, thus negating the 'already done' and living only from the new. But it is a freedom with which no memory interferes, a freedom upon which no past weighs.[16]

This freedom involves a rupture not just with the past, but with the immediate givens of the present, in a systematised, institutionalised suspicion of the self-evident, which is driven by 'the exigency of an extreme lucidity'.[17] But, increasingly, the process of this self-reflection, or interior dehiscence of self-differentiation from the past, or from the past in the present, is detemporalised, accelerated to the merest flicker, in which knowledge and present self-identity annul in advance all possibility of what lies before or beyond them.

> As knowledge, thought bears upon the thinkable called being; bearing upon being, it is outside of itself, to be sure, but remains, marvelously, in itself. The exteriority, alterity, or antiquity, of what is 'already there' in the known, is taken up again into immanence: the known is at once the other and the property of thought. Nothing preexists: one learns as if one created. Reminiscence and imagination secure the synchrony of what, in experience bound to time, was doomed to the difference between the old and the new. The new as modern is the fully arranged state of the world.[18]

Where Hegel claims to hold together history and its transcendence, Levinas argues that the modern, pledged as it appears to be to the excitement and exigency of emerging time, in fact abolishes time. Thus, as in Lyotard's argument, but for different reasons, the secularising institutional knowledges of modernity somersault bizarrely into a mythic or sacred timelessness:

> Does not time itself – which for everyday consciousness bears all events, and renders possible the play of the old and the new, the very aspiration for the new in the aging of all actuality – lose for modern humanity its innovating virtue and its peremptory powers? What can modern humanity expect from a future which it believes is held in the present of its absolute knowledge, where nothing is any longer exterior to consciousness?[19]

Levinas therefore ends up arguing for a present deprived of temporal dimension. But where, for some, the present is impossible because it is insufficiently nourished by, or open to history, for Levinas, it is impossible because it is so saturated by temporality. The present is stalled because there is no history that it does not consummate, no possible future that it will not have consumed. Once, the present was emptied out by time; now the present is glutted and engorged with it. Rather than being the dimensionless membrane that separates times and tenses, the present envelops all times and tenses; the already of the aorist, the projective possibility of the future, become merely subordinate modalities of that tense we might call the 'present perfect'. From now on, in this dispensation of the modern, time can no longer move, but only, so to speak, *dilate*:

> Time is not a succession of novelties which are made old and aged, but a history where everything comes and goes into a time progressively constituting the truth. It is an edification of the true whose completion is like a novelty which does not pass. The novelty of the modern is not, to be sure, the end of everything unknown, but an epoch where the unknown to be discovered can no longer surprise thought with its new alterity. Thought is already fully conscious of itself and of all the dimensions of what is reasonable in reality.[20]

Elsewhere, Levinas laments the 'degradation of the instant' in philosophy, its failure to acknowledge the radical autonomy of the present, in its desire to find anticipation and recompense for it in temporal extension.[21] Levinas's paradoxical argument is that such reparation is itself a forgetting or reduction of the present:

> Retribution in the future does not wipe away the pains of the present. There is no justice that could make reparations for it. One should have to return to that instant, or be able to resurrect it. To hope then is to hope for the reparation of the irreparable; it is to hope for the present.[22]

For Levinas, in other words, the commanding plenitude of the modern present, the violent lucidity of its ends and purposes, results, not in a loss of history or extension, but in the impossibility of being-in-the-present. Since, for Levinas, as we will see a little later on, the authentic movement of time is a movement of dislocation and dissociation, to be able to recover the disconnectedness of the present from the past and the future would in fact not be to refuse time, but to refuse the refusal of time that is at the heart of the subject-centred temporalities of modern philosophy and modernity more generally.

The present is often characterised as pallid and fatigued, in the withdrawal of its cathexis of the past and the future, its loss of moral and political tone and commitment and its swoon into indifference and apathy. Terry Eagleton, for instance, opposes the emptied contemporary present to that agitated, ambivalent state which is the characteristically modernist experience of presentness:

> If modernism lives its history as peculiarly, insistently present, it also experiences a sense that this present moment is somehow of the future, to which the present is nothing more than an orientation; so that the idea of the Now, of the present as full presence eclipsing the past, is itself intermittently eclipsed by an awareness of the present as deferment, as an empty excited openness to a future which is in one sense already here, in another sense yet to come.[23]

It is as though postmodernity had borrowed from the modern its capacity for breaking with the past, its quality of self-possession, while losing all of its forward impulsion. The past is abandoned, without the vocation towards a future. The flattened, or decompressed condition of the present is an effect, it seems, of amnesia combined with acedia, or future-fatigue — a systematic forgetting of the given and growing resignation or indifference to the imminent.

However, the idea of the indifference of the present to the future fails to register the extraordinary intensity of the present's colonisation of the past and future. David Harvey provides ample evidence of the operationalisation of the principles of speed in the contemporary economic world, organised as it is around the attempts both to stimulate and to master change. His account is reinforced both by Paul Virilio's aesthetics of acceleration[24] and Lyotard's reflections on the transformations wrought by capital not just through time, but on time itself, with time having become not just the measure of value, but itself a commodity to be speculated upon. For Lyotard, contemporary time — strange phrase, flickering between oxymoron and tautology — is best viewed as the struggle to take possession of time, the negentropic impulse to conserve and concentrate memory and continuity against change or loss.[25]

All of this is evidenced, of course, in the distension of the present by retrospection and anticipation: in the electronic museum of contemporary film and TV, which keeps the represented past and the past of representation permanently accessible, in the rolling archive of styles and fashions in clothing, lifestyle, sport, thought and politics. The enlargement of these mnemic resources cooperates closely with the alleged debilitation of memory or contraction of attention-span in the contemporary world. For when the world has developed such a faculty of prosthetic recollection, in the vast and versatile random-access-memory of contemporary information and reproductive technology, what further need is there to correlate the memory and time-span of the individual subject with that of the culture as a whole, or to think any longer of the memory of a culture in terms of that individual subject?

For Fredric Jameson, the postmodern present has been shorn of the depth and extension that a vital relationship to the past can ensure. The enhanced and accelerated representability of the past through the developments of reproductive technologies means for Jameson that we have lost the possibility of access to the past in itself. Ours is a short-circuit historicity, in which history is hot-wired to yield us the narcissistic gratification of discovering ourselves and our preoccupations wherever we look:

> The historical novel can no longer set out to represent the historical past;
> it can only 'represent' our ideas and stereotypes about that past (which
> thereby at once becomes 'pop' history). Cultural production . . . can no
> longer gaze decently on some putative real world, at some reconstruction
> of a past history which was once itself a present; rather, as in Plato's cave,
> it must trace our mental images of that past upon its confining walls.[26]

For Jameson, the 'waning of our historicity' also makes the present in some wise strange or unavailable to itself, and 'endows present reality and the openness of present history with the spell and distance of a glossy mirage'. The enormity of the loss of the past to an eternal present of recirculating historical simulacra is dwarfed by the greater enormity of 'a situation in which we seem increasingly incapable of fashioning representations of our own current experience'.[27]

And yet this does not seem quite right. For (to repeat) the present is surely characterised not only by what Jameson calls an 'omnipresent, omnivorous and well-nigh libidinal historicism',[28] but is also narcissistically concerned to appropriate and consume *itself*. Nowhere is the quality of the present so apparent as in the intensity of the desire to make the present known and available to itself, in that quickening desire to grasp and outstrip the accelerating instant of our instantaneity which at once imparts velocity to the present and, in T.S. Eliot's nice archaism, 'prevents us everywhere'.[29] Our desire to know and understand the present is never far from our desire to consume it as image or spectacle, such that our disinterested, academic reflection on the present becomes the very metabolism of a gratification. As such it mimes the very accelerations of consumption, in which satiety stops the momentary gaping of desire so swiftly as almost to seem to precede it. To borrow an advertising slogan used by a credit-card company a few years back, the present is becoming a machine for taking the waiting out of wanting.

It may seem strange to make such a claim in a context seemingly characterised by the awed awareness among those employing a Christian calendar of impending disaster or millennial transformation. But perhaps, following Baudrillard, we ought to see the seemingly intense cathexis of the end and the beginning in millennium-fever as the last attempt to precipitate a relation to a future time exterior to the present, which would not already be encompassed and programmed in advance. Baudrillard takes the digital clock on the Pompidou Centre in Paris which ticks off the seconds to the end of the millennium as emblematic of a reversal of time, in which time is counted, not progressively, and by accumulation, but by subtraction, backwards from an end. But, where the first millennium looked towards the advent of the Kingdom of God, we have no real prospect of ending, since our end will have been so thoroughly preceded by its simulation:

> Exactly the opposite of the end of history, then: the impossibility of finishing with history. If history can no longer reach its end, then it is no longer properly speaking a history. We have lost history and have also, as a result, lost the end of history. We are labouring under the illusion of the end, under the posthumous illusions of the end. And this is serious, for the end signifies that something has really taken place. Whereas we, at the height of reality – and with information at its height – no longer know whether anything has taken place or not.[30]

II UNTIMELINESS

Faced with this sense of the saturated present, the only proper response seems to be to loosen the temporal dominion of the modern, to distress the scansion of the omnicompetent present. In Levinas, this is attempted through a return to the work of Bergson, the great, largely unacknowledged resource for different versions of the postmodern politics of time.

> Against the encompassing, accumulating and organizing consciousness of the system through knowledge, against the tendency to equalize the new, as if it were only an unknown to know and not the other to desire in its unassimilable alterity – that is to say, to love rather than to equalize by knowledge – against this pan-logical civilization Bergson brings to bear an inestimable message. It perceives the essential – if one can say – of the psychism in change, in an unceasing passage to the other which does not stop at any identity; it teaches us time in primordial change, not as a 'mobile image of immobile eternity' – what is has been in the whole history of Western thought: simply the forfeiture of the permanence of being, a privation of eternity – but as the original excellence and the very superiority of mind.[31]

Thomas Docherty has pointed, in ways that perhaps cohere with Levinas's account, to the powerful structural correspondence between the continuous and the instantaneous in modernity, arguing that the unfolding of time in modernity turns out to depend upon and express itself through the fixing or spatialising of time, and similarly urging a postmodern opening to Bergsonian duration, and anachronism:

> The project of modernity is based upon the timely correspondence: action provoking appropriate reaction at the appropriate moment for the construction of a situational nexus in which power is formulated or articulated in terms of oppression or control. In aesthetic terms, the project of modernity leads to the realization of an essential object (the work of art) which is in timely correspondence with its social formation . . . [Modernity] depends upon punctuality, upon the timely correspondence between subject and object available to phenomenology; postmodernism, as in the thinking of Lyotard, Baudrillard, Virilio, Deleuze and others, is more interested in the maintenance of eventuality, of the untimely or anachronistic introduced into the power relations produced through phenomenology and its deconstruction.[32]

Docherty's ideal of anachronism may relate closely to the value of what Levinas calls 'diachrony'. 'Diachrony' derives from the Greek preposition *dia*, 'through', and is to be distinguished from 'synchrony' in the sense that it evokes movement through time rather than the correlations between times (the Greek preposition *syn* means 'between'). But Levinas's use of the term perhaps arouses some of the other meanings of the Greek *dia*, which include 'apart' and 'across'. For Levinas, diachrony is an ethical principle of openness to the other, who can never be assimilated to thought or knowledge. In moving apart from itself, through time, diachrony moves across to the other, in their time. Diachrony is 'non-coincidence, dispossession itself: a way of "being avowed" prior to every act of consciousness and more profoundly than consciousness, through the gratuitousness of time'.[33] Diachrony 'does not signify pure rupture, but a non-in-difference and concordance that are not founded on the unity of transcendental apperception'.[34]

In his opening of and on to the untimely, Levinas's work may be compared with that of Michel Serres. Against the modern ideal of linear or classically geometrical time, Serres's preference is for a topological or 'crumpled' time:

> If you take a handkerchief and spread it out in order to iron it you can see in it certain fixed distances and proximities. If you sketch a circle in one area, you can mark out nearby points and measure far-off distances. Then take the same handkerchief and crumple it, by putting it in your pocket. Two distant points suddenly are close, even superimposed. If, further, you tear it in certain places, two points that were very close can become very distant. The science of nearness and rifts is called topology, while the science of stable and well-defined distances is called metrical geometry.[35]

Like Levinas, and unlike most critical philosophers of our century, Serres is an irenic thinker, a philosopher of peace rather than of war. Serres's work declines the martial, exterminating logic of linear time, which he sees as 'a trajectory of the race for first place – in school, in the Olympic Games, for the Nobel Prize. This isn't time, but a simple competition – once again, war. Why replace temporality, duration, with a quarrel? *The first to arrive, the winner of the battle, obtains as his prize the right to reinvent history to his own advantage.'*[36]

Such an approach to time is consonant with that argued by Serres's interlocutor in the conversations from which this judgement emerges, Bruno Latour. For Latour, the idea of a sudden rupture in which modern (abstract, universal, non-contradictory) time tears itself out of preexisting rhythms and durations, is an illusion. Time has always allowed, or required, the meeting of different times. For Latour, modern time, the time of steady, universal progress from one unified temporal condition to another, has given way to an awareness of all the many exceptions and unclassifiable anachronisms in 'modern life'.

> No one now can categorize actors that belong to the 'same time' in a single coherent group. No one knows any longer whether the reintroduction of the bear in the Pyrenees, kolhozes, the Green Revolution, the anti-smallpox vaccine, Star Wars, the Muslim religion, partridge hunting, the French Revolution, service industries, labour unions, cold fusion, Bolshevism, relativity, Slovak nationalism, commerical sailboats, and so on, are outmoded, up to date, futuristic, atemporal, nonexistent, or permanent.[37]

Seen from the point of view of our impossible dream of modern time, such temporal turbulence may seem to bring time slewing sickeningly to a halt: 'Like a great ocean liner that slows down and then comes to a standstill in the Sargasso Sea, the moderns' time has finally been suspended.'[38] But Latour proposes a different relation to this mixed temporality, in a helical model of time in which progression and recurrence are coiled together:

> Let us suppose, for example, that we are going to regroup the contemporary elements along a spiral rather than a line. We do have a future and a past, but the future takes the form of a circle expanding in all directions, and the past is not surpassed, but revisited, repeated, surrounded, protected, recombined, reinterpreted and reshuffled. Elements that appear remote if we follow the spiral may turn out to be quite nearby if we compare loops. Conversely, elements that appear quite contemporary, if we judge by the line, become quite remote if we traverse a spoke. Such a temporality does not oblige us to use the labels 'archaic' or 'advanced', since every cohort of contemporary elements may bring together elements from all times. In such a framework, our actions are recognised at last as polytemporal.[39]

The collapse of faith in long, or universal temporalities has produced in other areas of thought a similar 'anachronistic' sense of the competing multiplicities of times, time-scales, and temporal syntaxes. An example here would be the debates concerning the gendering of temporality. Many of the arguments here have as their point of departure Simone de Beauvoir's position about the sexually privative nature of temporal domination, in her claim that 'Man's design is not to repeat himself in time: it is to take control of the instant and mould the future. It is male activity that in creating values has prevailed over the confused forces of life; it has subdued Nature and Woman.'[40] De Beauvoir aims, if not actually to promote woman to the position of subduer of time, then at least to shift her from the position of identification with time, considered purely as object, obstacle or inertia. But another tradition of critique, announced by Julia Kristeva's 'Women's Time' (1979), has sought to imagine a different kind of rapprochement between the rapacious time of modernity and the repetitious, or monumental times of the body, of maternity and of myth. Kristeva's essay is a rich resource for a politics of the temporal, in that it urges not just a melancholy acknowledgement of the existence of different temporal rhythms, durations, velocities and periodicities (the anthropological acknowledgement of such is melancholy because it is so often the prelude to their extinction), but also a sense of their emergent and unpredictable affiliations, or, as I will want before long to call it, their 'contemporality'. To be sure, acknowledging the unpredictability of these affiliations has some perturbing consequences, since there seems no guarantee that one can pick and choose one's temporal company. Thus Kristeva points, not only to the solidarity between certain forms of radical feminism and the 'obsessional time' of hysteria, or the times of 'marginal groups of spiritual or mystical inspiration', but also to certain contemporary scientific and economic discourses of time which might seem far from natural associates for a feminist temporality:

> Is it not true that the problematic of a time indissociable from space, of a space–time in infinite expansion, or rhythmed by accidents and catastrophes, preoccupies both space science and genetics? And, at another level, is it not true that the contemporary media revolution, which is manifest in the storage and reproduction of information, implies an idea of time as frozen or exploding according to the vagaries of demand, returning to its source but uncontrollable, utterly bypassing its subject and leaving only two preoccupations to those who approve of it: Who is to have power over the origin (the programming) and over the end (the use)?[41]

Peter Osborne is concerned that, insofar as it seems to offer only a spatialised account of such temporal affiliations, Kristeva's essay fails to guarantee any decisive breach with or step beyond the world-historical time enforced remorselessly by global capitalism – fails, indeed, to take seriously enough the rupture proposed by feminism itself, at least the 'first-generation' feminism represented perhaps by such as Simone de Beauvoir:

The success of such demands can . . . only be thought in terms of the 'parallel existence' or 'interweaving' of different (already established) times with women's experience; rather than as a genuinely transformative movement which would leave neither women's time nor historical time (neither 'women' nor 'history') unchanged.[42]

Osborne's clear preference for the strenuous transcendence of revolutionary transformation over the torpid inertia of 'parallelism' and 'interweaving' makes it hard to resist the charge that he is as guilty as Kristeva of leaving the definitional contrast between 'women' and 'history' unmolested. Against this, it seems necessary to urge a more complex sense of the interrelations between the spatial and the temporal, and in particular, of the complexity of temporal forces in any instance of the spatial, in something of the manner recommended by Doreen Massey:

Seeing space as a moment in the intersection of configured social relations (rather than as an absolute dimension) means that it cannot be seen as static. There is no choice between flow (time) and a flat surface of instantaneous relations (space). Space is not a 'flat' surface in that sense because the social relations which create it are themselves dynamic by their very nature. It is a question of a manner of thinking. It is not the 'slice through time' which should be the dominant thought but the simultaneous existence of social relations that cannot be conceptualized as other than dynamic.[43]

The difficulty seems to lie in describing, or predicting, or securing the kind of syntax of relations which might hold together this dynamic experience of contemporality without thereby petrifying it. John Frow suggests that we would do better to replace the notion of a synchronicity of different times, or *Gleichzeitigkeit*, with the idea of *Ungleichzeitigkeit*, or non-synchronicity. The idea of synchronicity posits a pure presence, a now which anthologises and connects the different temporalities of the world; the idea of *Ungleichzeitigkeit* makes available an idea of asynchronic diversity which is not referred to a more comprehensive temporal framework.

Ungleichzeitigkeit (non-synchronicity, the uneven layering of times within any historical formation) seems to me in fact to provide a more adequate way of understanding the *unequal* relations that hold within a synchronic framework characterized by uneven development and a global division of labour . . . [I]t is not necessary to posit a common human experience of time in order to speak of the interlinkage of political and economic destinies.[44]

This formulation does not seem to come out quite right, even in Frow's own terms. For we cannot avoid noticing that the idea of synchronicity that the idea of *Ungleichzeitigkeit* is supposed to help us do without springs straight back in that characterisation of *Ungleichzeitigkeit* as the '*unequal* relations that hold within a synchronic framework characterized by uneven development and a global division of labour'. Frow states that it is not necessary 'to posit a common human experience of time in order to speak of the interlinkage of political and economic destinies'. 'Destinies'? If the idea of asynchronicity is to mean anything, it must surely mean that not all ways of living in and ordering time involve destiny. There seems little to distinguish such a view from the evolutionary universalism of the nineteenth century, which acknowledged other times only by reference to the advancing, but always punctual 'mean time' of metropolitan imperialism.

And yet, if this is a failure of tact on Frow's part, a somewhat impolite forcing of the linear ideas of development and destiny on other cultures, it also registers two important points. Firstly, it gives us cause to suspect that it may in fact be impossible to measure any form of difference in time-scale or temporal experience except by reference to some kind of shared temporal scheme, some kind of synchronisation. When Michel Serres imagines time as a crumpled topology, rather than a racetrack, he nevertheless has recourse to a spatialising metaphor which both disorders time and holds it together; his handkerchief is put into a pocket. The question is, what and where is this pocket that produces the crumpling of time?

Here, Frow's account seems to blurt out a bitter truth: economic globalism does now indeed set the clock identically everywhere, making temporal variations variations upon a single, governing temporal framework. The problem with the different versions of the politics of untimeliness, polytemporality, or anachronism here reviewed is that they mimic so closely one of the most remarkable features of our saturated present, namely its capacity precisely to register and regulate a multiplicity of time-scales and rates of change. Global capitalism, with its associated drives and technologies, is the pocket that crumples up the fabric of time. There seems no way of guaranteeing the contrast between punctuality and eventuality that Docherty employs to validate the work of Lyotard and others, since it is precisely the characteristic of our present that it can assemble multiple times into singularity: the principle of universal domination under the identity-principle expressing itself through ever more versatile syntaxes of temporal consumption. No more powerful model of the unregulated, but powerfully regulating force of temporal conjuncture possessed by modern commodity capitalism can be imagined than Latour's spiral of time, for example. For Fredric Jameson, the deathly paradox achieved by the generalisation of modern temporality into its global, postmodern condition is the conjuncture of absolute change and absolute stasis. Given the continuous and unabating demand for change both in consumption and in media, 'even the relative meaning allowed by uneven development (or "nonsynchronous synchronicity") is no longer comprehensible, and the supreme value of the

New and of innovation, as both modernism and modernization grasped it, fades away against a steady stream of momentum and variation that at some outer limit seems stable and motionless'.[45]

In the condition of universal tele-presence, as Paul Virilio has called it, everything occurs at once, in a generalised 'real time'. Real-time live broadcasting ought to provide precisely the conditions for the folding or plaiting together of different dates and calendars. But, for Virilio, the fact that we live so much in the 'real time' of mediated representation means that chronological relations of succession and emergence (before, during, after) give way to 'chronoscopic' conditions of relative visibility or exposure (underexposure, exposure, overexposure). When every time can be made present to every other time, by 'real-time live broadcast', there is literally no time like the present:

> [T]he instantaneous duration of the 'real moment' now dominates duration, the extensive and relatively controllable time of history – in other words, of that long term that used to encompass past, present and future. This is in the end what we could call a temporal commutation, a commutation also related to a sort of commotion in present duration, an accident of the so-called 'real' moment that suddenly detaches itself from the place where it happens, from its here and now, and opts for an electronic dazzlement (at once optoelectronic, electroacoustic and electrotactile) in which remote control, this so-called 'tactile telepresence', will complete the task of the old telesurveillance of whatever stays at a distance, out of reach.[46]

III CONTEMPORALITY

Let us retrace our steps, to check that we have not missed the turning that would lead elsewhere than to this generalised terminus. The expansive energies of nineteenth-century capitalism brought about encounters between Western powers and their 'archaic' others, encounters which were managed by the theory of universally evolving time. Spatial distance was correlated regularly with temporal remoteness (thus the regular claim that the most geographically remote people of all, taking London and Greenwich Mean Time as a starting-point, the Australian aboriginals, were the most primitive, and therefore temporally as well as geographically antipodean). The map of imperialism and modernisation was the diagram, a race perpetually being won by the present. However, by the second half of the twentieth century, those very same expansive energies had begun to produce a simultaneous flattening and crumpling of the map, as it became less and less possible to maintain relationships of distance and proximity.

If it is the case that the no-time of the present is the culmination of modern synchronicity, then no real alternative is to be expected from the grasping or invention of new kinds of synchronisation or temporal synthesis looked for by Peter Osborne. On the other hand, there would be little to be hoped for either from the rumpling or corrugation of the present by different temporalities, since anachronism, the bringing together of disjunct times, is now the effect and expression of universal synchronisation.

It is tempting to give up on all attempts to totalise, summarise, or synthesise, in the hope of thereby releasing some measure of spontaneous or unadministered time. This is what Lyotard attempts to do in his different attempts to specify the nature of the nonsynthetic here and now of the aesthetic 'event', in the essays that make up *The Inhuman*. But even this is bound to fail (as Lyotard duly says it is), in so far as it seems to acquiesce to the powers of universal administration in contemporary time. For it is impossible to live in time spontaneously. Michel Serres says that people mistake the measurement of time for time itself. But it is mistaken to see the necessity of measuring time as an avoidable mistake; time is nearly nothing else but the measurement of time.

But if we must measure time, perhaps we could begin to measure it in different ways. What if we were to get into a companionable habit of looking at our watches to ask, not *what* time it is, or *where* we are in time, but whose time it is? Present time would then be an effect of contemporality. Being in the present would be a matter of contemporal being, alongside others in time, in their time as filtered through our time, in our time as folded into theirs. 'Our time' might become a way of keeping time and company, with others, with other times, with others' times. If time is nearly nothing other than the measuring of time, and time without measurement is as inconceivable as music without instruments, we will continue to need time-pieces. But, just as we are seeing in music the proliferation of instruments, actual and virtual, and perhaps soon of music not scored in advance for specific instruments, but capable of inventing and actualising those instruments as it goes along, so we might imagine a way of living and measuring time through different organs and instruments, as they are improvised, modified and exchanged between the players.

One limitation of many of the evocations of untimeliness – of anachronism, or polytemporality – that I have reviewed in this essay is that they seem to constitute no more than a clustering together of *dates*, or date-stamped objects. 'It is not only the Bedouins and the !kung who mix up transistors and traditional behaviours, plastic buckets and animal-skin vessels', says Bruno Latour, for whom however the mixing-up of modern time remains a matter primarily of adopting a different system of sorting or classi-fication of objects.[47] Fredric Jameson is sensitive to the startling exchanges of temporal priority characteristic of postmodern global capitalism – whereby, for example, so dominant is the need to modernise that 'nothing but the modern henceforth exists in Third World societies', even as the demodernisa-tion and deindustrialisation being undertaken in the West means that 'the Third World has entered the interstices of the First one'. Nevertheless, he is unable to conceive the exchanges of temporality involved in these processes except as 'some essential spatialization [in which] everything we have here been trying to work out in terms of temporality will necessarily have passed through a spatial matrix to come to expression in the first place'.[48]

But to conceive the polytemporality of the present either in terms of a vast warehouse stored with objects marked with the signs of their different temporal provenance, or as the result of a process of passing time through a singular spatial matrix, is far from exhausting the options. Rather, we could try to get better at conceiving polytemporality in terms of processes of reciprocal filtering, or (Michel Serres's word) 'percolation'. For, in con-temporality as I conceive it, there is never a simple batching of datelines, or coordination of calendars, nor yet a simple, one-way conversion of time to space. If time is inevitably caught up with the spatiality of mensuration, then the new mathematics ought to have taught us more about the com-plex nature of the resulting phase-spaces and topologies shaped by the interrupted elapsings of times. The correlation of times should be thought of, not as a topical, but as a topological phenomenon; it too takes time, and is taken up in time. In contemporality, the thread of one duration is pulled constantly through the loop formed by another, one temporality is strained through another's mesh; but the resulting knot can itself be retied, and the the filtered system also simultaneously refilters the system through which it is percolating. The scoring of time constituted by one temporality is played out on temporal instruments for which it may never have been intended, but which give it its music precisely in the way they change its metre and phrasings, and remix its elements.

It may be that literary texts provide some useful examples of the way in which this contemporality, or holding-together in representation of differ-ent, competing temporalities, may usefully disturb the identity-principle of the impossible present. Out of a number of possible literary examples of this process, which might well include the work of Angela Carter, Ben Okri, J.M. Coetzee, Marianne Wiggins or many others, I isolate for alleg-orical purposes only one, well-known example, Salman Rushdie's *The Satanic Verses* (1988). This is a text which goes beyond the particularised and coherent spatio-temporal dispositions of *Midnight's Children* (1982) and

Shame (1983), to develop a complex model of the necessary contemporality of different times in the crammed, turbulent present. Impinging on and transforming each other in the novel are the now-historical time of the novel's present, in the representation of 'contemporary' Britain; the mythical dream-time of the founding of a culture in Gibreel Farishta's involuntary vision of the inauguration of Islam; the account of the pilgrimage of Ayesha, set in the quasi-contemporary region of Peristan, which belongs both to secular time and to legend; the time of cultural fantasy embodied in Rosa Diamond's dream of colonial South America, which is transmitted, like the time of the founding of Islam, to Gibreel's porous dream-self; the accelerated time of global capitalism represented by Hal Valance with his ambition to sell everything to everybody; and the 'air-time' both of contemporary media and mass cultural forms and, more literally, of contemporary air-travel, that interterritorial, suspended time which nevertheless submits the earth and its politics to a certain kind of schedule. The most striking aspect of these different temporalities in the novel is not so much their agitated impingement upon one another, as the 'transferential' relationship that they have one to another. This is to say, they are transmitted like messages in the bodies and consciousnesses of particular persons, who are both displaced from one time to another, and communicate different times to each other. Under such conditions of transference, temporalities not only clash, but invert, adapt and mutate. Temporalities cross over and interfere both in the disordered consciousness of Gibreel Farishta and in the mutative temporal consciousness of the book itself, which seems to be constructed like a magnified version of the 'All-India Radio' which is Saleem Sinai's teeming telepathic receptivity in *Midnight's Children*. Temporality is transferential in something of the psychoanalytic sense, too, for temporalities are projected, assumed and multiplied in the novel, in what may seem an uncanny anticipation of the process of reading and misreading the novel that continues to be acted out during the *Satanic Verses* 'affair', with the 'modern' and 'archaic' temporalities of the West and its reputed Other(s) reciprocally defining and to some degree identifying with each other.

   That *The Satanic Verses* in no sense provides a programme for reconciling different, competing temporalities is so evident from the history of its readings and misreadings as scarcely to need stating. But the kind of interpretative conflict the book has incited – in common with many other contemporary texts that have not in actual fact incited political violence, but which make similar kinds of claim upon our temporal attention – has precipitated our time into a reflection on its own nature and responsibilities with regard to other times and the alterity of time as such. The book exemplifies, and is itself caught up by what Levinas calls the powers of temporal 'intrigue' against the inertia of temporal 'concordance', powers which make it possible to begin imagining the conditions under which a kind of justice may be framed and effected, a justice in and to our own time, as well as to the other times, that bear upon it – in short, to the contemporality of the contemporary.

NOTES

1. Jacques Le Goff, *Time, Work, and Culture in the Middle Ages*, trans. Arthur Goldhammer (Chicago: University of Chicago Press, 1980), pp. 29–42.
2. David Gross, 'Temporality and the Modern State', *Theory and Society* 14 (1985), p. 56.
3. Fernand Braudel, 'Histoires et sciences sociales: le longue durée', *Annales: Economies, Sociétés, Civilisations* 4 (1958), pp. 725–53.
4. Edward Thompson, 'Time, Work-Discipline, and Industrial Capitalism', *Past and Present* 38 (1967), pp. 79–97; Benedict Anderson, *Imagined Communities: Reflections on the Origin and Spread of Nationalism* (London: Verso, 1983).
5. Johannes Fabian, *Time and the Other: How Anthropology Makes its Object* (New York: Columbia University Press, 1983).
6. Peter Osborne, 'Modernity is a Qualitative, Not a Chronological, Category: Notes on the Dialectics of Differential Historical Time', in Francis Barker, Peter Hulme and Margaret Iverson, eds, *Postmodernism and the Re-Reading of Modernity* (Manchester: Manchester University Press, 1992), p. 32.
7. Gross, 'Temporality and the Modern State', p. 76.
8. David Harvey, *The Condition of Postmodernity: An Enquiry Into the Origins of Social Change* (Oxford: Blackwell, 1989). See especially 'From Fordism to Flexible Accumulation' and 'Time-Space Compression and the Postmodern Condition', pp. 141–72, 284–307.
9. Jean-François Lyotard, *The Postmodern Condition: A Report on Knowledge*, trans. Brian Massumi and Geoff Bennington (Manchester: Manchester University Press, 1984), p. 22.
10. Carol Greenhouse, 'Just in Time: Temporality and the Cultural Legitimation of Law', *Yale Law Review* 98 (1989), p. 1635.
11. Greenhouse, 'Just in Time', p. 1637.
12. Greenhouse, 'Just in Time', p. 1637.
13. Greenhouse, 'Just in Time', p. 1636.
14. Theodor Adorno, *Negative Dialectics*, trans. E.B. Ashton (London: Routledge, 1973) p. 331.
15. Michel Serres and Bruno Latour, *Conversations on Science, Culture and Time*, trans. Roxanne Lapidus (Ann Arbor: University of Michigan Press, 1995), p. 50.

16. Emmanuel Levinas, *Time and the Other*, trans. Richard A. Cohen (Pittsburgh: Duquesne University Press, 1987), p. 124.
17. Levinas, *Time and the Other*, pp. 125–6.
18. Levinas, *Time and the Other*, p. 125.
19. Levinas, *Time and the Other*, p. 126.
20. Levinas, *Time and the Other*, p. 127.
21. Emmanuel Levinas, *Existence and Existents*, trans. Alphonso Lingis (The Hague: Nijhoff, 1978), p. 73.
22. Levinas, *Existence and Existents*, p. 91. For a fuller account of Levinas's understanding of the ethics of the present, see Tina Chanter, 'The Alterity and Immodesty of Time: Death as Future and Eros as Feminine in Levinas', in David Wood, ed., *Writing the Future* (London: Routledge, 1990), pp. 137–54.
23. Terry Eagleton, 'Capitalism, Modernism and Postmodernism', in *Against the Grain: Selected Essays, 1975–1985* (London: Verso, 1986), p. 139.
24. Paul Virilio, *Vitesse et politique* (Paris: Galilée, 1979).
25. Jean-François Lyotard, 'Time Today', in *The Inhuman: Reflections on Time*, trans. Geoffrey Bennington and Rachel Bowlby (Cambridge: Polity Press, 1991), pp. 58–77.
26. Fredric Jameson, 'Postmodernism: Or, the Cultural Logic of Late Capitalism', *New Left Review* 146 (1984), p. 71.
27. Jameson, 'Postmodernism', p. 68.
28. Jameson, 'Postmodernism', p. 66.
29. 'East Coker', *The Complete Poems and Plays of T.S. Eliot* (London: Faber and Faber 1969), p. 181.
30. Jean Baudrillard, 'The End of the Millennium, or the Countdown', talk given at the Institute of Contemporary Arts, London, 8 May 1997.
31. Levinas, *Time and the Other*, p. 129.
32. Thomas Docherty, *After Theory: Postmodernism/Postmarxism* (London: Routledge, 1990), pp. 9–10.
33. Levinas, *Time and the Other*, p. 137.
34. Levinas, *Time and the Other*, p. 118.
35. Serres and Latour, *Conversations*, p. 60.
36. Serres and Latour, *Conversations*, p. 49.
37. Bruno Latour, *We Have Never Been Modern*, trans. Catherine Porter (London: Harvester Wheatsheaf, 1993), p. 74.
38. Latour, *We Have Never Been Modern*, p. 77.
39. Latour, *We Have Never Been Modern*, p. 75.
40. Simone de Beauvoir, *The Second Sex*, trans. H.M. Parshley (Harmondsworth: Penguin, 1972), p. 97.
41. Julia Kristeva, 'Women's Time', trans. Alice Jardine and Harry Blake, in *The Kristeva Reader*, ed. Toril Moi (Oxford: Blackwell, 1986), p. 192.
42. Osborne, 'Modernity is a Qualitative, Not a Chronological, Category', p. 43, n. 11.
43. Doreen Massey, 'Politics and Space-Time', *New Left Review* 196 (1992), p. 81.
44. John Frow, *Time and Commodity Culture: Essays in Cultural Theory and Postmodernity* (Oxford: Clarendon Press, 1997), p. 9.
45. Fredric Jameson, *The Seeds of Time* (New York: Columbia University Press, 1994), p. 17.

46. Paul Virilio, *Open Sky*, trans. Julie Rose (London and New York: Verso, 1997), p. 14.
47. Latour, *We Have Never Been Modern*, p. 75.
48. Jameson, *The Seeds of Time*, pp. 20–1.

CHAPTER THREE
The politics of time

Peter Osborne

> The simple possibility that things might proceed otherwise . . . is sufficient
> to change the whole experience of practice and, by the same token, its
> logic.
>
> Pierre Bourdieu, *The Logic of Practice*

The simple possibility that things might proceed otherwise is something in
which there has been depressingly little belief of late. For all the intellectual
enthusiasm for change manifest in the debates about postmodernism, there
is probably at present less of a sense that things might actually 'proceed
otherwise' in Western capitalist societies (otherwise than they are) than at
any time since the early 1950s. This situation has been reflected theoretically in a number of ways: from the 'realisation of nihilism' of Francis
Fukuyama's conception of the end of history, via the 'realisation of pos-
itivism' of Fredric Jameson's postmodernism, to a series of more diffuse
analyses of the end of politics and the crisis of the future.[1] It is a distinctive (although generally disavowed) feature of these scenarios that they all
embrace that hitherto discredited nineteenth-century genre, the *philosophy
of history*, albeit in predominantly negative or inverted forms.[2] Indeed, so
unorthodox would this seem to be that the mere fact that Fukuyama crafts
his argument at this level has been enough for some on the Left to identify
him as their ally: an agent of the State Department's secret discontent with
its own rule, perhaps.[3]

Personally, I am less persuaded that the philosophy of history belongs
intrinsically to the Left than I am of the dystopian character of its more
recent manifestations. Dystopias may once have functioned to raise an
emancipatory alarm about the present; today they all too readily confirm
the 'worst case scenarios' of the policy planners – using the imagination to
undercut, rather than underpin, the possibility that things might proceed in

another way. Grand narrative forms of the philosophy of history have migrated to the Right. To declare the genre dead is simply to reproduce it in its presently most pervasive, if paradoxical form.[4]

In Hegelian terms, this state of affairs appears as a crisis in the historical experience of 'reason'. Yet the fact that a certain literature continues to view the crisis from this standpoint (the standpoint of 'reason') is perhaps less significant than what it reveals about the temporal dimension of the conception of reason at stake. For the historical present does not just resist interpretation along the lines of any of the currently available Hegelian models, it positively mocks them, and not for the first time.

I   DIFFERENCE AGAINST DEVELOPMENT

There is a range of opinions about precisely which events this century have been most destructive of the classical Hegelian perspective on history as the *demonstrable* realisation of the idea of reason as freedom – as opposed to those heterodox variants which demand no more than a logical basis for a speculative hope. These views reflect the experiences of a number of political generations across a variety of social groups: from the horrors of the First World War, through European fascism, the Holocaust, Hiroshima, and the prospect of a global nuclear annihilation, to an increased awareness of the role of genocide and racial slavery in the constitution of Western culture, the ecological crisis of the planet, and the collapse of historical communism: a veritable 'slaughter-bench', as Hegel himself once described history, 'at which the happiness of peoples, the wisdom of states, and the virtue of individuals have been sacrificed'.[5] Yet in this case without the promise of reconciliation at its end.

Most decisive, perhaps, has been the cumulative impact of these events on a form of historical consciousness – narrative totalisation of history from the standpoint of a realised reason – which has at the same time been progressively eroded from within, by the power of temporal abstraction at work in the social processes of capitalist modernity. This is perhaps the most far-reaching cultural consequence of commodification: the destruction of 'lived' historical narratives by the instantaneity of the image. What appears in Habermas, in quasi-Romantic form, as the 'colonisation' of the life-world by the system is but one aspect of a more pervasive dehistoricisation inherent in the temporality of 'modernity' itself.[6]

Few, I think, would disagree with Ricoeur today when he writes that:

> It now seems as though Hegel, seizing a favourable moment, a *kairos*,
> which has been revealed for what it was to our perspective and our
> experience, only totalised a few leading aspects of the spiritual history of
> Europe and of its geographical and historical environment, ones that, since
> that time, have come undone.

What has come undone, Ricoeur continues, is 'the very substance of what
Hegel sought to make into a concept'. Difference, he insists, 'has turned
against development, conceived as a succession of stages'. Difference has
turned against development conceived, at the level of world history, as
a succession of stages.[7] The European spirit can no longer find itself in
the 'absolute dismemberment' to which Hegel refers in the Preface to the
Phenomenology, however hard it may continue to try. 'Contemplating the
negative face to face', it can dwell there no longer.[8] What Horkheimer
described as 'the *logical* difficulties that understanding meets in every thought
that attempts to reflect a *living* totality', have been so compounded by the
concrete *historical* difficulties listed above as to appear insuperable.[9] Both
forms of difficulty primarily concern the future: a conceptual tendency to
enfold the future back into the present, in the first case – to deny its
fundamental openness; a specific 'experience of the future' (present futures)
as a blockage or impediment to freedom, and hence as a barrier to a true
(qualitatively differential) futurity, in the latter.

From the point of view of the European philosophy of history, the
current situation is thus not unlike the late 1930s, when Horkheimer's
famous essay set the Frankfurt School on the road which would eventually
lead, by the 1960s, to the impasse of Theodor Adorno's negativism. If the
theoretical critique of the temporal dimension of Hegelian philosophy (its
'immobilisation of time') had been expounded in more or less completed
form as early as 1839 (in Feuerbach's 'Towards a Critique of Hegelian
Philosophy'),[10] the Hegelian philosophy of history nonetheless acquired a
new lease of life in the 1920s with the Marxist addition of a *practically*-based
futurity. Once the empirical basis of this newly practical, but nonetheless
hypothetical, futurity began to be undermined, however, in the 1930s,
Marxist Hegelianism was increasingly forced back onto the purely *conceptual*
resources of Hegelian logic, from which it constructed a correspondingly
utopian philosophy of history. It thereby became vulnerable, once again, to
Feuerbach's theoretical critique.[11] It is not history, but the philosophy of
history, which moves in cycles of repetition here.

But does the renewed implausibility of Hegelianism, in its broadest
sense, as a structure of historical experience (within which I include the
philosophy of history implicit in the political culture of the Communist
tradition) rule out the possibility of a totalising historical consciousness *per
se*? Or does it, rather more taxingly, demand a change in our conception of

its form? Are historical temporality and the standpoint of eternity *absolutely* opposed, as the critique of Hegelianism supposes, for example? Or is there some other way of understanding the constitutive role of timelessness (the standpoint of eternity) in cognitive experience; some other way than as a sign of the reified and detemporalised conceptuality of an idealist logic?

One thing which is at issue in these questions, among others, is the progressive political legacy of the metaphysical tradition: the capacity of human reason to mediate social experience in such a way as to foster, in a sufficiently concrete manner, the rational belief that 'things might proceed otherwise'. Since the beginning of the nineteenth century, the fate of this tradition has hung on its capacity to think 'history' in the collective singular – to transform historical experience into what, following Adorno, one might call 'philosophical experience', and vice versa – and thereby to provide political culture with a temporal horizon appropriate to the project of large-scale social transformation. The philosophy of history may not 'belong' to the Left, in the sense in which some of Fukuyama's admirers like to think, but it is a field upon which a certain socialist tradition depends, intellectually, for its credibility. This includes any development which would draw on the history of Marxism as one of its resources; Marx's critique of Hegel notwithstanding. The crisis in the category of history manifests itself within this tradition as a crisis in the conception of political experience.

What follows are some reflections on the temporalisation of history which argue the theoretical virtues of continuing to cultivate the terrain of the philosophy of history (the field of historical totalisation) by rethinking its terms, in order to overcome the conceptual difficulties of its classical Hegelian form, by way of what I shall call a *philosophy of historical time*. The idea has a number of precursors – foremost among whom one might name Walter Benjamin and the later Sartre – but it is expounded here, for the most part, independently of its relation to these writings.[12] Given the scope of the issues, the argument which follows is of necessity both summary and abstract.

II   HISTORICAL TIME: THE TOTALISING TEMPORALISATION OF HISTORY

What does the idea of history gain by a turn to the apparently even more abstract idea of time? Or to put it the other way around: what is added by the qualification 'historical' to the general idea of time?

39

It has become conventional, philosophically, to distinguish three main perspectives on time, associated with three different kinds of time: the objective or cosmological perspective (concerned with the time of nature); the subjective, lived or phenomenological perspective (concerned with duration or individual time-consciousness); and the intersubjective or social perspective (associated with a historical multiplicity of forms of time-consciousness which together make up the time of history or 'historical time'). This third perspective or 'kind of time' is generally taken to come in some disputed way between cosmological and phenomenological time. Ricoeur, for example, in his monumental *Time and Narrative*, sees what he calls 'properly historical time' as the product of narrative inscriptions of lived time onto cosmic time.[13]

Each perspective or kind of time is identified with a particular canonic literature. Thus, cosmological, objective, or natural time is identified paradigmatically with Aristotle and the discussion of time in Book IV of the *Physics*: specifically, the famous definition of time as 'the number of motion in respect of "before" and "after"'. Its main characterstics there are the *subordination of time to movement* (a reflection of the primacy of astronomy in Greek thought), and an image of time as an *infinite succession of identical instants*, split in relation to any one instant into a before and an after, an earlier and a later. This is what Martin Heidegger calls the 'ordinary' conception of time; what Benjamin refers to as 'empty homogeneous time'; and what Althusser describes as the 'ideological' conception of time as a homogeneous continuum.[14] It is essentially a way of measuring movement.

If we update the idea of nature beyond Aristotle's simple cosmological scheme, we may include within a significant broadening of this category the *periodic* times of various biological cycles and the complex and contradictory *relational* times of more recent astronomical and sub-atomic physical theory. These are very different times from Aristotle's, but they claim a broadly equivalent status, ontologically.

Phenomenological time, on the other hand, is generally taken to have its philosophical origins in Book XI of Augustine's *Confessions*, although one might trace it back further, to Plotinus.[15] It is paradigmatically associated with Husserl and his *Lectures on the Phenomenology of Internal Time Consciousness* (1905, published 1928). It is further developed by Bergson and Heidegger. Its main characteristics are *subordination of time to consciousness or human existence* (what Heidegger terms *Dasein*, or 'Being-there') as a dimension of its self-constituting activity, based not on the relation of before and after an instant, but on the permanently shifting, *self-differentiating*, *tripartite temporal division of past/present/future*. Past/present/future cannot be considered equivalent to before/present, instant/after, for two main reasons, each of which has to do with the specificity of the phenomenological present.

First, the concept of the present is not grasped by the Aristotelian idea of the instant because, as Augustine famously pointed out, it actually contains not just one, fleeting dimension of time but all three together. Past and future are not differentiated by their absence as opposed to their presence to consciousness, as Aristotle implied, but by the *form* of their presence as objects of memory and expectation, rather than attention, respectively. The present is actually a *'three-fold' present*: a present past, present present and present future. Secondly (and this was Bergson's and Husserl's point), the 'present present' is not a point-like instant, but an *expanded, longitudinal* present, which must retain elements of the recent past through projective identification if a continuity of experience is to be possible. The lived present has *duration*. It endures. It also includes certain expectations about the future. Projected futures are a central part of the existential structure of any present moment. Most importantly, famously, for Heidegger, is the anticipation of *death* as the transcendental horizon of human temporality, such that human existence is essentially defined as Being-towards-death. On this model, what we call 'time' is the reified result of an ongoing process of temporalisation, part of the *active (self-) production* of a particular kind of being, rather than a merely given form. For Heidegger: 'There is no nature-time, since all time belongs essentially to *Dasein*'.[16]

Finally, the multiple social times of history provide the object of a tradition of historiographic literature about calendars, clocks, and social time-consciousness which emphasises the social determination and historical variety of forms of collective time-consciousness. This work has often focused on struggles over the units of labour-time at various stages in the transition to capitalism (the day? the hour? the minute?) and the role of religious institutions in introducing scheduling into social life. It is represented by the tradition of the Annales School in France (such as Le Goff's classic, *Time, Work and Culture in the Middle Ages*), and in England by E.P. Thompson's 'Time, Work-Discipline and Industrial Capitalism'. More recently, Frederick Cooper's 'Colonising Time' essay has extended this kind of analysis of the temporal consequences of the imposition of wage-labour to the study of colonial Mombasa.[17]

The main feature of this type of time is its *social composition through struggle* over the conflicting rhythms of different definition of social practice (right down to the micro level of struggles over television schedules in domestic living-rooms), or the *objectification of subjective, phenomenological forms of time in collective, institutionalised forms*. It is manifest in the regulation of the calendars by holidays and feast days, for example, but also in the increasingly generalised (and subsequently 'naturalised') imposition of standard units for the measurement of time through navigational systems and the development of the railways. These developments are very recent. Clock time as we know it – that is, as a substitute for solar time – did not come into being until 1780, in Geneva. And it wasn't until 1966, for example, that the US Congress finally passed its Uniform Time Act. In the nineteenth century the time-reckoning in colonised countries tended to work differently depending on whether the colonisers came from the East or the West. And although there has been a World Standard Time since the Meridian Conference of 1884, it wasn't until 1940 that a country as central to modern European history as Holland synchronised itself with the rest of the world.[18]

This literature includes the historiography of historical consciousness (historical accounts of the emergence of different ideas of history) and the semantics of historical time, as the past is extended longitudinally, in various ways, back beyond the memory of the living to embrace the community of the dead through tradition, and the future is extended forwards to include the expectation of various different ends to history and hence to historical time: Doomsday, the Last Judgment, Communism.[19]

So, it would seem that not all time is 'historical'; at least, not in the technical sense, or so the literature would have it. However, as will perhaps already be evident, there are actually two rather different kinds of time at issue under the general heading of 'historical time' here. There are the *multiple* temporalities associated with the historical and geographical diversity of social practices,[20] and there is the *single overarching* temporality – the time of History with a capital H – through which these multiple temporalities are unified, *if* they are unified, into a single complex stream. It is the relationship between the two which lies at the heart of debates about the concept of history. It is the latter (emphatic) sense of historical time that I am concerned with here – the time of history in the collective singular – and its philosophical justification; or rather, as I would prefer to put it, the implications of its inescapability. For if we accept the early Heidegger's account of the phenomenological unity of temporalisation (independently of the deeply problematic reduction of history to 'historicality' which it follows in the text of *Being and Time*), we may infer that, phenomenologically at least, some kind of totalisation of social times into 'history' cannot be avoided.

The key to this argument lies in the internal relations between the ideas of *temporalisation, totalisation and narrativity*. All temporalisation is of phenomenological necessity an ongoing process of differentiated unification of three temporal ecstases (past, present and future) through which human existence is constituted as something 'outside-of-itself' and hence open to history.[21] In this sense, what we call 'time' is the idealised horizon of 'the totalisation of existence'.[22] Conversely, totalisation is of phenomenological necessity a temporal process which operates with only projected closures of the temporal horizon. Yet such closures are necessary if events are to be endowed with meaning. Time acquires meaning by taking on the structure of a narrative. Narrative is the meaningful unification of temporal relations. The attempt to avoid such temporal relations through the structuralist methodology of synchronic analysis serves only to underline their point, since its artificial negation of time places the results of such analyses, in principle, beyond the horizon of any possible practice, until they are mediated with experience through some process of temporalisation.

Furthermore, just as according to Heidegger, the anticipation of death is a condition, existentially, for the temporalisation of 'time' in general, so the projection or anticipation of some historical end is a condition, hermeneutically, for the constitution of a temporal horizon beyond the generational reach of a living individual. The phenomenological structure of temporality – to which all time must at some level conform, in order to be mediated with experience – dictates that there be *no historical experience without the implicit anticipation of an end of history*.

This is to say at once a great deal and very little, depending on one's point of view. From the standpoint of some great debate between opponents and defenders of the possibility of historical totalisation, it is a decisive intervention. It cuts the Gordian knot of the epistemological struggle between identity and difference, returning the deconstruction of time to the methodological position of a second reflection, from which its less enthusiastic adherents have never sought to displace it. The 'temporising detour of deferral' registered by Derrida's concept of différance *constitutes*, rather than challenges, the movement of totalisation. Its 'infinitesimal [yet] radical' displacement of Hegelian discourse is precisely that: a displacement of Hegelianism, not an end to totalisation. If this argument is sound, then all disputes about historical totalisation must be read as arguments about specific forms of totalisation and their limits, without generalisable implication for the idea of totalisation *per se*.[23]

From the standpoint of those for whom the debate was always about specific *forms* of totalisation, their meanings and limits, however, we have merely a new point of departure from which a number of arguments can set out anew. There is no space to embark on this journey here, except to note that, since the 'end' in question cannot be posited as the realisation of an immanent telos without negation of the differential constitutive of temporality itself, totalisation will have to find another standpoint – in some kind of 'exteriority' perhaps.[24] If the critique of historicism places Benjamin in the unlikely company of both Althusser and Popper, his insistence on an alternative standpoint for the totalisation of history distances him from them, definitively.[25]

The early Heideggerian provenance of this line of thought distinguishes it in principle from the temporality of Hegelianism in at least two crucial respects. On the one hand, the acknowledgement of the *finitude* of human existence at the centre of Heidegger's discussion of *Dasein* places strict hermeneutical limits on the epistemological status of historical interpretations, however successful they might be (this has particular significance for the cognitive status of historical 'ends', and their relations to the historical present). On the other hand, however, if pursued in another direction, this stress on human finitude opens up the phenomenology of historical time-consciousness to the material of both the natural and social sciences, demanding an integral account of the three kinds of time referred to above ('natural', 'phenomenological' and 'socio-historical'): the totalisation of social times into 'historical time' requires the totalisation of all three kinds of time – the totalisation of time – as history. Such an approach departs radically from Heidegger's association of time with the question of the meaning of Being in general, in favour of the establishment of theoretical connections with the development of various positive knowledges, in the spirit of a renewal (but by no means a mere repetition) of the trajectory of Frankfurt School Critical Theory.[26]

III POLITICS AND EXPERIENCE

How do these abstract theoretical matters bear, concretely, upon the comprehension of history, let alone anything which might appear under the heading of a *politics* of time? What is implied for the idea of politics by a rethinking of the philosophy of history from the standpoint of the philosophy of time?

The connection lies in the concept of experience, and more specifically, in the possibility of '*historical experience*', using this phrase in the doubly emphatic sense of history (history as a whole, history in the collective singular, the totalisation of time) and an emphatic sense of experience (*Enfahrung* as opposed to *Erlebnis* – something which is acquired and learnt from, as opposed to merely 'lived through'). This is a sense of experience which has little in common with dominant empiricist conceptions, although it is connected to one of E.P. Thompson's usages of the term.[27] In Benjamin's writings, the concept of experience is developed in increasing proximity to the concept of history and its political significance is determined, above all, by its temporal structures. For it is through experience that different categories of historical totalisation – such as 'modernity' and 'tradition', 'progress' and 'decline' – are lived as *socially produced forms of*

time-consciousness through which history is made (or forgotten). If structural
categories of historical analysis like 'capitalism' are to be rendered effective
at the level of political experience, they will need to be mediated by these
phenomenologically more fundamental categories of historical time through
which history is lived as an ongoing temporalisation.[28]

Two main points can be extracted from Benjamin's writings at this
point. The first concerns the centrality of *totalising temporalisations of history*
to the structure of *everyday experience* in capitalist societies. This is the object
of Benjamin's own distinctive sociology of modernity: excavation of the
competing totalisations of history (competing forms of temporal totality)
built into the interpretive structures of our social practices at a variety of
levels. The second is the rather more problematic redefinition of 'the
political' as a *mode of temporalisation*, such that the terms 'political experience' and 'historical experience' (in the doubly emphatic sense referred to
above) become more or less equivalent.[29] For the fundamental categories of
historical experience – categories like 'progress' and 'reaction', 'revolution',
'crisis', 'conservation', 'stagnation' and 'the new' – are not the products of
different totalisations of historical material across a common temporal frame.
They are not just based on different *selections* of which historical material is
significant. They are alternative temporal structures, alternative *temporalisations
of 'history'*, which structure experience temporally – offering alternative
articulations of historical pasts, presents, and futures – in what are, politically, significantly different ways.

It is in this sense that I write of a 'politics of time' – indeed, of all
politics as centrally involving *struggles over the experience of time*. How do the
forms of the social practices in which we engage structure and produce,
enable or distort different senses of time? What kinds of experience of
history do they make possible or inhibit? Whose future do they ensure?
Conversely, all temporalisations involve specific orientations to *practice*, since
they provide alternative structures through which past, present and future
may be fused together to define the temporal structure of action. A politics
of time would attend to the temporal logic of these structures insofar as
they open onto, or foreclose, specific historical possibilities, in distinctive
temporal modes. It would rethink the political significance of social practices from the standpoint of their temporal forms. Think, for example, of
the way in which the political significance of the level of unemployment
in capitalist societies is determined by the horizon of expectation within
which it is received; and of how that horizon is related to broader forms
of historical consciousness.

This brings me, in conclusion, back to the quotation from Bourdieu
with which I began: the idea that 'the simple possibility that things might
proceed otherwise . . . is sufficient to change the *whole experience of practice*

and, by the same idea, its logic'. For this is a possibility which must not only be *lived* as a possibility, but, thereby, *produced* as possibility, for Bourdieu's point to hold true. What appears initially in Bourdieu's text as a comment about the probabilistic logic of social laws, only becomes a point about practice if uncertainty is internalised as the basis of strategy: 'substituting the dialectic of strategies for the mechanics of the model, but without falling over into the imaginary anthropology of theories of the "rational actor" '.[30] Just as possibility (as a category of action) depends upon the internalisation of uncertainty as the basis of strategy, so politics (in the classical sense)[31] depends upon what we might call the *social production of possibility* at the level of historical time-consciousness.

'Possibility' is produced by and as the temporal structure of particular types of action, it is sustained by others, and eroded and undermined by others still. And it is produced in a variety of temporal forms. It is in this deep structural sense that there is a crucial political significance to culture – culture as formation, not culture as value – and a need for a left cultural politics which would engage in the willed transformation of the social forms of subjectivity at their deepest structural levels. For it is these forms, including the form of the 'political' itself, which determine (and ration) the social production of possibility. 'The simple possibility that things might proceed otherwise' must be produced as experience if the otherwise is to proceed.

NOTES

This is a revised version of a talk given at the *Radical Philosophy* conference, 'The Politics of Experience', at Birkbeck College, University of London, on 13 November 1993. It was originally published, in a slightly different form, in *Radical Philosophy* 68 (Autumn 1994). It deals with arguments which are treated in greater detail in Peter Osborne, *The Politics of Time: Modernity and the Avant-Garde* (London: Verso, 1995).

1. Francis Fukuyama, *The End of History and the Last Man* (Harmondsworth: Penguin, 1992); Fredric Jameson, *Postmodernism, or the Cultural Logic of Late Capitalism* (London: Verso, 1991).
2. See Lutz Niethammer, *Posthistoire: Has History Come to an End?*, trans. Patrick Camiller (London: Verso, 1992) for an account of both the structure and the history of this inversion.
3. See, for example, Joseph McCarney, 'Endgame of History', *Radical Philosophy* 62 (Autumn 1992) and 'Shaping Ends: Reflections on Fukuyama', *New Left*

Review 202 (Nov.–Dec. 1993); Gregory Elliott, 'Cards of Confusion: Historical Communism and the End of History', *Radical Philosophy* 64 (Summer 1993).

4. I am thinking of Jean-François Lyotard's *The Postmodern Condition*, trans. Geoffrey Bennington and Brian Massumi (Minneapolis: University of Minnesota Press, 1984). Fukuyama might be read as countering Lyotard's Left Nietzscheanism with a more geo-politically realistic, Hegelian Nietzscheanism of the Right.

5. G.W.F. Hegel, *Reason in History: A General Introduction to the Philosophy of History*, trans. Robert S. Hartman (Indianapolis: Bobbs-Merrill, 1953), p. 27.

6. Jürgen Harbermas, *The Philosophical Discourse of Modernity*, trans. Frederick Lawrence (Cambridge, Mass.: MIT Press, 1987), ch. 1, and *The Theory of Communicative Action, Volume Two, Lifeworld and System: A Critique of Functionalist Reason*, trans. Thomas McCarthy (Cambridge: Polity Press, 1987), ch. 6 and 8. For a discussion of the distinctive abstractness of 'modernity' as a form of 'historical time-consciousness', see my *The Politics of Time*, ch. 1, 'Modernity: A Different Time'. I take the opposition of historical temporality of narrative to the instantaneity of the image from the work of Walter Benjamin. However, for a critique of the undialectical and ultimately unsustainable character of Benjamin's treatment of this opposition, see *The Politics of Time*, ch. 4, pp. 134–59.

7. Paul Ricoeur, *Time and Narrative*, vol. 3, trans. Kathleen Blamey and David Pellauer (Chicago: University of Chicago Press, 1988), pp. 204–5.

8. G.W.F. Hegel, *Phanomenologie des Geistes* (Frankfurt: Ullstein, 1970), p. 29. *Hegel's Phenomenology of Spirit*, trans. A.V. Miller (Oxford: Oxford University Press, 1977), p. 19. Translation altered.

9. Max Horkheimer, 'Traditional and Critical Theory' (1937) in *Critical Theory: Selected Essays*, trans. Matthew J. O'Connell *et al.* (New York: Herder and Herder, 1972), p. 238.

10. Ludwig Feuerbach, 'Towards a Critique of Hegelian Philosophy', trans. Zawar Hanfi, in *The Fiery Brook: Selected Writings of Ludwig Feuerbach* (New York: Anchor Books, 1972).

11. For a recent variation on this critique, under the more precise heading of the 'eternalisation of the present', see Ricoeur, *Time and Narrative*, vol. 3, ch. 9, 'Should we Renounce Hegel?'.

12. For a reading of Benjamin's cultural criticism as the working out of a philosophy of historical time *in concreto*, see my 'Small-Scale Victories, Large-Scale Defeats: Walter Benjamin's Politics of Time', in Andrew Benjamin and Peter Osborne, eds, *Walter Benjamin's Philosophy: Destruction and Experience* (London: Routledge, 1993). Sartre's position is strikingly reminiscent of Benjamin's: 'Marxism caught a glimpse of true temporality when it criticised and destroyed the bourgeois notion of "progress" . . . But – without ever having said so – . . . renounced these studies and preferred to make use of "progress" again for its own benefit'. Jean-Paul Sartre, *Search for a Method* (1960), trans. Hazel Barnes (New York: Vintage Books, 1968), p. 92. However, it is not clear that after 1,200 pages of the *Critique of Dialectical Reason* Sartre got any closer to the 'true temporality' of history himself. Symptomatically, his most extensive remarks on the subject are to be found in the notes assembled as the appendix to the unfinished second volume. Jean-Paul Sartre, *Critique of Dialectical Reason, Volume Two (Unfinished): The Intelligibility of History*, trans. Quinton Hoare (London: Verso, 1991). In the text itself, Sartre returns repeatedly to the totalising structure of individual action, the exposition of which is progressively deepened, but he breaks off before 'the advent of history'.

13. Ricoeur, *Time and Narrative*, vol. 3, p. 99. See also Cornelius Castoriadis, 'Time and Creation', in John Bender and David E. Wellbury, eds, *Chronotopes: The Construction of Time* (Stanford: Stanford University Press, 1991). Oscillation between the languages of 'perspectives' and 'times' is a distinctive feature of most recent philosphical literature on time. It is as initially productive as it is ultimately problematic.

14. Martin Heidegger, *Being and Time* (1927), trans. John Macquarrie and Edward Robinson (Oxford: Basil Blackwell, 1969), division 2, part 6; Walter Benjamin, 'Theses on the Philosophy of History', trans. Harry Zohn, in *Illuminations* (London: Fontana, 1973); Louis Althusser, 'The Errors of Classical Economics: An Outline for a Concept of Historical Time', in Louis Althusser and Etienne Balibar, *Reading Capital* (1968), trans. Ben Brewster (London: Verso, 1979). The Heideggerian roots of Althusser's discussion of differential temporality are rarely appreciated.

15. See Genevieve Lloyd, *Being in Time: Selves and Narrators in Philosophy and Literature* (London: Routledge, 1993).

16. Martin Heidegger, *The Basic Problems of Phenomenology* (1927), trans. Albert Hofstader (Indianapolis: Indiana University Press, 1982), p. 262. Translation altered.

17. Jacques Le Goff, *Time, Work and Culture in the Middle Ages*, trans. Arthur Goldhammer (Chicago: Chicago University Press, 1989); Edward Thompson, 'Time, Work-Discipline and Industrial Capitalism', *Past and Present* 38 (1967); Frederick Cooper, 'Colonising Time: Work Rhythms and Labour Conflict in Colonial Mombasa', in Nicholas B. Dirks, ed., *Colonialism and Culture* (Ann Arbor: University of Michigan Press, 1992). See also Eviatar Zerubaval, 'The Benedictine Ethic and the Modern Spirit of Scheduling', *Sociological Review* 50 (1993).

18. The examples are taken from Eviatar Zerubaval, 'The Standardisation of Time: A Sociohistorical Perspective', *American Journal of Sociology* 88:1 (1988). For a broader developmental perspective on time as the 'symbol of a socially learned synthesis', see Norbert Elias, *Time: An Essay*, trans. Edmund Jephcott (Oxford: Basil Blackwell, 1992).

19. Herbert Butterfield, *The Origins of History* (London: Methuen, 1981); Reinhart Koselleck, *Futures Past: On the Semantics of Historical Time*, trans. Keith Tribe (Cambridge, Mass.: MIT Press, 1985).

20. Western anthropology has traditionally read socio-spatial distance as temporal, for a critique of which see Johannes Fabian, *Time and the Other: How Anthropology Makes its Object* (New York: Columbia University Press, 1983).

21. Heidegger, *Being and Time*, p. 377.

22. Ricoeur, *Time and Narrative*, vol. 3, p. 66. Cf. Jean-Paul Sartre, *Critique of Dialectical Reason, Volume One: Theory of Practical Ensembles*, trans. Alan Sheridan-Smith (London: Verso, 1976), p. 53. For all his interest in the social, Sartre's mistake, following Heidegger, was to conceive of such totalisation as an irreducibly 'individual' rather than an intersubjective process.

23. Jacques Derrida, 'Différance', in *Margins of Philosophy*, trans. Alan Bass (Hemel Hempstead: Harvester, 1982), p. 14; Gayatri Spivak, 'Remembering the Limits: Difference, Identity and Practice', in Peter Osborne, ed., *Socialism and the Limits of Liberalism* (London: Verso, 1991). For the notion of philosophy as second reflection, see Theodor Adorno, *Negative Dialectics*, trans. E.B. Ashton (London: Routledge, 1973).

24. See Osborne, *The Politics of Time*, ch. 3–5.

25. For an attempt to use Althusser and Benjamin *together*, see Susan Buck-Morss, 'Fashion in Ruins: History after the Cold War', *Radical Philosophy* 68 (Autumn 1994). Popper's hostility to historical totalisation per se – which is not unlike that of much contemporary postmodernism – derived from a scepticism about historical prediction. His distance from Benjamin on the question of historical knowledge could hardly be greater.

26. Cf. Ricoeur, *Time and Narrative*, vol. 3, 'Towards a Hermeneutics of Historical Consciousness'. However, my position differs from Ricoeur's in three important respects: 1) in extending the notion of totalisation to the unity of all temporalisations, and thus to 'narrative' in its most fundamental structural form (Ricoeur arbitrarily restricts his use of the term 'totalisation' to the Hegelian form); 2) in reading his 'narrative' mediation of cosmological and phenomenological forms as being of ontological as well as poetic significance; 3) consequently, in continuing to insist on the practical significance of the philosophical attempt to totalise time, beyond the (essentially religious) consolation of the contemplation of its mystery.

27. For a discussion of which, see Perry Anderson, *Arguments within English Marxism* (London: Verso, 1980), ch. 2. Compare Adorno's reminder that for Hegel: 'Nothing can be known "that is not in experience"', *Hegel: Three Studies*, trans. Shierry Weber Nicholsen (Cambridge, Mass.: MIT Press, 1993), p. 54.

28. I take this to be the point of Susan Buck-Morss's extension of the concept of fashion to the analysis of epochal transformations such as the collapse of historical communism, in her 'Fashion in Ruins'.

29. This strategy can be traced back to Benjamin's reception of Surrealism. See 'Surrealism: The Latest Snapshot of the European Intelligentsia', in *One-Way Street and Other Writing* (London: New Left Books, 1979).

30. Pierre Bourdieu, *The Logic of Practice*, trans. Richard Nice (Cambridge: Polity Press, 1990), p. 99. Translation altered.

31. Jürgen Habermas, 'The Classical Doctrine of Politics in Relation to Social Philosophy', in *Theory and Practice*, trans. John Viertal (London: Heinemann, 1974).

CHAPTER FOUR

Now, here, this

Thomas Docherty

I

The question of 'the contemporary' is, almost by definition, a problem of representation. A presentation of the present must always involve a re-presenting, which has the effect of marking the present moment with the passage of time. 'The contemporary' (the 'with-time'-ness of the present) thus has the effect of introducing an element of heterogeneity and difference into what is or should be homogeneous, self-identical, the self-present as such. There is a second complication to 'the contemporary'. The term operates as a deictic, shifting its sense depending on where and when it is spoken. It therefore requires a Subject of consciousness, an 'I', in relation to which something can be proposed precisely as the contemporary of the 'I'. Contemporaneity 'happens' when an 'I' is produced as a Subject sharing a time – even a moment – with an event, and producing in that relation a specific solace of identification, by which I mean to say that contemporaneity in such circumstances produces a fiction of the Self as an entity persisting in time across the various events which make up that Self's history or biography.[1]

We can see this most clearly at work, perhaps, in that most deictic of literary forms, the confession. When Auerbach considered the problem of representation in *Mimesis*, he turned to the *Confessions* of Augustine. This is a text in which, necessarily, the Subject of the discourse appears to be present, 'here, now'. In Book 10, Chapter 3, Augustine writes:

> What does it profit me, then, O Lord . . . I ask, also to make known to
> men in your sight, through this book, not what I once was, but what I
> am now? I know what profit I gain by confessing my past, and this I have
> declared. But many people who know me, and others who do not know

me but have heard of me or read my books, wish to hear what I am now,
at this moment, as I set down my confessions.[2]

Auerbach notes in this text a new attitude to time, an attitude which we
can see clearly replicated at the beginning of an emergent modernity in the
eighteenth-century novel, whose concerns were to be a kind of 'writing to
the minute', a journalistic identification and description of present or modern times.[3] First, Auerbach indicates the stylistic break which Augustine
makes from the erstwhile normative classical traditions, a stylistic break into
a modernity of sorts. Considering a passage from Book 6, Chapter 8 (in
which we have a description of Alypius going to a gladiatorial contest),
Auerbach notes the prevalence of what he characterises as a specifically
'Christian' style of parataxis (a linking of narrated events by 'and then . . .
and then'):

> Instead of the causal or at least temporal hypotaxis which we should
> expect in classical Latin . . . [we get] a parataxis with *et* [*and*]; and this
> procedure, far from weakening the interdependence of the two events,
> brings it out most emphatically: just as in English it is more dramatically
> effective to say: He opened his eyes and was struck . . . than: When he
> opened his eyes, or: Upon opening his eyes, he was struck.[4]

This modernising style of 'Christian' parataxis produces a new and different
conception of time, argues Auerbach. It necessitates what he calls 'figural'
interpretation, in which events are seen to be linked not by cause and effect
and not even in a necessarily linear chronological fashion. Events, rather, are
connected when 'occurrences are vertically linked to Divine Providence,
which alone is able to devise such a plan of history and supply the key to
its understanding'.[5] That is to say, events are linked by dint of the fact that
their significance always depends upon a single referent which acts as their
self-evident and single horizon of interpretation. In its literary manifestations, 'figural' time constructs the position of an omniscient narrator whose
single point of view on the ostensibly divergent elements of the narrative
guarantees the univocal meaning of the entire story. To put it in the terms
I have used above, events are linked by the fact that the Subject position
which marks their temporality is that of a transcendent God, who sees all
'contemporaneously'. The result, as Auerbach points out, is *homogenisation*
of time and, as a corollary, the production of what becomes known as a
'Universal History', a history in which all events are fundamentally a part of
the same monolithic story.

It is perhaps for this reason that Jean-François Lyotard can take a specific
interest in Augustine, and that he can claim him as a paradigmatic example
of a certain version of modernity. Like Auerbach, Lyotard considers 'the
modern' to be a matter of mood and attitude (or 'Subject-position') rather
than a simple indicator of temporality or contemporaneity. For him, the

modern is not a period (and thus, by extension, neither can the postmodern be thought of as simply that which comes 'after' the modern). Lyotard adds to the discussion of Augustinian temporality a further specifically 'modern' element, derived from the philosophy of the early modern European period. He adds the Subject-position in that other great 'confessional' text, Descartes's *Discourse on Method*. That Subject-position ascribes to itself precisely the mastery implicit in Augustine's notion of 'Divine Providence', and enables thereby the production of the specific literary form of omniscient, plot-dominated narrative, such as we have it developed and extended in the novel from the eighteenth century onwards. The culmination of this combination of temporal attitude and masterful Subject upon whom the meanings of history itself are seen to depend is in the production of the *Bildungsroman*, a form in which the horizon of interpretation, and thus the ultimate refer-ent, is not a form of Divine Providence but rather a unified (if fictional) human Self, a human Subject thought to persist across time. (That is to say, it produces the human Subject in the form of a transcendent monotheistic – indeed Christian – God.)

Auerbach indicates quite clearly what happens in this state of affairs to the notion of the contemporary, or the now:

> the here and now is no longer a mere link in an earthly chain of events, it is simultaneously something which has always been and which will be fulfilled in the future . . . This conception of history is magnificent in its homogeneity.[6]

We might set alongside this passage an interesting comment from Lyotard's essay on 'Time Today', in which he addresses Leibniz's *Monadology*. From this text, Lyotard points out that:

> God is the absolute monad to the extent that he conserves in complete retention the totality of information constituting the world. And if divine retention is to be complete, it must also include those pieces of information not yet presented to the incomplete monads, such as our minds, and which remain to come in what we call the future. In this perspective, the 'not yet' is due only to the limit on the faculty of synthesis available to the intermediary monads. For the absolute memory of God, the future is always already given. We can thus conceive, for the temporal condition, an upper limit determined by a perfect recording or archival capacity. As consummate archivist, God is outside time.[7]

The function fulfilled in relation to time by God for Augustine is analogous to the function fulfilled by forms of information technology today: it is the eradication of historicity. Lyotard goes on:

> Complete information means neutralizing more events. What is already known cannot, in principle, be experienced as an event. Consequently, if one wants to control a process, the best way of so doing is to subordinate

the present to what is (still) called the 'future', since in these conditions
the 'future' will be completely predetermined and the present itself will
cease opening onto an uncertain and contingent 'afterwards'. Better: what
comes 'after' the 'now' will have to come 'before' it.[8]

This collocation of Auerbach and Lyotard helps strengthen the claim
that a Universal History is, paradoxically, peculiarly devoid of historicity.
In its homogeneity and implicit simultaneity, its time is oddly 'empty',
empty of events; and in its 'magnificent homogeneity', its time is also
extraordinarily anti- or non-social. If the ultimate referent of the now is
always the transcendental, be it God or a fictional transcendental Subject,
then the now as experienced by specific human agents is always entirely
isolated from the temporal existence of all other human agents. Emmanuel
Levinas indicates the contradiction implicit in this conception of temporality
when he shows, in *Le Temps et l'autre*, that 'time is not something made by
a singular and isolated subject . . . rather it is the very relation of a subject
with others'.[9]

In what follows I shall indicate first the contradictory philosophy of
identity at work in this conception of homogeneous time; and secondly, I
shall advance the case for a different order of temporality.

II

Aesthetic modernism, by which I mean that explosion of aesthetic experimentation across Europe from 1848 to 1939, infiltrating America at the
turn of the century, advances a specifically new conception of the priority
of the human Subject of consciousness. In some ways, the conception of
this Subject is extremely optimistic, in the weak sense of that term: the
Subject's individuality, considered to exist prior to its historical construction or enactments, is seen as a bolster for the emergent modern democracy
in which an individual autonomy is the condition of social existence.[10] Yet
it is exactly such an autonomy which – in its deviation into the validation
of individualism and of the priority of the Subject over the objects of an
exterior world – eradicates historicity precisely at the moment when it
appears most fully to be internalising the movement of history itself.

Put more bluntly: the human Subject is no longer seen as simply the
victim of a history to which it is subjected, as an emergent bourgeois
democracy claims the principle of Subjective autonomy and the possibility
of active intervention and determination of history by the individuated

Subject of consciousness. 'I' am/is free precisely to the extent that I am 'I', or, axiomatically, the modern Subject is free to shape and determine its history. Yet this, while seeming to offer the Subject the possibility of internalising the movement of history (and thus controlling it, subduing it to the identity of the self), does so at the cost of that very heterogeneity which is of the essence of historical change. Instead of history as event (in the Lyotardian sense of the event as the non-predetermined), we have history as narrative, in which the identification of the Subject of the narrative is of paramount importance and in which such an identification makes the Subject omniscient, transcendent, and therefore expelled from the movement of history itself. Modernism claims and denies history simultaneously: it generates the 'scandal' or threat of human diversity in order to forestall the possibilities of genuine, fundamental historical change.

This is clear in the thinking of T.S. Eliot. Like Augustine, he too pondered the question of time, both in his poetry and in his criticism. While in *Four Quartets* he appeared to be able to conceptualise a present moment which is rendered non-self-identical through the irruption in the present of time past and time future, in his criticism such a state of affairs seems to elude him. The most obvious theoretical site for discussion here is his essay on 'Tradition and the Individual Talent' in which he argues – seemingly at one with the thought of the later *Four Quartets* – for the necessity of acquiring 'tradition', an acquisition that requires a specific critical mood or attitude. It is part of the work of a critic, argues Eliot, to see literature whole, rather like the way in which history might appear to Divine Providence in Auerbach's description of 'figural' interpretation, and, writes Eliot, 'this is eminently to see it not as consecrated by time, but to see it beyond time; to see the best work of our time and the best work of twenty-five hundred years ago with the same eyes'.[11]

Yet this tradition, like the historical sense which Eliot claims is so crucial to it, is not inert. He writes that

> the historical sense involves a perception, not only of the pastness of the past, but of its presence . . . The historical sense, which is a sense of the timeless as well as of the temporal and of the timeless and of the temporal together, is what makes a writer traditional. And it is at the same time what makes a writer most acutely conscious of his place in time, of his contemporaneity.[12]

For Eliot, of course, the point of acquiring such tradition is in order to facilitate the becoming of the 'individual talent', a talent marked by a specific *identifiable* consciousness whose validation or legitimation lies not (as Eliot indicates at length himself) in personality, but rather in the Subject as the *medium* for poetry and for the tradition itself. In this arrangement, history (or the tradition) becomes dependent for its articulation (or its narration) on the identity of the Subject of consciousness in whose grasp (or voice) it is recorded or archivally maintained. Eliot, thus, sees tradition as instrumental in the construction of a philosophy not of personality but of identity; and such a philosophy is inimical to temporality itself. It is for this reason that Eliot can comfortably claim in his poetry that easy intimacy among past, present, future: all three are dependent upon the logical priority of the identity of the Subject who narrates – in 'figural' fashion – their interrelations or their fundamental identification with each other. Identity – and this is the meaning of Levinas – is the counter to history; and the formulation, thus, of a history based upon the priority of the modern autonomous Subject is inherently anti- or non-historical. I do not claim that this state of affairs is anything other than paradoxical, even counter-intuitive.

Walter Benjamin would seem, at first glance, to be an ally in countering the figural or sacred interpretation of history implicit in Eliot's position. In Benjamin's 'Theses on the Philosophy of History', he is at some pains to distinguish historical materialism (which is good) from historicism (which is bad). He writes that '[h]istoricism rightly culminates in universal history', and goes on to argue that '[u]niversal history has no theoretical armature. Its method is additive; it musters a mass of data to fill the homogeneous, empty time.'[13] That additive principle of parataxis – with its concomitant product, homogeneous and empty time – reappears here. For Benjamin – more restless, less optimistic, than Auerbach in these matters – such a time is not yet and cannot yet be history: 'Materialist historiography, on the other hand, is based on a constructive [i.e. not additive] principle. Thinking involves not only the flow of thoughts, but their arrest as well.'[14]

It is such an 'arrest' that is to be taken up in later philosophy as the 'event': that irruption into a theoretically comprehensible schema or order of things of some unforeseeable item which demands, but which cannot have, its recuperation into the predetermining theory which has produced its possibility in the first place. This 'arrest-event' is that which makes no sense according to the terms, conditions and norms of the very theory or history that has produced it for our inspection. 'Auschwitz' has become a classic example of this for some postmodern thinkers in that Auschwitz ostensibly cannot be explained by the terms of modernity and enlightenment, even if it has been produced by the very same reason that shapes enlightened modernity as such.[15] The irruption of the event is thus the interruption of our norms by something rather 'singular' (idiosyncratic, *purely* and literally autonomous); and insofar as it is singular in these terms, this event is the introduction of – or, better, *presentation* of – that which was not promised or foreseen, and thus of that which was not always already *represented*.[16]

The idea of a 'contemporary' which would be a 'real presence' – not implicitly subject to representation – is important to Benjamin. He argues for the necessity of a *Jetztzeit*, a 'now-time' in Thesis 14, claiming that '[h]istory is the subject of a structure whose site is not homogeneous, empty time, but time filled by the presence of the now'.[17] So far, this appears to be the demand for a different order of time from that enjoyed by Eliot. Benjamin appears to criticise historicism on the grounds not only that it represents history as seen from the point of the view of the victors in those struggles constitutive of history itself, but also – and more fundamentally – on the grounds that it *represents* at all. The *Jetztzeit* in its full 'nowness' is inimical to the Eliotic principle that time past is contained in time future, or that past, present and future all commingle under some sacred sign or horizon of interpretation. And yet in Appendix A to his 'Theses', Benjamin comes so close to Eliot as to be almost indistinguishable from him. It is in this appendix that he argues for a complexity in the notion of historical cause and effect. He rejects simple linearity, describing that as a way of telling history like telling rosary beads (in 'Christian' fashion), and argues instead that the historian must 'grasp the constellation which his own era has formed with a definite earlier one. Thus he establishes a conception of the present as the "time of the now" which is shot through with chips of Messianic time.'[18]

This ostensible indecision between two contrasting notions of time is perhaps resolved slightly more clearly in Thesis 16. There, Benjamin argues for the indispensability of a concept of the 'now' which is not merely a transition, a now in which time has, as it were, stopped. In the argument, we get an especially vigorous metaphor, which is all the more striking or 'eventful'/arresting for the fact that nothing elsewhere in the theses prepares the reader – or indeed Benjamin – for it:

> Historicism gives the 'eternal' image of the past; historical materialism supplies a unique experience with the past. The historical materialist leaves it to others to be drained by the whore called 'Once upon a time' in historicism's bordello. He remains in control of his powers, man enough to blast open the continuum of history.[19]

The first sentence here is unsurprising, and strengthens the claim that there are two competing conceptions of history in contest: the universal and homogenising set against the discrete, particular and heterogeneous. But from where does the metaphor which suddenly follows this sentence emerge? What we have here is not an argument as much as a characterisation of the historical materialist: a fictional Self or Subject in a narrative situation. Benjamin produces, through the metaphor, a construction of the historical materialist as a character in a tale: he is identified as the austere and manly master of the Self or of his own Subjectivity. He is the autonomous Subject, unthreatened, unseduced by any dissolution of his material corporeal Self, a Self dedicated to itself, determined to open a future rather than dwell in the arms of a female past of 'Once upon a time'. Yet the effect is, nonetheless, that of the narrative which begins 'Once upon a time, there was a historical materialist who, though tempted by the seductions of the world, yet remained above them, the austere Subject of consciousness in control of his Objects or those Others against whom he defined and maintained himself in readiness for action'. This self-dramatising is a re-run of Descartes, the modern philosopher doubting the external world and then refiguring it entirely based upon his own *dubio* and *cogito*. It is Augustine the paratactician who wanted to resist the seductions of the world – but 'not yet'; it is Eliot the sacred critic, austerely denying personality (and thereby indirectly gaining it).

What remains constant throughout these examples is the construction of a philosophy of identity (in fact or more precisely a philosophy of Subjectivity) which, as I have indicated, is not only modernist but also non-secular (Christian, Messianic, sacred) and hence profoundly anti- or non-historical. The 'now' in modernity does not – cannot – exist as such. The function of history in these terms is to bolster the illusion or fiction of the self, a self which had been threatened by temporality itself right from the moment in the Enlightenment when Hume argued against any philosophy based on the foundational principle of a stable selfhood. In what follows now, I shall look at a counter-position to what I have described as the denial of history that is the modern.

III

For Levinas, time is the condition of our relation with alterity – that is to say, it is the condition of our being and our sociality – as such. I want to extend this slightly and to make the case that the now – or contemporaneity – can occur as a historical event if and only if it is marked by an intrinsic heterogeneity: now cannot happen now, so to speak.

In the 'figural' view of the now as described above, history is homogenised: the singularity of the historical event is lost under the sign of representation as the historian, ideally omniscient, constructs a universal history in which the single event makes sense as the representation of another event in relation to which it constructs its horizon of interpretability, or in which semiotic constellations are constructed, to be mastered by the individual consciousness of the Subject of history, the human and individually identified agent. I propose here a different notion of contemporaneity, one which demands the necessity of precisely attending to singularity and to the heterogeneity of the events constitutive of historical activity, agency and being. The philosophy which lays this most bare is perhaps that of Clément Rosset, who argues that the real is real if and only if it cannot be duplicated, and hence that an event is real (or 'historical', to put it in the terms of my argument) if and only if it is inimical to a primary representation, if and only if it is conditioned by its idiosyncracy and its unimaginability.[20]

While the source of an offensive modernity such as that described earlier might be found in Augustine's Christian parataxis, we might find an alternative – I am tempted to say postmodern – attitude or mood in the thinking of Duns Scotus. I do not propose here an in-depth engagement with Scotist philosophy; rather, all I wish to retain from his thinking is the importance of *haecceitas* or 'thisness': that attention to specificity which is recapitulated not only in the philosophy of Rosset but also in that of Deleuze, Agamben, and other recent 'anatheoretical' thinkers.[21] Instead of prioritising the individuality of the Subject (as in the modern), Scotus prioritises the individuality of the Object of cognition, in an uncanny prefiguration of the 'fatal strategies' of Baudrillard.[22] For Scotus, the world consists of singularities; and, for the poet who was most directly and overtly influenced by Scotist philosophy, Hopkins, such an attitude resulted in a peculiar warping of language. There is no prevalence of parataxis in Hopkins's poetry, but rather the attempt to render everything in an object at once: its presence or nowness.

The peculiarity of Hopkins's language is increasingly apparent in some more recent writing. There is a stylistic feature developing, influenced if not by Hopkins then by poets such as William Carlos Williams and Wallace Stevens. In this style, we find increasing attention to what we can see as 'not ideas about the thing but the thing itself' and an increasing belief in a specific materialism or empiricism which suggests that there are 'no ideas but in things'. There is a post-Heideggerian poetry of 'the Thing' itself; and this, while at one level simply a matter of style, carries with it a philosophy as well.[23]

Some examples of the style are to be found in the recent poetry of Heaney, most obviously in the collection called *Seeing Things*, where we read, for instance, of '[t]he deep, still, *seeable-down-into* water' (emphasis added) in a phrase clearly reminiscent of Hopkins. Or consider, for another paradigmatic example from this collection, lines such as:

Willed down, waited for, in place at last and for good.
Trunk-hasped, cart-heavy, painted in ignorant brown,
And pew-strait, bin-deep, standing four-square as an ark
   . . . cargoed with
Its own dumb, tongue-and-groove worthiness
And un-get-roundable weight.[24]

American prose would also carry its own examples of this, perhaps more immediately indebted to the American imagist traditions than to Hopkins or Scotus. Yet the effect is the same. A good example is in Harold Brodkey's *Runaway Soul*:

> I mean the unabstraction, not of a field but of THAT FIELD OVER THERE . . . You can daydream as you bike about being a great baseball player – normal but famous – you can project this mental light of daydream on the landscape like my shadow on the ditch and then on the field and down the side of the steeply banked causeway. The narrow highway is crossing a bit of flood plain. Your mind can enter the shadow world and close out the real one. Illogic of that sort can do nothing but be imaginary. It does not dare ally itself with the real.[25]

The intertext in that example would probably be the heavily overdetermined metaphors of Richard Brautigan, or the extended conceits of John Ashbery. In such examples, we witness a renewed attention to the material otherness of the real world. The importance for these writers, conditioned as they are by a new empiricism, is no longer in the exploration of the Subject's consciousness, but rather in the exploration of the material sensuality or sensuousness of the object itself in all its resistant and recalcitrant materiality, a materialism deemed to be unamenable to representation or even to semiotics at all. Contemporary literature is playing out one of Baudrillard's fatal strategies, going over to the world of the object in the interests not of preserving some philosophical principle of reality but rather in the interests of finding out what might be the real in all its heterogeneity, in all its unavailability for human consciousness or for the Subject.

A similar thing had been attempted before this in some European cinema, in which the vision of alterity began to supersede the exploration of the point of view itself. It is clear in Alain Resnais's *L'Année dernière à Marienbad* (*Last Year in Marienbad*), for instance, where narrative gives way to the fixed stare of the camera on things, even to the point of rendering the human characters of the status of objects themselves. We find such priorities also in the cinema of Robert Bresson, where an attention to the ostensibly trivial object defuses the characterological or subjectivist interest of the film, and stresses instead what it might mean to 'see' an object. For Bresson and some of his contemporaries, such seeing must be of the nature of an event: that is to say, the object of sight resists comprehension as a semiotic counter in some grander 'vision' that the Subject may have. In other words, the thinginess of the world resists theorisation.

The philosophical stakes of this are perhaps best revealed, not entirely surprisingly, in a literary as opposed to an abstract philosophical text. Ian McEwan's *The Child in Time*, though perhaps romanticising to some extent the notion of an infantile attitude to the world, nonetheless hits on the effect which I am aiming to describe in this alternative contemporaneity. At one moment in this text, Stephen, the father of the disappeared child, Kate, imagines in her absence how she might see the world before him:

> It needed a child, Stephen thought, succumbing to the inevitable. Kate would not be aware of the car half a mile behind, or of the wood's perimeters and all that lay, beyond them, roads, opinions, Government. The wood, this spider rotating on its thread, this beetle lumbering over blades of grass, would be all, the moment would be everything. He needed her good influence, her lessons in celebrating the specific, how to fill the present and be filled by it to the point where identity faded to nothing. He was always partly somewhere else.[26]

What Stephen appreciates is a seduction of the Subject by the objects that constitute the Subject as a consciousness at all. The result is the loss of a sense of progressive linear time, and its replacement by a 'now' which is not part of a larger schema of history, a now that cannot be narrated. It is a now which, in its attention to alterity or heterogeneity, allows the very possibility of the experience of an event in time at all. The modern would be the Stephen who is 'partly somewhere else', but this is Stephen, now and here, Stephen who has lost identity to become this, an event in which he is a constituent part but which he does not control in an act of subjective appropriation.

The now, the here, the this are all deictics which depend for their significance, value or meaning on the Subject in relation to which they exist. The modern – let us call it 'figural' – attitude to this is the attitude that breeds a philosophy of identity in which the now, the here, the this are thought to exist *for* the Subject of consciousness; and as such, therefore, they have no existence in their own right. Their *haecceitas* is stripped from them as they are reduced to the status of an element in the constitution of a specific Subject who thus enjoys, courtesy of this reification of the now, here and this as commodities, the solace (actually of course a fiction) of identity and mastery. The non-figural attitude is one which, by contrast, returns to the deictic its own specificity, even to the point of endangering that 'solace of good form' – that identity – of the Subject of consciousness.[27] It is in this latter state that contemporaneity can take place. Paradoxically, the modern, then, knows no contemporaneity: it is only what we might now more comfortably call the postmodern, in its

openness to the undetermined, that can make the contemporary happen
or be an event.

NOTES

1. The modern Subject requires such a *fiction* precisely because of one effect of
    Hume's sceptical philosophy which, in its refusal to found thinking of truth
    upon a stable self, opens a specific antifoundationalism whose effect is to
    produce various strategies of containment advanced in the name of fiction
    rather than truth. Fictions of the self – in those biographical fictions of the
    eighteenth century, say – thus answer to an anxiety that there might not be a
    self in the first place: the fiction constructs, and proposes as normative, that
    which it pretends merely to describe. Temporally, the novel predicts – or
    'foretells' – a history, thus making the future into the past, while its present
    remains curiously void, empty.
2. Augustine, *Confessions*, trans. R.S. Pine-Coffin (Harmondsworth: Penguin, 1961),
    p. 209.
3. 'Writing to the minute' is Samuel Richardson's phrase describing the supposed
    transcription of *Clarissa*. For a good exploration of the issues involved in such
    'contemporaneous' writing, see Lennard J. Davis, *Factual Fictions* (New York:
    Columbia University Press, 1983).
4. Erich Auerbach, *Mimesis* (1946), trans. Willard R. Trask (New Jersey: Princeton
    University Press, 1968), pp. 70–1.
5. Auerbach, *Mimesis*, p. 74.
6. Auerbach, *Mimesis*, p. 74.
7. Jean-François Lyotard, *The Inhuman: Reflections on Time*, trans. Geoffrey
    Bennington and Rachel Bowlby (Cambridge: Polity Press, 1991), p. 60.
8. Lyotard, *The Inhuman*, p. 65.
9. In the original, 'le temps n'est pas le fait d'un sujet isolé et seul, mais . . . il est
    la relation même du sujet avec autrui'. Emmanuel Levinas, *Le Temps et l'autre*
    (Paris: Quadrige/PUF, 1991), p. 17. Author's own translation.
10. Jürgen Habermas has recently asserted that it is precisely this principle of
    autonomy as a constituent element of the movement of Enlightenment that
    Lyotard 'has not understood'. The assertion was made to me in conversation in
    University College Dublin, 14 April 1994. Part of the present argument origin-
    ates from a consideration of this claim, which Habermas also asserted as the
    basic philosophical – and not political – difference between Lyotard and him-
    self. For a fuller exploration of the implications of this, see the essays in Seyla
    Benhabib, ed., *Democracy and Difference* (New Jersey: Princeton University Press,
    1996).
11. T.S. Eliot, *The Sacred Wood* (London: Methuen, 1966), pp. xv–xvi.
12. Eliot, *The Sacred Wood*, p. 79.
13. Walter Benjamin, *Illuminations*, ed. Hannah Arendt, trans. Harry Zohn (London:
    Fontana, 1973), p. 264.

14. Benjamin, *Illuminations*, p. 264.
15. For an interesting discussion of this, see Zygmunt Bauman, *Modernity and the Holocaust* (Oxford: Polity Press, 1989).
16. The kind of singularity in question here is that described by Clément Rosset in his many texts, but most pertinently in *L'Objet singulier* (Paris: Minuit, 1979).
17. Benjamin, *Illuminations*, p. 263.
18. Benjamin, *Illuminations*, p. 265.
19. Benjamin, *Illuminations*, p. 264.
20. See Rosset, *L'Objet singulier, passim*.
21. For a fuller description of what I call 'anatheory', see my recent studies, *After Theory* (Edinburgh: Edinburgh University Press, 1996) and *Alterities: Criticism, History, Representation* (Oxford: Oxford University Press, 1996).
22. Jean Baudrillard, *Fatal Strategies*, trans. Philip Beitchman and W.G.J. Niesluchowski (London: Pluto, 1990).
23. With respect to Hopkins, the single most significant ostensible parataxis is the 'AND' that appears in 'The Windhover' and that actually fails to operate paratactically. The silent allusions in the rest of this paragraph are to Wallace Stevens, 'Not Ideas about the Thing, but the Thing Itself', in *Collected Poems* (London: Faber and Faber, 1984), p. 534; William Carlos Williams, *Paterson* (Harmondsworth: Penguin, 1983), p. 6 and *passim*; Martin Heidegger, 'The Thing', in *Poetry, Language, Thought*, trans. Albert Hofstadter (New York: Harper Colophon, 1975), ch. 5.
24. Seamus Heaney, 'Seeing Things' and 'The Settle Bed', in *Seeing Things* (London: Faber and Faber, 1992), pp. 16 and 28. For a fuller discussion of this 'new empiricism' in Heaney, see my chapter on 'The Modern Thing' in my *Alterities*.
25. Harold Brodkey, *The Runaway Soul* (London: Vintage Books, 1992), pp. 40–1. See also pp. 29–31 of this text, which address almost directly the question of *haecceitas* and the ontology of the real.
26. Ian McEwan, *The Child in Time* (London: Picador, 1988), p. 105.
27. Jean-François Lyotard, 'Answering the Question: What is Postmodernism', in *The Postmodern Condition*, trans. Geoffrey Bennington and Brian Massumi (Manchester: Manchester University Press, 1984), p. 81.

CHAPTER FIVE

Melancholic modernity and contemporary grief: the novels of Graham Swift

Wendy Wheeler

I POSTMODERNITY AS MOURNING AND MELANCHOLIA

In 1996 Graham Swift's *Last Orders* won the Booker Prize. The novel is a skilful and moving allegory of contemporary life which borrows both from Geoffrey Chaucer's *Canterbury Tales* and from William Faulkner's *As I Lay Dying*. Both of these pilgrimage texts attempt to domesticate, through small narratives, the sublime and *unheimlich* ('unhomely') narrative of human mortality. Swift's borrowings indicate his long absorption in the task of doing justice, in novel form, to history and change in a post-Romantic secular world. In this world religion no longer offers universal succour, and neither art nor romantic love seem capable of salving the isolation of the modern self. One might surmise that the reward of the Booker was recognition that *Last Orders* had finally solved the problem of aesthetic and cultural coherence – that is, a fit between form, content and context – towards which all Swift's earlier novels have been directed. This essay charts Swift's engagement with that problem throughout his work, and does so in relation to his constant themes of love, loss, nostalgia and grief.

Broadly speaking, modernity can be understood as the attempt, since the sixteenth and seventeenth centuries, to understand the world – philosophically and scientifically (the distinction between philosophy and science is, itself, born of modernity) – without recourse to religious or mystical accounts. But, in doing away with God, and in replacing Him with man as the source of all knowledge about the world, modernity opened within itself a sort of abyss of meaninglessness. The joy offered by reason's escape from superstition was accompanied also by the particularly modern terror induced by the apprehension of an utterly meaningless world. To put it another way, those human needs and feelings which had been more or less securely held and provided for by religious and traditional narratives of man's meaning and place in the cosmos no longer worked. In their place was something like a conceptual void – an infinitely empty place where God had been.

Enlightenment science was in many ways very successful in filling out the void which it had created. It offered compelling explanations of the physical laws of the universe and the workings of nature, and many saw (as some still see) God's hand in these. Nonetheless, there was something ruthless and impersonal in this God of physical laws. The eighteenth-century interest in the category of the sublime testifies to a cultural attempt to name that which had become distant, frightening in its impersonal force. The sublime is that vastness which can be *conceived*, but which always exceeds the possibility of any complete *representation* of it. For example, one can conceive of vast numbers, or of infinity, but the mind fails before the possibility of actually representing these adequately.

Although, by the early decades of the nineteenth century, both philo-sophical and scientific narratives of modern progress had appeared, whether mechanical, as in the successes of the Industrial Revolution, or philosoph-ical, as in the great synthetic thesis offered by Hegel's *Phenomenology of Spirit*, the nineteenth century remained largely culturally anxious and mel-ancholic. Many worried about the rise of a mechanistic philosophy,[1] and much of the literature and culture of the mid-century and beyond is funereal and preoccupied with the difficulty of encountering mortality and with mourning it.[2]

Charles Baudelaire's perception of the funerary nature of nineteenth-century modernity, and his quest to discover the aesthetic capable of repres-enting modernity in all its fevered and fashionable transience,[3] allow us to understand the extent to which the burden which religious representations (narratives and visual art) had once borne was transferred, throughout the eighteenth and nineteenth centuries, onto secular art more broadly. It is, as Jay Bernstein argues, in art that mourning is to be accomplished (if at all) in the modern world.[4]

II SWIFT AND MOURNINGFUL DREAMS

Graham Swift's work offers an exemplary case of the artist who attempts to come to terms with, and to represent, both the possibility and the difficulty of really mourning modernity's losses. These might be seen as the loss of traditional forms of knowledge with the advent of the absolutely *new*, and the loss of the solaces of a personally revealed God. From the first to the last, Swift's novels explore the failure of romantic conceptions of meaningfulness – whether in Hegel's story of history as the gradual unfolding of spiritual knowledge towards the perfect and mutually recognising community, or in romantic art's conception of aesthetic knowledge as offering a moment of healing transcendence in the mystery of symbolic unity.

There are, Freud says, two responses to loss: one is the crazy mourning in which the madness of grief (and it *is* a madness: a form of psychosis) can be gradually transformed into some accommodation with reality, and into some kind of renewal of the lifeful forces of eros (or the life drives) against the depredations and compulsive repetitions of entropy which Freud named the death drive.[5] The other response to loss – in which mourning becomes pathological and impossible – Freud called melancholia.[6] In melancholia, loss is perceived not simply as the loss of some other – whether a person or a cherished idea – but, due to the incorporation of the object in order to preserve it, as *the loss of the self*. In mourning, the bereaved and shattered self learns to let go of what has made its world meaningful, to forgive the lost object for leaving, and to make a different world and future. In melancholia, bereavement consists in *not* letting go, in hanging on to the object by internalising it, and in punishing it for going. Clearly, the structure of melancholia thus consists in forms of *self*-punishment in which what is nostalgically sought is a past satisfaction, and sense of wholeness or self-completion in which the cherished object is preserved, rather than a radically changed future in which both self and world are utterly transformed in the castrating experience of permanent loss.

The task which Swift sets himself is that of discovering how the self-destructive melancholias of modernity can be turned into the healthy mournings of something that we might call *post*modernity. Since what we call the postmodern seems to consist in the struggle between melancholia and mourning – between nostalgic turns to the past, and a masochistic sense of social fragmentations, on the one hand, and the attempt to imagine differently reconsituted communities and selves on the other – we might say that the *outcome* of postmodernity, seen as the attempt to live with loss and uncertainty as a permanent condition, might be the discovery or invention of ways of being in the world which move beyond the harsh individualism of utilitarian modernity, and towards a different way of accounting for and valuing human needs. It is this problem, the problem of inventing an aesthetic form capable of telling us something about the invention of new cultural, social and political forms – a '*new* modernity' or 'second Enlightenment'[7] – which drives Swift's work. His central preoccupations lie in the aesthetic imagining of cultural mourning as a form of erotic (that is to say lifeful and loving) and, in the end, *communal*, not individualistic, labour in the world. This would be a sort of *good work* in the world akin to what the philosopher Gillian Rose has called 'love's work'.[8] Swift only finally achieves this full communality of working voices in his latest novel *Last Orders*.

Lack of space prevents me from offering detailed readings of all of Swift's six novels; here I will deal, in differing amounts of detail, with a symptomatic selection beginning with the first, *The Sweet Shop Owner* (1980), moving to the third, *Waterland* (1983), and concluding with the fifth and sixth, *Ever After* (1992) and *Last Orders* (1996).

III I'LL NEVER, EVER, LET YOU GO – *THE SWEET SHOP OWNER*

No reader of Graham Swift will have any difficulty in recognising the very English nostalgia and melancholy present in his novels. This is particularly true of his first novel, *The Sweet Shop Owner*.[9] Although the fictional chronology extends back to 1937, the book is largely taken up with the careful domestic detailing of South London petty bourgeois life in the period from the Second World War up to 1974.

The Sweet Shop Owner's central character is Willy Chapman, and he is the first manifestation in novel-length form of what will come to be a regular theme in Swift's writing, that of the 'weak' (and often phlegmatic) English father. These 'failed fathers' come to take on an increasingly obvious allegorical weight in Swift's fiction. They function as signs of the failure of cultural and historical continuity, the failure, in psychoanalytic terms, of the 'paternal' function of bearing and transmitting the cultural 'law', but also as figures of a divine Father who no longer 'works'. In *The Sweet Shop Owner*, the allegorical dimension remains embryonic, however, and it is only retrospectively that the reader of Swift's work will be in a position fully to appreciate the significance of Willy as husband and father as he is inscribed over a series of South London high street *tableaux* during the course of thirty years.

Willy seems to represent simply the pattern of order – and of an essentially unreflective English way of life: 'He had planned nothing. Not for himself. And yet he knew: plans emerged. You stepped into them' (24). In a larger sense, this pattern, and Willy's unthinking confidence in it, signifies the phlegmatic and domestic conservatism of 'England' in the 1950s. This particular kind of Englishness – a phlegmatic and domestic order which Alison

Light sees as developing during the 1930s, extended by post-war consensus and the welfare state[10] – is the Englishness from which Swift attempts to break free with *Waterland*. It represents a kind of wilful and conservative blindness to the forces of history and culture, an attendance to the pattern of an eternal present – a 'forever England' – which seeks to hold off change.

The *point* of the novel is to show that Willy's unreflective romanticism – his attempt, in staging his own death, to force the symbolic unity which will be signified by his estranged daughter Dorry's return home on *her* birthday and *his* deathday – does not work. Willy's romantic fantasy is that, with Dorry's response to the nostalgic commitment to return home, the 'pattern' – and historical and cultural transmission – will be assured. 'She would go down, weep, clasp his knees, as though she were clasping the limbs of a cold, stone statue that stares out and beyond without seeing. He would be history' (10). In the absence of this, all Willy's devotion to maintaining the pattern will have amounted to nothing, and he will have failed to establish his proper paternal and symbolic relation to history. The novel closes with this failure: its failed closure thus inaugurates Swift's search for a form and content capable of giving full expression to a *post*-romantic, *post*-modern cultural experience.

For Swift, the transmission of culture is seen as the symbolic, paternal task in a modern culture in which the paternal fiction (an authoritative and unifying cultural narrative) no longer has the power to command assent (Dorry's doctoral thesis is, significantly, on 'Romantic Poetry and the Sense of History' [216]). Swift thus initially comes at the problem of bourgeois Romantic individualism – and the unifying of subjective and objective worlds in a disinterested aesthetic contemplation which is 'like' romantic love inasmuch as each seems to overcome alienation – from the point of view of the post-romantic who clings to the pattern of an idea long after its content has proved to be insubstantial. In *Waterland*,[11] the paternal task will come to be presented as overwhelmingly difficult and, formally, Swift's concern with cultural history and the means for handing it on will move from the critical vestiges of Romantic symbolism towards the complex layering – and more open-ended – form of allegory.

IV *WATERLAND*: LETTING GO OF THE SAVIOUR OF THE WORLD

The Fens are not the first place which springs to mind when one thinks of 'Englishness'; they are decidedly unpretty. Swift's imaginary Fenland town of Gildsey is, however, umbilically tied to Greenwich (England's imperial 'mean') by the line of zero degrees longitude which passes through both. The homeland imagined here is both something and nothing, and the landscape of the Fens is, appropriately, sublime. Not only is it a vast flatness where the light of an extensive sky drowns all other scales, but its very contourlessness drives men beyond reason:

> To live in the Fens is to receive strong doses of reality. The great, flat monotony of reality; the wide empty space of reality. Melancholia and self-murder are not unknown in the Fens. Heavy drinking, madness and sudden acts of violence are not uncommon. How do you surmount reality, children? (15)

Waterland's narrator, Tom Crick, is fifty-three, lives in Greenwich and is a history teacher in a local South London comprehensive. His 'A' level class on the French Revolution is interrupted by Price:

> Children, it was one of your number, a curly-haired boy called Price . . . who once, interrupting the French Revolution and voicing the familiar protest that every history teacher learns to expect (what is the point, use, need, etc., of History), asserted roundly that history was 'a fairy-tale'. (A teacher-baiter. A lesson-spoiler. Every class has to have one. But this one's different . . .)
> 'What matters,' he went on . . . 'is here and now. Not the past. The here and now and the future.' (The very sentiments, Price – but you didn't see that – of 1789.) And then – alluding rapidly to certain topics of the day . . . and drawing from you, his class-mates, a sudden and appalling venting of your collective nightmares – he announced, with a trembling lip that was not just the result of uttering words that must have been (true, Price?) carefully rehearsed: 'The only important thing . . .' 'Yes, Price – the only important thing – ?' 'The only important thing about history, I think, sir, is that it's got to the point where it's probably about to end.' So we closed our textbooks. Put aside the French Revolution. So we said goodbye to that old and hackneyed fairy-tale with its Rights of Man, liberty caps, cockades, tricolors, not to mention its hissing guillotines, and its quaint notion that it had bestowed on the world a New Beginning.
> I began, having recognised in my young but by no means carefree class the contagious symptoms of fear: 'Once upon a time . . .' (6)

The fairy-tale Crick tells is of the Fens. Tom is faced with redundancy in a Thatcherite Britain dedicated to the most superficial utilitarianism: 'We're cutting back on history . . . You know how the cuts are biting. And you know the kind of pressure I'm under – "practical relevance to today's real world" – that's what they're demanding' (19). He is also faced with a mad wife who is driven to stealing a baby to replace the child she could never conceive following a teenage abortion in 1943. His response is to turn away from the 'grand Narrative' of History (53), which tells everything on a grand public scale but explains nothing of intimate experience, and begin to recount the tale of his own family origins.

The 'fairy-story' of the Fens and of Tom Crick's family is offered as an allegory of the French Revolution's tale of the ways in which 'progress' can lead to terror. The Revolution itself stands as a synecdoche of Enlightenment modernity, and of a false notion of progress. Tom's story is a sustained critique of Price's belief that something sublime called 'the here and now' ('which brings both joy and terror' [52]) can ever be grasped. The Here and Now in Tom's tale is pure event – a reality of such immediacy as to be, strictly speaking, intolerable – and a thing which, unless tamed by narratives, drives people mad. Crick's story does not give up on the idea of progress, but it offers a different model for thinking the 'here and now' and a different goal for historical, philosophical, political and, implicitly, literary narratives.

The novel is delivered as a series of 'lessons' to Crick's class. Each 'lesson' has to be read – like sediments of silt – allegorically against all the others. An archaeology and genealogy of land and family builds up as the novel progresses. In Chapter 3, 'About the Fens', the reader learns that the history of the reclamation of the Fens is congruent with the rise and consolidation of early entrepreneurial capitalism in England in the seventeenth century. Whilst the paternal Cricks acquire the English virtue of phlegm – and 'outwit reality' by telling stories (15) – the maternal Atkinsons outwit reality by acquiring ideas and land: 'While the Atkinsons made history, the Cricks spun yarns' (15).

One of the meanings of the domestication of the Fens is thus to offer an allegory of modern development, and of the modern 'English' character, as both entrepreneurial and phlegmatic. But 'The Fens were formed by silt. Silt: a word which when you utter it, letting the air slip thinly between your teeth, invokes a slow, sly, insinuating agency. Silt: which shapes and undermines continents; which demolishes as it builds; which is simultaneous accretion and erosion; neither progress nor decay' (7). Undermining their first meaning, the Fens (and capitalist progress and 'English' identity) now become less substantial: 'The chief fact about the Fens is that they are reclaimed land, land that was once water, and which, even today, is not quite solid . . . Strictly speaking, they are never reclaimed, only being reclaimed' (7–8).

The story of *Waterland* concerns the local causes and effects of the murder and then drowning, in the summer of 1943, of the adolescent Tom Crick's friend Freddie Parr. Uncovering the meaning of the (unrecognised) murder – the coroner's verdict is 'Accidental Death' – means uncovering the history of the Cricks and Atkinsons and their various historical relationships to the Fens. It also means uncovering the present meaning of Mary Crick's descent into madness, overwhelmed by the 'here and now'. These little local histories, intimately tied to the history of the Fens, are offered as an allegory of the transformation of a sublimely ungraspable 'nothing' into the 'something' of the everyday – as ways of making the vast nothing of the Fens into a local and knowable something, and as a way of quelling the 'restless thoughts' of Tom's frightened 'children' (6).

The Atkinsons are brewers. In the course of their business they build canals and drain ditches, all of which must be regulated by locks and dredged of silt. These latter tasks fall to the Cricks. Whilst the Cricks labour, phlegmatically, at the business of keeping the Fenland solid, and of tending – via locks and stories – to the symbolic limits which must be set upon a maddening nothingness, the Atkinsons labour at the business of providing it, overwhelmingly, with an undermining and dissolving liquor. The story of the Fens, and the Atkinsons and Cricks, is, then, a history which is also a many-layered allegory which formally enacts its own thesis concerning the difficulty of keeping things (land, water; truth, fiction; something, nothing) separate.

Initially drawn to History because it seems to offer real answers, Tom Crick gradually comes to understand that History is not reality, and that reality is sublime. History is the sense we make of the terrifying reality which always threatens to escape our orderings and to overwhelm us with its awful vacancy: 'Reality's not strange, not unexpected. Reality doesn't reside in the sudden hallucination of events. Reality is uneventfulness, vacancy, flatness. Reality is that nothing happens . . . I present to you History, the fabrication, the diversion, the reality-obscuring drama. History and its near relative Histrionics' (34). All that there is are 'stories in which each actor, even if he has missed the grand repertoire of history . . . imitate[s] . . . in miniature its longing for presence, for feature, for purpose, for content' (34–5).

The drama which the murder-mystery story in *Waterland* acts out centres on a series of misconceptions about the meaning of love. Following the burning down of the Atkinson brewery in 1911, Tom's maternal grandfather, Ernest, convinced that there will be war and that the world will be visited by unprecedented calamity, withdraws with his daughter Helen to the isolation of Kessling Hall where, in 1915 and because they love each other, father and daughter enter upon an incestuous relationship.

After the Great War, the Hall is turned – at Helen's suggestion and in order to distract her father from his increasing desire for a son from her who will be 'the Saviour of the World' – into a home for shell-shocked soldiers. It is here, in 1922, that Helen meets Tom's father, Henry Crick, and that they fall in love. Henry's Fenlander capacity for telling stories has been shattered by the experience of war ('He thinks: there is only reality, there are no stories left' [17]), but gradually love and stories from Helen restore him to health, memory, narrative and home. Helen sees in this the opportunity to assuage her father's desire and also to become free. She agrees to become pregnant by her father provided that Ernest consents to her marriage to Henry. This accomplished, Helen gives birth in March 1923 to Tom's elder (half) brother, Dick. But the saviour of the world turns out to be 'a potato head' (200), who, although sometimes giving the impression of 'lofty and lucid' contemplation, is 'irreclaimable' (32).

Dick is a monstrous personification of the resistant sublimity of the Fens. Of prodigious (not to say sublime) phallic proportions, he is a figuration of the will to seize hold of reality and to 'save the world'. At home on land or in water, Dick is the vacant-faced 'here and now' made flesh: 'Not a saviour of the world. A potato-head. Not a hope for the future. A Numbskull with the dull, vacant stare of a fish' (209). As the murderer (whose weapon is a bottle of the ale of 1911 bequeathed by his father/grandfather), Dick is the 'nothing' *grounds* of the history which follows. Nevertheless he cannot become a *part* of history. He is the sublime 'reality' upon which History is acted out. Himself the result of a culturally unbinding act, Dick cannot understand 'love' – which is a form of historical binding up – and finally returns to the sublime and watery nothingness from which, symbolically, he emerged.

Ernest Atkinson is the most desperate and vivid example yet of Swift's many troubled fathers. His attempt to father a new saviour out of the paradise of Helen is 'like tying up into a knot the thread that runs into the future, it's like a stream wanting to flow backwards' (197). Its result – Dick – has all the vacant sublimity of the Fenland silt with which he is continually associated. Dick's conception, and his association with nature and silt, mark him out as the failure of the symbolism of love in Swift's work: 'Love. Lu-love. Lu-lu-love. Does it ward of evil? Will its magic word suspend indefinitely the link between cause and effect?' (259). For Swift, love and the art of telling stories is what humans do to ward off the fearful sublimity of natural existence. Dick murders Freddie because he does not understand the complexity of narratives and love. When Dick learns the truth he throws himself into the River Ouse: 'Obeying instinct. Returning. The Ouse flows to the sea . . .' (310).

Mary Crick's 'problem' is her inability to turn her fascination with the sublime Here and Now (a happening in the face of nothing, a prodigiously sized and fascinating phallus which is 'too big') into a narrative:

> First there is nothing; then there is happening; a state of emergency. And after the happening, only the telling of it. But sometimes the happening won't stop and let itself be turned into memory. So she's still in the midst

of events . . . which have not ceased. Which is why it's impossible to get through. Which is why she cannot cross into the safe, sane realm of hindsight and answer the questions of the white-coated doctors: 'Now tell us, Mrs Crick, you can tell us everything, you can tell . . .' (284)

The story (as opposed to the novel) ends with Tom Crick's valedictory address to his school. Contained in Chatper 49, 'About Empire Building', his speech addresses both the fantasy of the paternal fiction (killing bad fathers and needing better ones) and the 'fiction' of modernity as a New Beginning. In place of these, Crick offers history and progress according to the model of the *reclamation* of the Fens: 'My humble model for progress is the reclamation of land. Which is repeatedly, never-endingly retrieving what is lost. A dogged and vigilant business. A dull yet valuable business. A hard, inglorious business. But you shouldn't go mistaking the reclamation of land for the building of empires' (291).

V BUT IF I LET GO FOR *EVER AFTER*, HOW CAN I TAKE MY LIFE?

Ever After[12] is a novel very much concerned with different kinds of loss, with mourning, and with coming to terms with the 'simulations, fabrications, biographical conjurations . . . the . . . wilder delusions, the subterfuges, superstitions of grief' (255).

William Unwin was once a lecturer in English, and then the manager of his successful actress wife Ruth Vaughan. Following her death from cancer some eighteen months before the time of the narrative, Bill, paralysed with grief, is 'appointed' to the Ellison Fellowship at a Cambridge college. The Fellowship has been endowed by Bill's American stepfather, 'Uncle Sam' Ellison, from the fortune amassed from his plastics business and on the discreet understanding that Bill will be its first beneficiary. Appropriate to the conventions of its elegiac form, the story is narrated from the pastoral setting of the Fellows' Garden during the long vacation where Bill sits recovering from the suicide attempt he made three weeks previous to the narrative 'present' and some twelve odd months after his appointment. Bill is supposed to be writing a book based around the mid-nineteenth-century notebooks of a distant maternal relative – Matthew Pearce – which came into his hands on the death of his mother nine months earlier.

The notebooks, written intermittently over a six-year period from 1854 to 1860, concern Matthew's gradual loss of faith following the death of his third child, Felix, in 1854. Matthew himself cites the moment of doubt which the child's death retrospectively activates in an experience ten years earlier, in June 1844, when he stumbled across the fossil of an ichthyosaur. From an intimation that Man is not the central purpose of God's creation, Matthew begins to think that there might indeed be no God at all but only an endless series of evolutionary struggles.

Matthew is a young man who, emerging from Oxford in 1840, remains entirely convinced of the literal truth of the Bible as a foundation of meaning and of nature's design as evidence of God's. 'It meant that the profounder questions of existence were settled and one was free to go out on to the surface of the world and do good, practical work. And the surface of the world only brought you back to the central fact: nature's handiwork, and man's too since it exploited the unchanging laws that were part of nature's design, was evidence of God's' (92). The ichthyosaur, Felix's death and the publication of Darwin's *Origin of Species* in 1859 will bring about the loss of faith that Bill Unwin, using the 'original data' of the Pearce notebooks, will supposedly make the centre of his research. What Unwin actually writes is the story of his own life and loss. The two stories – which both tell of the vertiginous experience of stumbling upon the sublime 'real' in all its appalling resistance and nauseating emptiness – thus resonate across each other, one from the side of the entirely domestic in the loss of a cherished wife, and the other from the side of modernity as a huge collective confrontation with the loss of faith.

Both Bill Unwin and the ancient university, which was once supposed to be the defender of authentic civilised values and Enlightenment 'rising like some fantastical lantern out of the miasmal fens and out of the darkness of dark ages' (9), now owe their existence to that apparently most inauthentic (because entirely imitative) of things: plastic. Plastic is a substitute for the real stuff, but, insists Bill's 'Uncle Sam', 'the real stuff is running out, it's used up, it's blown away, or it costs too much. You gotta have *substitoots*' (7).

The university, once the site of 'the true, real, permanent thing', is now 'artificial and implausible, like a painstakingly contrived film set. It is everything that is beyond real . . . Out there . . . the world is falling apart; its social fabric is in tatters, its eco-system is near collapse. Real: that is, flimsy, perishing, stricken, doomed' (2). But most significantly, the 'real stuff' which Unwin believed he had – his love for his actress wife Ruth – is also made of endless fabrications: the fabrications of art and human love. Up to the point when he discovers the truth of his *real* paternity (that he is the son of a nameless engine driver on Brunel's Great Western railway which, surveyed by Matthew Pearce in the mid-nineteenth century, was the site of Bill's own 'paternal' identifications in the mid-twentieth century),[13] Bill remains unfashionably committed to the notion that literature is good because it is 'beautiful', because it transforms the everyday into the sublime (70) and thus provides access to an intimation of, a moment of stumbling upon – albeit retrospectively – the truth of reality.

But with Ruth's death, it is the 'commonplace' obviousness of the real, the real in all its vulgar everydayness, which Bill faces:

> And nothing is left but this impossible absence. This space at your side the size of a woman, the size of a life, the size – of the world. Ah yes, the monstrosity, the iniquity of love – that another person should *be* the world. What does it matter if the world (out there) is lost, doomed, if there is no sense, purpose, rhyme or reason to the schemeless scheme of things, so long as – But when she is gone, you indict the universe. (256)

In *Ever After*, the quest for the father, and his truth, is finally abandoned. What moves to the fore in its place (the 'inauthentic' place of 'ever after') is the question of the adequate symbolisation of loss itself. In other words, Swift's question increasingly becomes one which is concerned with the relationship between aesthetic form and ethical content. The form must be one which is capable of properly symbolising the trauma of loss. Uncle Sam, Bill's plastics millionaire step-father, says 'You gotta have *substitoots*' (7) and as Peter Sacks points out, the work of elegy is precisely that of substitution of the melancholic's narcissism by the processes of symbolisation: 'primary desire never attains its literal objective except in death, or in a deathlike loss of identity. The only object that such a desire can possess in life will be a sign or substitute for what it cannot have.'[14] That the language of substitution should issue from such a source (the resonantly named 'Uncle Sam' fulfils the role of Claudius in Bill's identification with Hamlet) merely lends strength to Sacks's contention that elegy stages a work of mourning which attempts to recapitulate the resolution to the Oedipal drama.

Bill's father killed himself apparently because of his wife's adultery with the young Sam Ellison in 1945 when Bill was nine years old. Bill Oedipally identifies himself with the melancholic Hamlet whose dilemma is to be 'actuated, or immobilised, by two questions: 1) is there or is there not any point to it all? 2) Shall I kill Claudius? Or to put it another way: shall I kill Claudius or shall I kill myself?' (5). In other words, the symbolic value of the father's bequest lies not in his life but in his death, at which point symbolic transformation, mediation and exchange become possible. Bill's life is dominated by his mother's seductiveness and his father's death, by understanding the cause and meaning of the latter, and by his unfulfilled desire for revenge upon Sam.

In the end, however, Bill gives up on the melancholic's desire for revenge. It isn't, finally, what matters:

> I read up on Brunel; but I do not research my own father. I summon
> up Matthew, but I do not try to know my own father. My nameless,
> engine-driving, killed-in-the-war father. And why should I when I never
> got to know the living, breathing man I took to be – ? What difference
> does it make? The true or the false. This one or that one. (204)

The novel's concluding chapter opens with an ambivalent restatement of the theme in a way which also refers the reader back to the famous Oedipal ambivalence of Hamlet: 'It's not the end of the world. It is. Life goes on. It doesn't. Why seems it so particular with thee?' (249). And it is precisely this ambivalence associated with art which, as it were, resolves by not resolving.

So, what kind of allegorical 'solution' does Swift offer? The novel closes with a return and a repetition. In the final chapter Bill remembers the carefully planned occasion of the first time he and Ruth made love and nakedly presented themselves and their lives to each other. Bill tells Ruth what he has never told anyone, that his father killed himself ('That he took his life' [260]), and remembers 'how strange, how incomprehensible . . . How unreal' (261) the phrase sounded then to two young people in love. The novel ends with 'How impossible that either of these young people, whose lives, this night, have never been so richly possessed, so richly embraced, will ever come to such a pass. He took his life, he took his life' (261).

The final sentence is ambiguous. Does the pronoun refer to the father or to the son or to both? The repetition and the content suggest the re-emergence of the double (Bill Unwin is, after all, his own 'plastic' imita-tion) with which the novel opens, and this directs us towards the repetitions and uncanniness of the death drive which lies behind and beyond the pleasure principle motivating the lovers. Another reading is possible, how-ever, in which the deathly sense of the verb is read erotically – as, indeed, Bill and Ruth have just taken each other. In this sense 'he took his life' signifies acceptance of life as it is – both terrible and banal, sublime and domestic, at the same time – rather than suicide. This ambiguity – a sort of agreement not to close off, or possess, the meaning of the object – suggests a desire to tolerate anxiety and ambivalence which is part of the relinquish-ment of narcissistic melancholia. But the move from the narcissisms of the child to the sociality of the adult consciousness involves labour and com-munity with others in the world. It is to these themes that Swift turns in *Last Orders*.

VI *LAST ORDERS*: TO BE WHAT WE'RE MADE OF

Last Orders[15] is a pilgrimage. Like *The Canterbury Tales*, it starts at a pub in Southwark in April from where a group of friends make their journey, via Canterbury, to Margate to scatter the ashes of their butcher friend Jack Dodds (I take the name Dodds to be an amalgamation of Dads and Gods) upon the sea. As with *The Canterbury Tales*, the narrative consists of the tales of each of these pilgrims, although in line with the 'protestant' conventions of the English novel, these tales largely take the form of private, inner narratives. Swift's continual preoccupation with the relationship between fathers and sons reappears in *Last Orders*, but this time it is not with a father who fails to acknowledge a son, but with an adopted son who will not acknowledge a father. As with the traditional elegy, the novel's drive is towards re-establishing the order in which the symbolic father, as dead father, is acknowledged by the 'son' who comes after. As Peter Sacks says, in order to succeed, the elegy must re-establish reverence for the father and the law.[16]

In *Ever After*, Swift explored erotic romantic love, and asked whether this is enough to help us survive ever after. His conclusion there was maybe, maybe not: it depends on how you understand the verbs 'to love' and 'to take'. In *Last Orders*, the emphasis seems to fall upon the spirit with which a person finally takes command of, or orders, him or herself in their loving. Here, the messiness and contingency of human lives are subsumed within a last kind of order, but it is one *discovered* in the pilgrimage rather than imposed at the start and rigidly enforced. Jack's last orders seem to be the *first* orders of the day of the pilgrimage, but they are shifted in the comedy of experience, and truly *become* last orders in the remains of the day.

Throughout the novel, characters follow the commands of love, not as desire, but rather as a kind of acknowledgement of obligations. From the same root as ligature, obligation means a binding-up, a tie. And what the pilgrimage allows each to discover is that the order expressed in last rites – in proper mourning in other words – is precisely the *same* order which is expressed in the ties of love. As in Hegel's *Phenomenology*, the movements of spirit which trace out all the follies and detours of the stages of the encounter with Death and mourning turn out, in the end, to be the work of mutual recognition and obligation which is love (*caritas*) as *work* in the social and political commitments and activities of the day to day – 'activity beyond activity' as Gillian Rose puts it, and the bindings-up of labouring communality.

Much could be said about Swift's intricate and reverberating novel. Perhaps one of the most interesting things is the way in which, beneath the ordinary Bermondsey voices and lives, another language surprisingly emerges: the symbolic language of the spirit and the soul. No elevated language here, but, nonetheless, a glimpse of the sacred and the enchanted. This pilgrimage passes beyond Canterbury to, of all places, Margate. This was where Jack and Amy Dodds took a belated honeymoon in 1939 and where, fifty years later, Jack orders his friends to bury him 'at sea'. But if the faded seaside town, and the lights of Dreamland and Marine Parade, represent a tired dream of England, it is nevertheless from that tacky fantasy of the pleasures of mass consumption, rather than from the cathedral mass at Canterbury, that symbolic salvation must be found. The Miracle Worker in this novel is the name of an outsider running at 33–1. Jack, dying in hospital and in debt, asks Ray, the lucky gambler, to place a bet. When Ray's chosen horse, The Miracle Worker, wins, Jack knows that his wife Amy (from 'ame', meaning love or soul) will be safe, and he dies leaving only the last orders for his burial at sea.

It is the paying of *this* debt, rather than the financial one, that will do the work of mourning. Any modern fool recognises the nature of money debts, but it is only in the folly of other kinds of obligation (the novel is full of 'fool's errands' and 'detours' in the service of memories and memorials) that the nature of the debt, the significance of the human comedy, and the work of mourning, will be symbolically realised. Amy does not go on the pilgrimage. That is because she is attending, as she has done for fifty years, to her own pilgrimage in the regular beat of the visits to the idiot daughter June, to whom Jack has refused to acknowledge any obligation. The friends undertake the pilgrimage *for* Amy – who has her own. In *Last Orders*, postmodern realism works through the community of ordinary lives in order to realise the soul and to inaugurate mourning *for her* and on her behalf. The dead father is mourned, and in the labour of the day reverence is not only re-established for him, but for the mother-soul also. In this, dead Jack *and* living Amy 'become what we're made of':

> The wind takes it, it's gone in a whirl, in a flash. Now you see it, now you don't. Then I take the jar in both hands again, giving a quick peek inside, and say, 'Come on, come on'. They all huddle round to take another scoop. There isn't much more than four men can scoop out twice over. They dip in again, one by one. Lucky dip. And I dip and we all throw again, a thin trail of white, like smoke, before it's gone, and some seagulls swoop in from nowhere and veer off again like they've been tricked . . . One handful, two handfuls, there's only two handfuls. I say, 'Goodbye Jack' . . . Then I throw the last handful and the seagulls come back on a second chance and I hold up the jar, shaking it, like I should chuck it out to sea too, a message in a bottle, Jack Arthur Dodds, save our souls, and the ash that I carried in my hands, which was the Jack who once walked around, is carried away by the wind, is whirled away by the

wind till the ash becomes wind and the wind becomes Jack what we're made of. (294–5)

Swift's purpose is not to argue simply for community, or 'immediate ethical experience in place of the risks of critical rationality', as Gillian Rose puts it.[17] The invocation of order, of last orders, and of commands to the labour of last rites, says otherwise. What Swift is ever after here, is the recognition that the order of reason and death and the disorder of human contingency and difference displayed in the histories of the Bermondsey community, *must* be thought in the same place at the same time: the obligations imposed by the dead *are* the obligations we discover and re-negotiate in life.

What Swift's pilgrims come to on their fool's errand, with its constant memorial detours, is the remembrance, rediscovery and renegotiation – beyond the city walls where the ashes of the dead are left – of boundaries, and of what binds us. These are what Gillian Rose has called the boundaries of the city and the soul. Discussing Poussin's painting 'Gathering the Ashes of Phocion', Rose reminds us that the Athenian law which had the virtuous Phocion cremated by an alien without the city walls was a tyrannical law – 'tyranny temporarily usurping good rule in the city'[18] – not a just one.

In *Last Orders* the bleeding heart of the modern city is Smithfield – 'Life and death' says Jack the butcher. In his life Jack did not do justice to his obligations to June, Amy, the soul, or love. In his *death*, by what he obliged his friends to do, for *themselves* and for *her*, he did do it, and mourning became them. Within the modern city just now – as in the Athens of Phocion – the soul and the city are ruled by butchers; but beyond the city wall, in Margate of all places, the soul becomes a trope, or trick, of the wind which whirls around the ashes until 'the ash becomes the wind and the wind becomes Jack what we're made of'. Upon this note of *symbolically rich* secular communion, the novel ends.

NOTES

1. See Raymond Williams's charting of these anxieties in *Culture and Society* (London: Chatto and Windus, 1958).
2. See Peter Sacks, *The English Elegy: Studies in the Genre from Spenser to Yeats* (London: Johns Hopkins University Press, 1985) on the increasing difficulty of writing mourning poems from the seventeenth century onwards. See too Foucault's references to Baudelaire's 'funerary' nineteenth century in 'What is

Enlightenment', in *The Foucault Reader*, ed. Paul Rabinow (Harmondsworth: Penguin, 1986).

3. Charles Baudelaire, *The Painter of Modern Life and Other Essays*, trans. J Mayne (London: Phaidon, 1964).

4. Jay Bernstein, *The Fate of Art: Aesthetic Alienation from Kant to Derrida and Adorno* (Cambridge: Polity Press, 1992).

5. Sigmund Freud, 'Beyond the Pleasure Principle', *Pelican Freud Library*, vol. 11 (Harmondsworth: Penguin, 1984).

6. Sigmund Freud, 'Mourning and Melancholia', *Pelican Freud Library*, vol. 11.

7. 'New modernity' is the term used by Albrecht Wellmer, *The Persistence of Modernity: Essays on Aesthetics, Ethics, and Postmodernism*, trans. D. Midgely (Cambridge, Mass.: MIT Press, 1991). 'Second Enlightenment' is taken from Gerald Edelman, *Bright Air, Brilliant Fire: On the Matter of the Mind* (Harmondsworth: Penguin, 1992).

8. Gillian Rose, *Love's Work* (London: Chatto and Windus, 1995).

9. Graham Swift, *The Sweet Shop Owner* (London: Penguin, 1983). All references in text.

10. Alison Light, *Forever England: Femininity, Literature and Conservatism Between the Wars* (London: Routledge, 1991).

11. Graham Swift, *Waterland* (London: Picador, 1984). All references in text.

12. Graham Swift, *Ever After* (London: Picador, 1992). All references in text.

13. For a more detailed account of Bill Unwin's Freudian paternal identifications, see my 'After Grief? What Kinds of Inhuman Selves', *New Formations* 25 (Summer 1995).

14. Sacks, *The English Elegy*, p. 17.

15. Graham Swift, *Last Orders* (London: Picador, 1996). All references in text.

16. Sacks, *The English Elegy*, p. 301.

17. Gillian Rose, *Mourning Becomes the Law: Philosophy and Representation* (Cambridge: Cambridge University Press, 1996), p. 22.

18. Rose, *Mourning Becomes the Law*, p. 25.

CHAPTER SIX

Memory recovered/recovered memory

Roger Luckhurst

I

Three 'contemporary' scenes:

Rachel Whiteread, the sculptor, wins the competition to build a Holocaust memorial for Vienna's Judenplatz. Local shopkeepers complain the memorial will deprive their customers of parking. Undaunted, the Viennese Jewish community, supported by Simon Wiesenthal, the famous 'Nazi-hunter', push the project through city planning meetings. As soon as excavations begin, the earth reveals a secret: uncovered is the smoke-blackened floor of a synagogue burnt down in a pogrom in 1421. Vienna's chief rabbi withdraws support from Whiteread's memorial: 'For us, the excavations alone are very moving . . . no other monument is necessary'.[1]

Anthony Minghella, a script-writer and film-maker with a number of small film successes in England, spends four years convincing nervous financiers that his script of the 'unfilmable' novel, Michael Ondaatje's *The English Patient*, is a worthwhile investment. After continuous crises and disruptions to the production, the film sweeps the Oscars in 1997.

Whitley Strieber, a little known horror and fantasy writer, releases an autobiographical account of his life which propels him to the top of the bestseller list in America in 1988. His account announces that since the age of seven he has been repeatedly abducted by four-foot-tall grey aliens. The cover of *Communion* has an artist's impression of a 'little grey' alien.[2] Within ten years, this image becomes embedded in the cultural imagination around the world, and many become conversant with at least some aspects of the alleged phenomenon of alien abduction.

These apparently disconnected scenes each reveal a facet of the cultural politics of memory. Whiteread's memorial project enters the field not only of debates concerning the 'correct' means to remember and represent the Jewish Holocaust, but also of disputes over public and symbolic commemorations in general. Do monuments really incite remembrance, or do they *entomb* memory, fixing it in stone which by itself remains 'inert and amnesiac'?[3] What does a memorial remember, and what, given its single, monumental representation, does it choose to forget? Today, whenever a public memorial is commissioned, different interest groups with different memories and different interpretations of the event compete over what is to be remembered. Whiteread's case adds another twist: on the same site 1996, 1942 and 1421 come into painful collision. To memorialise one date is to erase another. Memory, then, is always contemporary, caught up in the politics of the present, and always con-temporal, bringing disjunct times together: 'The complex of practices and means by which the past invests the present is memory: memory is the present past'.[4]

Minghella's film of *The English Patient* opens up other aspects of memory. In terms of plot, memory is revealed as the index of identity, the provider of narratives of location, for without it the amnesiac patient is misrecognised and misplaced. Played out between remembering and forgetting, the success of the film is in part due to belonging to a larger wave of re-evaluations of the legacy of the Second World War. Contemporary texts continually circle back to the 1940s. Ghosts of murdered Jews haunt the French farmhouse in Michèle Roberts's *Daughters of the House*; a symbolic encounter with mythic forces of evil in 1946 connects to the orphaned identity of the contemporary narrator in Ian McEwan's *Black Dogs*; the placid narration of a butler's pre-war memories reveals the complicity of English ideals of servitude with the rise of Nazism in Kazuo Ishiguro's *The Remains of the Day*.[5] To confront the traumatic past, Freud suggested, was to pit *remembering* against the fateful and uncontrollable *repetition* of trauma.[6] At a moment when Europe unfreezes from the blocs of the Cold War it is as if the uncanny repetitions of ethnic rivalries and nationalist rhetorics suggest 'a pervasive, even perverse, sense that history repeats itself' and that 'circumstances compel us to regard our own contemporaneity in the language and imagery of a "past" that turns tradition into a turbulent reality'.[7] It is this that urges cultural narratives to fight repetition with remembrance.

Part of that fight is evidenced in the way *The English Patient* and the other texts mentioned here place the intensely interior and private act of memory in opposition to the public and collective narrative of history. Interstitial meanings and counter-memories are dislodged from History, for the fluid con-temporality of memory is felt to resist the way history 'closes the gaps' and 'forgets the heterogeneous'.[8] Memory's anamnesis resists History's selective amnesia. And Ondaatje's novel (far more so than Minghella's film) possesses a very contemporary concern to displace the nation as the locus of history and identity. Sri Lankan sapper, Canadian nurse and Italian-Canadian thief circle around an English patient whose memory finally reveals a distinctly un-English identity, and a story which blurs the categories of nation, ally or enemy. This, too, conforms to a larger movement of memory politics: 'Into the gap created by a retreat from history as a mode of relating to the past, and a retreat from the state as the primary referent for an understanding of collective political existence, there enter memory, recollection and remembrance and the discovery of new sites on which a commemorative relation to the past might be established'.[9]

Whitley Strieber's curious claims initially might seem out of place here. In fact, Strieber's memoir is dependent on an American-led revolution in psychotherapy, for Strieber's experiences of abduction are only accessed by hypnotic regression to retrieve 'forgotten' memories, much to his own initial incredulity and resistance. The emergence of a group of people who nominate themselves as 'abductees' is an effect of a transformation of the conception of the subject as the product of the interplay between memory and traumatic forgetting.[10] This very contemporary model of subjectivity teaches something valuable: memory is not a pre-given faculty, but is constructed by disciplines and transformed by institutional practices. This is to say that *memory has a history* and that at moments of transformation the disciplinary object of memory becomes visible as a cultural rather than innate artefact.

An as-yet unbuilt memorial, an Oscar-winning film and the memoirs of an abductee can thus indicate the extent of the terrain of what Andreas Huyssen has suggested is 'a memory boom of unprecedented proportions'.[11] But how is this to be squared with the influential view of the contemporary as 'postmodern'? Ever since Fredric Jameson's thesis, first presented in 1984, on postmodernism as the cultural logic of late capitalism, we have learnt to read the present as detemporalised; flattened out into the random spatial juxtapositions of images and simulations; a channel-hopping, tele-visualised world based on 'the structural exclusion of memory'.[12] The thematic of time and memory is a lost modernist concern; the 'distinctively spatial' problematic of postmodernism is premised on the view that 'memory has been weakened in our time, and that the great rememberers are a virtually extinct species'.[13] Famously, Jameson proposed schizophrenia as the privileged subjective experience, the schizophrenic 'reduced to . . . a series of pure and unrelated presents in time', whatever access to the past a rubble of 'dead styles and fashions'.[14]

Was this diagnosis plain wrong? 1984 was the year the French historian Pierre Nora began his collaborative seven-volume study, *Lieux de Mémoire* (*Sites of Memory*), a project so successful that by its completion in 1992, the title phrase had entered common parlance and France was gripped by commemorative fever,[15] in much the same time-scheme that produced the discourse of English Heritage in Britain. 1985 was the year German intellectuals fought the *Historikerstreit* (the historians' dispute) on the fortieth anniversary of Germany's defeat, conservatives and liberals arguing over the relative centrality or marginality of Nazism's legacy to contemporary Germany.[16] Didn't Jameson's amnesiac contemporary entirely miss this extensive memory-work? Over a decade later, it seems that memory has been recovered from a paradigm that failed to see its insistent presence.

It is easy to demolish Jameson's assertions, but in fact most memory theorists could accommodate Jameson's amnesiac culture in their work on memory. Pierre Nora maintains that this is an 'era of commemoration', but immediately suggests 'we speak so much of memory because there is so little of it left'.[17] The construction of national, regional or local sites of memory becomes vital once computers and videotapes store vast, undifferentiated quantities of 'memory' *outside* us, untouched by investiture of human meaning: '*Lieux de mémoire* originate with the sense that there is no spontaneous memory, that we must deliberately create archives, maintain anniversaries, organise celebrations . . . because such activities no longer occur naturally'.[18] And if Huyssen speaks of a 'memory boom', it is precisely because 'accelerating technological processes' are effecting 'the draining of time in the world of information and data banks'. 'Mnemonic fever', he suggests, is precisely attributable to 'the virus of amnesia that at times threatens to consume memory itself'.[19] Jean-François Lyotard's philosophical project of bearing witness to that which thought forgets, a fundamentally memorial project, is generated by the sense that specific ethnocultures, those heterogeneous and local traditions which serve as 'apparatuses for memorising information such that people were able to organise their space and time', are being busily destroyed by a global, technocratic system whose indifferent data systems contain, in the end, 'nobody's memory'.[20]

To think through the intensity of memory-work in the contemporary moment, it is important to see it as inextricably intertwined with an anxiety concerning systems that induce structural forgetting. But memory and forgetting are not opposing things; rather, they are an interplay of the same process. It was the peculiarities of what an individual forgets and the invention of a new pathology of amnesia, after all, that led Victorian psychologists to privilege memory as the locus of identity. Then again, for memory to work at all, forgetting is intrinsic to its function, for to remember everything would be to overwhelm the present with the past. Perhaps most importantly, though, for contemporary criticism that sees technology as accelerating forgetfulness, it must not be assumed that memory is automatically redemptive and forgetting a terror to be warded off. Memory can tyrannically bind you and impose a determining identity you might wish to resist; active forgetting can be a liberation from the dead weight of memorial history. Equally, memory can be *incited*, a compulsory injunction given to remember, and this is what Pierre Nora has in mind when he suggests we are being constructed as 'memory-individuals' in the service of memorial narratives we do not always control.[21] To recover memory, then, is not always an act of resistance against a culture of forgetting. To track the vicissitudes of contemporary memory it is vital to sustain the ambivalence of working between hypermnesia (too much memory) and amnesia (too little).

In what follows, I want to pursue these ambivalences in an arena which has hitherto failed to attract the kind of intense cultural concern of Holocaust studies or the focus on institutional remembering that has produced new disciplines such as Museum studies. 'One of the costs of the historical metamorphosis of memory has been a wholesale preoccupation with the individual psychology of remembering', Nora suggests.[22] Throughout the 1980s, whilst cultural criticism was installing the schizophrenic as the exemplary contemporary subject, the discourses of psychotherapy were producing a wholly different model of the subject, centred on a specific mode of memory. The theory of *recovered memory*, the therapeutic retrieval of 'forgotten' traumatic experiences, may have produced eccentric efflorescences such as Whitley Strieber's 'abductions', but it began with the deadly serious project of recovering memories of sexual abuse. It is the theory of recovered memory that most clearly articulates the simultaneity of the memorial and amnesiac narratives that run through accounts of the contemporary. It is also a specific structure of remembering, I want to suggest, that begins to emerge in contemporary literature at the beginning of the 1990s.

II

At the end of *The Radiant Way*, Margaret Drabble's somewhat awkward attempt to write a state of the nation novel for the 1980s, one of the central characters, Liz Headley, a psychiatrist, 'solves' the mystery of her father's absence from her childhood. After her mother's death, she uncovers news reports for her father's arrest for indecent exposure and suicide in 1939. Beyond this, she has fleeting images, at the very edge of memory, which suggest sexual abuse: 'Yes, she had sat upon her father's knee . . . giggling as he tickled her and played with her. Damp between her innocent infant's legs.'[23] In Shena Mackay's more recent *The Orchard on Fire*, April makes a

pilgrimage to the village of her 1950s childhood, only to confront memories of her best friend's physical abuse by her violent father, and her own
desperate attempts to avoid the pathetic desires of the abusive Mr Greenidge.[24]
In both cases, the bleakness of the present is a result of the effects of an
abusive past: Drabble's symbolic choice of 1939 suggests, even, that the
legacy of the war is best articulated through the trope of abuse.

Neither of these texts simply 'choose' abuse. This thematic is the product, rather, of a shift in awareness about the prevalence of sexual abuse and
an admission of its primary location: inside the family. One of the most
important social effects of feminism in the 1970s was to provide a context
for women to contest the silence surrounding incest-abuse, and this has had
positive and transformative effects. Towards the end of the 1980s, though,
a new addition to the abuse paradigm arrived. Hitherto, people were
struggling to resolve the invasive effects of remembered abuse; now, it was
claimed, sexual abuse could be so traumatic that the mind often resorted to
complete *erasure* of the event. Anguish was felt not through the presence
of memory but by its absence, by structural gaps or 'holes' in memory.
Hypermnesic trauma, the paralysing effect of intolerably present memories,
was replaced by amnesia, the experience of having no conscious memory
of the trauma *at all*. For the advocates of Recovered Memory Therapy
(RMT), the sign of a gap became the symptom of abuse. 'Survivors with
repressed memories are left with a disjointed sense of their own history and
suffer from a sense of incompleteness', the therapist Renee Fredrickson
explained, having proposed that 'millions of people have blocked out frightening episodes of abuse, years of their life, or their entire childhood'.[25]
RMT resituated the locus of subjectivity in an encrypted core of forgotten
trauma; at the same time it proposed that every event was 'recorded and
stored in the filing system in [the] brain' and could be recovered with
crystalline accuracy following correct procedures to 'access' the memory
bank.[26] If claims about the powers of the capacity to forget were being
radically extended, so, simultaneously, was the ability to remember.

The spread of RMT is usually associated with the publication of Ellen
Bass and Laura Davis's self-help book *The Courage to Heal* in 1988. Celebrity
confessions of recovered abuse followed: the chat-show host Oprah Winfrey,
comedian Roseanne Barr, and singer LaToya Jackson all revealed abused
childhoods in 1991. By 1992, a counter-pathology was proposed which
read the same events differently. Recovered memories were false memories, in this thesis, the urge to find memories of abuse implanted by therapists in the minds of those highly suggestible to the allure of uncovering an
instant secret motivation for life's ills, and the promise of a communitarian
identity as a 'survivor'. Recovered memory was iatrogenic, campaigners like
Richard Ofshe and Ethan Watters argued, the strategy of always affirming

memories producing efflorescences of stories of conspiratorial Satanic cabals and alien abductors.[27] The response to the naming of False Memory Syndrome was venomous; this was a denial of women's reality and seen as 'an instance of class consolidation against an internal threat' to the self-image of the middle-class family.[28] The Memory War had begun.[29]

Contemporary British and American literature has followed the shape of this dispute, although with interesting transatlantic differences of emphasis. The fascination lies in the emergence of a new structure of subjectivity, oscillating between memory and forgetting, with the prospect that another self, attached to a wholly occluded memory-chain, might lurk in the interstices of a life-story. In the instant of recovery, the technique proposes, we can become strangers to ourselves.

In 1991, at the peak of American awareness about recovered memory, Jane Smiley's novel *A Thousand Acres* was awarded the Pulitzer Prize.[30] A brilliant re-working of *King Lear*, transposing the fate of a kingdom to a mid-West farm divided amongst the patriarch Larry Cook's daughters, it was the *mechanism* of the revisionist reading that spoke to its time. At the play's pivotal moment – Lear's abandonment to the storm – Smiley shifts the focus back to the daughters, and Rose/Regan begins to excavate for Ginny/Goneril's forgotten memories. 'You don't remember how he came after us, do you? . . . When we were teenagers. How he came into our rooms . . . How can you not remember?' (188). The effect of this challenge follows the pattern recovered memory therapists outline: Ginny issues a flat denial, but the suggestion speaks to Ginny's sense of absence and disquiet. This is a fragile landscape with a brittle surface: she remembers staring down the farm drains, 'perched thoughtless on the filmiest net of the modern world, over layers of rock . . . layers of dark epochs' (47). The farm has buried secrets – Ginny's bloodied clothes from her last miscarriage, the mother's grave. Symptomatic gaps are already evident: why does Ginny hold no memories of her mother, even though she was fourteen when her mother died? Forty pages on from Rose's challenge, the forgotten trauma returns in a flash of image-memory: 'I knew that he had been in there to me, that my father had lain with me in that bed, that I had looked at the top of his head, at his balding spot in the brown grizzled hair, while feeling him suck my breasts' (228). The 'emergency phase', the catastrophic intrusion of occluded memories into an identity built on an excised version of the past, follows from this one memory ('I would feel a growing obsession to remember surging through me, seizing me, taking me into a danger that I could not endure yet' [231]). The abuse retrospectively explains the awkwardness of her marriage in symptomatic behaviours that become now 'obvious evidence [of] my midnight experiences with Daddy' (279). What Renee Fredrickson terms 'feeling memory' and 'bodily memory' accompanies the imagistic flashes that have evaded the censorious conscious memory, and Ginny arrives at the admission that 'one thing Daddy took from me . . . was the memory of my body' (280).

With one stroke Smiley re-writes the dynamics of *Lear*. The inexplicable motivations of Lear's daughters are given vital depth. The horror at the derangement of natural orders is resituated from the failure of daughterly duty to paternal incestuous desire. Lear's venomous disgust of female sexuality ('Down from the waist they are centaurs/ . . . There's hell, there's darkness, there is the sulphurous pit'[31]) is marked as projection from abuser to abused. And Cordelia's loving rapprochement with her father is here transformed into Caroline's complicitous refusal to confront abuse (363). This is more than just an ingenious exercise in revisionary intertextuality, however. Splitting open a canonical text aims at exploding the wider cultural attitudes that would instate *King Lear* as an exemplary humanist text, silencing its violent misogyny and discourse of property and chattel. Smiley's de-cryption of a sub-text of paternal abuse in *Lear* acts to counter a contemporary conservatism about the family that would precisely locate female insubordination as the greatest threat – that is, take Lear's part. As Kate Chedgzoy points out, however, 'the compelling narrative pleasures of Smiley's fiction are secured by a revision of the plot which does take the woman's part and which . . . refuses tragic closure'.[32] The truth of abuse that re-writes Shakespeare is also the truth that, for Smiley, discourses of the American family must confront.

Four years later, the model of recovered memory travels across the Atlantic, also to be found in an award-winning novel. It is significant, however, that Kate Atkinson's *Behind the Scenes at the Museum*[33] is not centred on abuse but the forgotten trauma of a family death. This perhaps reflects an English distance from the heat of a predominantly American debate over RMT; it certainly helps to detach the question of abuse from the argument over a *structure* of memory. The trauma of a hidden death is not incompatible with RMT, however, which, as Judith Herman points out in *Trauma and Recovery*, began with the treatment of shell-shock in the early twentieth century.[34]

It is only towards the close of *Behind the Scenes at the Museum* that the title begins to resonate with its full meaning. This sprawling, comic family saga, which tracks the generations of a dissolute family over a century, is apparently fulfilling a memorial project. The forward progress of the narration of Ruby's life from 1950s childhood to the present is repeatedly disrupted by footnoted scenes from the family's transgenerational history, narratives which are sparked almost involuntarily by the secret histories of objects surviving anonymously into the present. Tea-spoons, buttons, a rabbit's foot become fully con-temporal objects, hinting at uncanny repetitions across lost time, their inaccessible stores of memory impossibly voiced by a narrator who hovers peculiarly between Ruby and omniscience. These objectal histories seemingly act to recuperate all the lost familial lines that derive from the 'originating' maternal figure, and gradually animate the enigmatic photograph of Alice taken in 1888, a picture that has passed down the generations. This patchwork of disordered segments works to redeem individual histories of loss, disappointment and death.

This is one memorial narrative, but another belatedly intersects it and demands a retrospective revision of the family narrative. Only when Ruby is seventeen is she confronted with the repressed memory of her twin sister, Pearl, who drowned at the age of five. 'I could feel a dreadful, threatening pulse beating in my stomach, yet I had no recollection of this sister, could bring no image to mind. I had a strange flash of memory – as if caught in a photographer's flash – . . . but nothing more' (328). By a carefully staged process of hypnotic recovery (Atkinson displays her knowledge of recovered memory literature), Ruby has 'my twin, my double, my mirror' (331) returned to her. It is this process that goes *behind* the behind of the familial museum.

The tonal disjunction of a comic romp which nevertheless aggregates an alarming record of death and disappearance is thus revised as a symptomatic dissonance. The strange oscillation of narrative locus – Ruby, yet not, omniscient yet not – is readable as the product of a familial saga which is in fact constituted around a central traumatic core. Working to re-construct tangled family lines, the floor drops away from an implicit trust in the narrative voice, and the belated realisation of the repeated clues or signals that there is a 'hole' in the history virtually compels a second reading. In effect, Atkinson manoeuvres the reader into the position of the unknowing subject of repressed memory, subject to all the estrangements and dissonances a belated revelation of a hidden secret can produce.

Both Smiley and Atkinson use the structure of recovered memory as concealing a truth that, once confronted, can resolve divided memory. Smiley's cautious ending, suggesting a difficult route for Ginny out of the ruins of her memory, is more powerful than Atkinson's rapid assimilation of Pearl's death into a memorial narrative – merely another exhibit in the familial museum. By 1997, however, Nicci French's *The Memory Game* traverses the same psychological terrain only to explore the effects of the implantation of false memories.[35] The novel opens with a discovery that literally shakes the foundations of the Martello family. The architect daughter strikes ground for a new building in the grounds of her parents' house only to uncover a body: the corpse of her sister Natalie, who disappeared in 1968. Jane's initiation into the culture of recovered memory advocates and support groups follows her work with a therapist on retrieving the 'repressed' elements of her last memory of Natalie. It seems as if the familiar structure is operating here, Jane worrying at the disquiet that hovers over her memory: 'I've been thinking about my golden, golden childhood and a black hole in the middle of it . . . Somehow it's there, always on the edge of vision, but when I turn to look at it directly it's gone, gone to the edge again' (57). The results, however, are different. It is the persistence of her therapist's belief that the gap *must* contain an encrypted trauma, since Jane 'fits' the schema of symptoms of repressed memory, that leads her to uncover her father in the focal memory. After his imprisonment for the murder, Jane returns to the real scene only to realise the image she has worked on so intensely misremembers crucial details. The condensed finale exposes the false memory at work, and it is detective logic that identifies the brother as the real perpetrator.

This is a text programmatically written from arguments that recovered memories are no more than suggestions implanted by schema-driven therapists. Openness to suggestion in certain individuals has been well-documented since the discovery of 'magnetic sleep' (hypnosis); *The Memory Game* dramatises the view that therapists holding a conspiratorial belief in the extensiveness of familial violence and abuse, and possessing an extensive list of symptomatic signifiers of submerged trauma, can suggest an image a patient *ought* to hold, induce it and then confabulate fantasies which are affirmed as memory. If the novel has a strangely educative air, almost aiming to introduce its readership to an insidious invasion of a new and dangerous therapeutic method, this may be because the plot owes much to the real-life case of Eileen Lipsker, whose recovered memories which 'solved' a sixteen-year-old murder by identifying her father are still being contested in the American law courts. It is a case which advocates of False Memory Syndrome are fond of citing as evidence of the 'social harm' RMT is causing.[36]

Novelistic investigations, then, would seem to fall into the intractable positions of the recovered memory debate. As Ofshe and Watters have argued, 'the options for those taking sides in this debate are quite unambiguous: the mind either has the ability to repress vast numbers of events, as described by recovered memory therapists, or it does not'.[37] Although investigating the possibilities of the same structure of subjectivity, the projects behind *A Thousand Acres* and *The Memory Game* could hardly seem more incompatible in their sympathies. But if I end with Helen Dunmore's *Talking to the Dead*,[38] this is because her treatment of recovered memory refuses to stay *in* the debate.

The novel begins with Nina's arrival to help her elder sister Isabel through the first days following the birth, with complications, of Isabel's son. Nina is assailed by memories of childhood and Isabel's authoritative hold over the story of her early years; as she says, 'I'm in the habit of believing Isabel's version' (13). The air of tension, Chapter 8 belatedly reveals, is the unspoken absence of their younger brother, who died in infancy from cot-death. This is the core event on which the novel turns. At first its absent presence implies fears of repetition with the new child, but something else is moving in the traumatic scene. It is significant that immediately after the trauma's first narration Nina begins to interrogate the general tenor of her childhood memory: 'It's a safe story, well-worn and comforting . . . Perhaps I tell myself this story so loudly that I can't hear anything else' (58). The challenge becomes more urgent as the first explicit mention of the lost brother occurs between the sisters: memory surges, and begins to animate the frozen image of Colin's death. 'I want my past back. . . . But there's nothing', Nina realises, except 'Isabel's stories' (91). Just before the revelation Nina is unwittingly but perfectly defined as the 'gapped' subject of amnesia: 'There's something missing in you' (98).

As the sisters talk, Nina captures an image of Isabel pushing down on Colin's back, but at the brink of articulation, Isabel reverses the action and issues a contradictory injunction: 'Don't, don't. Don't remember. You were only four. It wasn't your fault' (100). Jealousy transfers agent: the authority of Isabel's narrative of their childhood has precisely served to occlude Nina's murderous act from herself. With that knowledge, a fragile self is shattered: 'uncertainty runs round me like ice . . . The iceberg hits the side of my ship, and I go down' (102–3). Dunmore therefore builds her plot from the phases of RMT: conscious recall of a placid childhood, edged by disquiet; a memory-image that becomes the focal point for retrieval; the recovery of the scene and entry into the 'emergency phase' as identity threatens to collapse.

But Dunmore refuses to let the traumatic scene become fixed. The scene speaks of deadly sibling rivalry, but so does the *context of the recovery* of the scene. As the dread gathers that contemporary events will compulsively repeat the past, the primal scene is entered once more, agency reverses itself again, and Nina this time relocates her sister, too late, as the murderous figure in the traumatic memory. By the end, following Isabel's suicide, Nina's conviction seems secure: 'It must have been hard to do . . . By the time he went still she must have hated him for taking so long to be dead' (204). Nevertheless, the text ends on an incomplete fragment of memory as Nina stands over her sister's grave. Reaching up to take Isabel's hand, the memory and text end on a question – 'Can I ask you something?' (214) – which now cannot be answered. Memory, which means talking to the dead, will be without final resolution, Dunmore implies.

This is Dunmore's innovation: it is not that the traumatic scene is either 'true' or 'false', but one which is set in motion by the imbrication of actual history, memory's imperfect and *interpretive* relation to that history, and the role of contemporary fantasy investments in the re-telling of the scene. This is what the recovered memory debate cannot contain. Both the defenders and detractors of recovered memory share the same assumption that the past is *determinate* and memory a mere re-presentation of the past that can be judged on an index of accuracy: true or false. But the historical past is irrecoverable; memory alone is the only access to it, and memory is a malleable narrative always open to retroactive re-description. The very existence of the recovered memory debate paradoxically displays this, for only instability in the conception of memory could allow such diametrically opposed positions to be simultaneously maintained. As Ian Hacking argues, 'the past becomes rewritten in memory, with new kinds of descriptions, new words, new ways of feeling', such that 'each of us becomes a different person as we redescribe the past'.[39] As the agency in the recovered scene circulates between Nina and Isabel, new subjectivities and new histories are being elaborated as memory submits to the impress of the sisters' competing investments. Between history, memory and desire 'the notion of "true" and "false" memory reduces out these indeterminate, intermediate points between knowing and not knowing and between the concrete and symbolic functions of memory'.[40]

Richard Terdiman summarises the 'memory crisis' in this way:

> All manner of reflection on our condition has sought to ground identity in our memory. What else could be its guarantor, what else seems constant as we change? Such views have been familiar over a long portion of the history of the West. Yet modernity puts this foundational idea into crisis. Suddenly memory does not ground us – it rather registers our drift.[41]

The contemporary version of this crisis is in the oscillation between the terrors of too little memory, or too much. The most intensive instantiation of this ambivalence is the amnesiac subject who buries a perfect, hypermnesic image at the core, poised to strike at the essence of identity. In many ways, it is clear that this new subject of memory is the product of the retreat from larger structures of memorial identity – history, nation, state – that I outlined earlier. The 'mundane, slow-moving institutional failure' of these supports, Charles Turner suggests, has led to a situation which 'throws individuals increasingly back upon themselves, and makes all of us sensitive to catastrophes of every sort'.[42] And how are those catastrophes inscribed? Both sides of the recovered memory dispute introject the object of contemporary anxiety: technology. RMT speaks of lost and retrieved files and replaying the memory 'movie' with its flashbacks, close-ups and zooms; detractors speak of the 'virus' of therapy, corrupted files and data manipulation. Both wish to stabilise memories as true or false by the very thing which, elsewhere, is seen as radically de-stabilising memory.

To historicise the argument over recovered memory is neither to deny the reality of sexual abuse nor refuse the argument that certain techniques might offer hidden trauma as a curiously consoling 'comprehensive cause-and-effect story . . . at those times when we seem unable to do this for ourselves'.[43] It is, rather, to suggest that the desire to stabilise memory as either true or false is an anxiety induced by a forgetfulness that the history of memory itself twists and turns, is subject to constant mutations and revisions.

NOTES

1. Cited by Lynn MacRitchie, 'The War Over Rachel', *The Guardian*, 5 November 1996, Arts p. 9.
2. Whitley Strieber, *Communion* (London: Arrow, 1988).
3. James E. Young, *The Texture of Memory: Holocaust Memorials and Meaning* (New Haven: Yale University Press, 1993), p. xii.
4. Richard Terdiman, *Present Past: Modernity and the Memory Crisis* (Ithaca: Cornell University Press, 1993), p. 8.
5. Michèle Roberts, *Daughters of the House* (London: Virago, 1993); Ian McEwan, *Black Dogs* (London: Picador, 1991); Kazuo Ishiguro, *The Remains of the Day* (London: Faber and Faber, 1989).
6. Sigmund Freud, 'Remembering, Repeating and Working-Through', in *Standard Edition*, vol. 12, trans. James Strachey (London: Hogarth Press, 1958).
7. Homi Bhabha, 'Anxious Nations, Nervous States', in Joan Copjek, ed., *Supposing the Subject* (London: Verso, 1994), p. 201.
8. Jean-François Lyotard, *Heidegger and 'the jews'*, trans. Andreas Michel and Mark Roberts (Minneapolis: Minnesota University Press, 1990), p. 8.
9. Charles Turner, 'Holocaust Memories and History', *History of the Human Sciences* 9:4 (1996), p. 46.
10. For more detailed analysis of this phenomenon, see my 'The Science-Fictionalisation of Trauma: Remarks on Narratives of Alien Abduction', *Science Fiction Studies* 25:1 (March 1998).
11. Andreas Huyssen, *Twilight Memories: Marking Time in a Culture of Amnesia* (London: Routledge, 1995), p. 5.
12. Fredric Jameson, *Postmodernism, or the Cultural Logic of Late Capitalism* (London: Verso, 1991), p. 71.
13. Jameson, *Postmodernism*, pp. 364–5.
14. Jameson, *Postmodernism*, pp. 27 and 286.
15. See Nancy Wood's excellent summary of Nora's project in 'Memory's Remains: *Les Lieux de mémoire*', *History and Memory* 6:1 (Spring/Summer 1994).

16. For a summary of the dispute, see Saul Friedlander, *Memory, History, and the Extermination of the Jews of Europe* (Indianapolis: Indiana University Press, 1993).
17. Pierre Nora, 'Between Memory and History: *Les Lieux de Mémoire*', *Representations* 26 (Spring 1989), p. 7.
18. Nora, 'Between Memory and History', p. 12.
19. Huyssen, *Twilight Memories*, pp. 9 and 7.
20. Jean-François Lyotard, *The Inhuman: Reflections on Time*, trans. Geoffrey Bennington and Rachel Bowlby (Cambridge: Polity, 1991), pp. 62 and 64.
21. Nora, 'Between Memory and History', p. 15.
22. Nora, 'Between Memory and History', p. 15.
23. Margaret Drabble, *The Radiant Way* (Harmondsworth: Penguin, 1988), p. 386.
24. Shena Mackay, *The Orchard on Fire* (London: Minerva, 1996).
25. Renee Fredrickson, *Repressed Memories: A Journey to Recovery from Sexual Abuse* (New York: Fireside, 1992), pp. 31 and 15.
26. Fredrickson, *Repressed Memories*, p. 88.
27. Richard Ofshe and Ethan Watters, *Making Monsters: False Memories, Psychotherapy, and Sexual Hysteria* (New York: Scribner's, 1994).
28. Elizabeth Wilson, 'Not in this House: Incest, Denial, and Doubt in the White Middle Class Family', *Yale Journal of Criticism* 8 (1995), p. 52.
29. Frederick Crews *et al.*, *The Memory Wars: Freud's Legacy in Dispute* (London: Granta Books, 1997).
30. Jane Smiley, *A Thousand Acres* (London: Flamingo, 1992). All references in text.
31. William Shakespeare, *King Lear*, IV.vi.124–8.
32. Kate Chedgzoy, *Shakespeare's Queer Children* (Manchester: Manchester Univeristy Press, 1996), p. 58.
33. Kate Atkinson, *Behind the Scenes at the Museum* (London: Black Swan, 1996). All references in text. Atkinson won the Whitbread Book of the Year, and the novel was reprinted sixteen times in 1996 alone.
34. Judith Herman, *Trauma and Recovery: From Domestic Abuse to Political Terror* (London: Pandora, 1992).
35. Nicci French, *The Memory Game* (London: Heinemann, 1997). All references in text. 'Nicci French' is the pseudonym adopted by the husband-and-wife writing team, Sean French and Nicci Gerrard.
36. Eileen Lipsker's case is summarised by Crews, *The Memory Wars*, pp. 168–81.
37. Ofshe and Watters, *Making Monsters*, p. 5.
38. Helen Dunmore, *Talking to the Dead* (Harmondsworth: Penguin, 1997). All references in text.
39. Ian Hacking, *Rewriting the Soul: Multiple Personality and the Sciences of Memory* (New Jersey: Princeton University Press, 1995), pp. 94 and 68.
40. Janice Haaken, 'Sexual Abuse, Recovered Memory, and Therapeutic Practice: A Feminist-Psychoanalytic Perspective', *Social Text* 40 (Fall 1994), p. 118. See, too, John Frow, who reiterates the view that memory's 'relation to the past is not that of truth but of desire', *Time and Commodity Culture* (Oxford: Oxford University Press, 1997), p. 229.
41. Terdiman, *Present Past*, p. 290.
42. Turner, 'Holocaust Memory and History', p. 58.
43. Ofshe and Watters, *Making Monsters*, p. 43.

CHAPTER SEVEN

'We come after': remembering the Holocaust

Nicola King

We come after, and that is the nerve of our condition.[1]

This essay analyses the ways in which some recent fiction represents the Holocaust, the event which, even after Cambodia, Bosnia, Rwanda, seems to stand, at least in the West, as the paradigm of atrocity. The Holocaust remains a contemporary concern not only for obvious reasons such as the rise of neo-Nazism, the prosecution of suspected war criminals and echoes suggested by 'ethnic cleansing' in Bosnia and Rwanda, but also because the event itself has come to represent a rupture in historical continuity, problematising the relationship between past and present and, according to Shoshana Felman, opening up a 'radical historical crisis in witnessing'.[2] Even naming the event is problematic: many dislike the term 'Holocaust', which means, literally, 'whole burning' and has connotations of sacrifice; Claude Lanzmann's choice, 'Shoah' or 'destruction', also has biblical precedents; the metonymical 'Auschwitz' seems to negate the experience of those who died by other means; the euphemistic 'Final Solution' replicates Nazi ideology. These terms are all, in different ways, metaphoric, and the use of metaphor in representation will be one of my main concerns. I discuss the ways in which fiction might be a 'site of memory' as the generation who directly experienced it begins to die out. As Anne Michaels has said, 'our generation have the advantage of time, even a small amount of time and distance . . . our responsibility is to find a different way of thinking about it, of moving on without forgetting'.[3]

Michaels's recent Orange Prize-winning novel, *Fugitive Pieces*,[4] will be the main focus of this essay. Her protagonist, Jakob Beer, is a Jewish child in Poland whose family are killed at the beginning of the narrative, and who is saved by a Greek archaeologist and brought up in Greece and Canada. He becomes a poet who inspires a younger man, Ben, himself the child of Holocaust survivors. Jakob and Ben thus belong to the generation marked by 'the compact void of the unspeakable', who have to 'recover the past by inventing it',[5] and the novel is a moving evocation of memory and love which enacts and enables the sharing of traumatic memory. I discuss two other novels more briefly. Emily Prager's *Eve's Tattoo*[6] is a cruder attempt at transmitting the memory of lives destroyed. Her protagonist is a New York journalist who discovers a photograph amongst her Jewish lover's possessions of another woman who bears a concentration camp tattoo. Eve has herself tattooed with the number – 'to keep her alive' – and uses peoples' questions about the tattoo as the opportunity for telling the stories of the women she might have been. Christopher Hope's *Serenity House*[7] is a black comedy in which Max Mountfalcon, an 'ethnologist' who worked in the Nazi camps, ends up in an old peoples' home in Britain. He is tracked down as a war criminal and threatened by a young American psychopath, Jack, who once worked in a Disney theme park: both institutions are developed as analogies to the concentration camp.

Those, like Elie Wiesel, who claim that the Holocaust cannot be compared with anything else (although, of course, it inevitably will be) insist upon its uniqueness, and it is elements of this uniqueness as described by Eberhard Jaeckel which constitute the shock to our sense of humanity and historical continuity effected by this event:

> the Nazi murder of the Jews was unique because never before has a state decided and announced, on the authority of its responsible leader, that it intended to kill in its entirety, as far as possible, a particular group of human beings, including its old people, women, children and infants, and then put this decision into action with every possible instrument of power available to the state.[8]

Jürgen Habermas describes this sense of shock and rupture:

> Something took place here which up until that time no one had even thought might be possible. A deep stratum of solidarity between all that bears a human countenance was touched here. The integrity of this deep stratum had, up until that time, remained unchallenged, and this despite all the natural bestialities of world history . . . Auschwitz has altered the conditions for the continuity of historical life-connections – and not only in Germany.[9]

This radical alteration includes, for many, a crisis in and of language and representation itself. Jean-François Lyotard has compared the Holocaust to an earthquake so powerful as to destroy all instruments that might have been capable of measuring it. Despite this, a 'complex feeling of something indeterminate having happened would stay in memory'. The signs that might refer to it, however, indicate 'that something which should be able to be put into phrases cannot be phrased in the accepted idioms . . . The silence that surrounds the phrase "Auschwitz was an extermination camp" is not a state of mind, . . . it is a sign that something remains to be phrased which is not, something which is not determined.'[10] Lyotard is here talking about the (im)possibility of writing a history of the Holocaust. Similar arguments can be brought into play in the analysis of fictional narratives. The best-known statement on the possibility of literary expression after the Holocaust is Adorno's maxim, 'After Auschwitz, to write poetry is barbaric'.[11] He later qualified this to say that *'literature must resist this verdict'* of silence,[12] a silence also paradoxically demanded by survivor and novelist Elie Wiesel: 'Silence, more than language, remains the substance and the seal of what was once their universe, and . . . like language, it demands to be recognized and transmitted'.[13] Lawrence Langer, in his analysis of oral testimony, explains why complete silence is not an option, at least for survivors: 'If "reality" is not accessible in language it will be made more fully accessible through blows. The Nazis themselves, prompted by the skeptical linguisticism of their own time, made the effort to reach beyond words with their ferocious strength.'[14]

But whose language – or silence – is being demanded or refused? Survivors may need to speak, or to write, and several are only now finding the voice in which to do so. Helen Lewis and Binjamin Wilkimorski have recently published testimonies which differ radically in their mode of bearing witness. Lewis, a young woman when she was imprisoned in Auschwitz, constructs a lucid, coherent, logical narrative which maintains a certain sense of distance from her experiences. She begins: 'As a young child, my only regret was that I had no little brother or sister to play with'.[15] Wilkimorski, a young child when he was deported to Majdanek, begins: 'I have no mother tongue, nor a father tongue either'. His memories are 'shards that keep surfacing against the orderly grain of grown-up life and escaping the laws of logic'. He bears witness to his experience 'exactly the way my child's memory has held on to it; with no benefit of perspective or vanishing point'.[16] The reader experiences this text as a sequence of visual fragments of half-understood and almost unbearable suffering: the child being given a crust of bread in the camp by his dying mother; two starving babies whose fingers are so frozen that they feel no pain when they gnaw them to the bone.

Wilkimorski has explained that many of his memories only returned in therapy, and the psychoanalyst Dori Laub has written of his own work with survivors that, because

massive trauma precludes its registration, . . . [t]he victim's narrative . . . does indeed begin with someone who testifies to an absence, to an event which has not yet come into existence . . . The trauma – as a known event and not simply as an overwhelming shock – has not been truly witnessed yet, not been taken cognizance of. The emergence of the narrative which is being listened to is, therefore, the process and the place wherein the cognizance, the 'knowing' of the event is given birth to.[17]

In this sense the experience of these survivors is still 'contemporary', and yet, paradoxically, still unreal. One of Langer's interviewees said: 'It can only be told, I think it is important to be told, but it cannot be experienced. I cannot even experience it.'[18] Laub claims that therapy, which he describes in terms of an act of witness, may enable a belated re-integration of memory and restoration of a sense of life continuity. 'The systematic destruction of self-identity of inmates in concentration camps was also the attempt to destroy their narrative of themselves.'[19] If it is the task of the therapist to restore that narrative, what is the responsibility of the writer of fictions who also wants to bear his or her own witness to this event?

In spite of Lyotard's claim that sign and referent have become detached in the wake of Auschwitz, historians and educators clearly do feel the responsibility to 'tell the story' of the Holocaust. What Lyotard demands is a form of writing that does not 'forget' the fact of the forgotten and the unrepresentable: his work is a radical critique of 'the limitations of all historicisms and "monumental" or memorializing histories that "forget" by having too certain, too definite, too representative, too narrativized (too anecdotal) a "memory"'.[20] The paradox here is that a certain kind of memorialising can constitute a *defence* against memory, or destroy its very possibility: even Primo Levi wrote that 'a memory evoked too often, and expressed in the form of a story, tends to become fixed in a stereotype, in a form tested by experience, crystallized, perfect, adorned, which installs itself in the place of raw memory and grows at its expense'.[21] If memorials, histories and even survivors' testimonies run the risk of totalising, fixing, 'memorialising', so do fictional narratives or other cultural representations. Gillian Rose has argued that Spielberg's *Schindler's List* falls, in its latter stages, into this trap by sentimentalising Schindler and enabling a too-easy identification with him on the part of the audience, imposing a comforting pattern of salvation and redemption.[22] This might be what Elie Wiesel meant by his claim that '[i]f it is a novel, it is not about Auschwitz. If it is about Auschwitz, it is not a novel.'[23] Lyotard explains that '[n]arrative organisation is constitutive of diachronic time, and the time that it constitutes has the effect of "neutralizing" an "initial" violence . . . of staging the obscene, of disassociating the past from the present, and of staging a recollection that must be a reappropriation of the improper, achronological affect'[24] – the 'achronology' which results from the shock of unassimilated traumatic experience. In spite of the risky nature of the enterprise, it may be the very freedom of fictional narrative which offers this possibility of representing 'the fact of the forgotten and the unrepresentable'.[25] It offers 'some sort of narrative margin which leaves the unsayable unsaid'[26] – the kind of silence which might seem irresponsible to the historian or unbearable for the survivor. After denying the possibility of poetry after Auschwitz, Adorno wrote: 'the abundance of real suffering . . . demands the continued existence of art [even as] . . . it prohibits it. It is now virtually in art alone that suffering can still find its own voice, consolation, without immediately being betrayed by it.'[27] Adorno does not here specify what form or genre of art he is thinking of, and it is clearly impossible to prescribe a mode of literary or artistic expression, or predetermine a reader's or a viewer's response. Adorno acknowledged that '[t]he so-called artistic representation of naked bodily pain, of victims felled by rifle butts, contains, however remote, the possibility of wringing pleasure from it',[28] and Berel Lang has suggested that 'what is presented [might] become an offense, an aggression, and may arouse such strong defenses that – in a profound way – we do not believe that what we are made to feel and see is part of reality'.[29]

Even those whose aims are clearly not those of trivialisation or sensationalism disagree about the appropriateness of different kinds of literary expression. Wiesel states that this subject 'must be approached with fear and trembling. And above all, with humility.'[30] Howard Jacobson claims the opposite: that '[t]he trap isn't too little reverence but too much . . . Our instinct to mock, precisely where we are most protective of what is sacred, is one of the oldest and soundest instincts we possess . . . It's precisely because the Holocaust is, perversely, sacred, that we must now let writers and artists do, perversely, what they choose with it.'[31] Hartman similarly wonders whether tragedy is an adequate interpretation of these events, or whether ' "the worst returns to laughter" in some new, as yet unrealised form closer to the grotesque'.[32]

Christopher Hope's *Serenity House* can be seen in these grotesque terms. Many of its effects, and even its basic premise, are clearly grotesque – Max, a former camp 'ethnologist' who created a new identity for himself after the war, is now a potential victim of advocates of (supposedly voluntary) euthanasia for the elderly. Jack is a modern and distorted equivalent of the fairy-tale Jack the Giantkiller, addicted to witnessing (or even perpetrating) violent deaths, who tracks Max down at the request of the antique dealers to whom he has taken Max's instruments, left after the war in the care of Marta, Jack's adoptive mother, who was forced to work with Max in the camps in order to survive. Jack later steals Max's fiercely guarded carpet-bag which turns out to contain more 'souvenirs', including his collection of human eyeballs. But this novel also attempts to address central questions such as the repression of memory on the part of the perpetrators and the question of responsibility. Max's son-in-law, a Member of Parliament, is determined to have him prosecuted as a war criminal. Max seems to have come to believe almost entirely in his second and deliberately created identity, and in his 'eventide refuge' *he* is becoming the victim both of Jack and of the owner of Serenity House, who turns a blind eye when many of the residents (who he calls, ironically, 'survivors') die in mysterious circumstances under Jack's care.

Marta's stories of atrocity reflect her need to witness – but the effect is only to feed Jack's violent fantasies. These are stories 'you could believe in', compared with the increasingly violent videos which now only make him laugh. Jack clearly does not have the problem of belief suggested by Berel Lang; his favourite, most 'believable' story is Marta's account of how prisoners were made to dig trenches, were shot in the head and then burned in them. When there was a shortage of fuel, '[t]he fat that comes from our own bodies, they collected it . . . in pails. And with these pails the fires in the trenches were fed.' Jack's response at this point in the story is to shout 'Snap! . . . Crackle, pop!' (86). This is a blackly comic paradigm of how Holocaust memory might now be dissociated from its context, fractured, difficult if not impossible to transmit, its effect impossible to determine. '[M]emory, after all', reflects Max, 'was not history, but more of a system of values' (153). Black youths in some US cities apparently responded with laughter and enjoyment to the scenes in *Schindler's List* where Amon Goeth takes pot-shots at Jews from his balcony – this was too close to their experience of life on the streets to evoke the expected reaction of horror. Hope's (possibly not entirely comic) equation of the Nazi murder of millions with the 'solution' of euthanasia to the problem of growing numbers of the elderly might seem facile, but, possibly, educative to those who do not know that, as Max puts it, 'the camps began in the hospitals . . . then the hospitals moved to the camps' (75). Max finally escapes from Serenity House with the help of his grand-daughter Innocenta, flies to Florida, and finds and kills Jack on one of his Disneyland rides. The reader is clearly being invited to take Max's side: earlier atrocities have been superseded by a contemporary addiction to mindless violence fed by the media and a soulless consumer culture.

Hope's comedy relies upon metaphor which seems at once too obvious (old people's homes and theme parks both having to deal with 'the problems of number') and too dissonant (nobody has to go to a theme park, and those who do presumably enjoy themselves; assisted death for the terminally ill does not necessarily lead to mass euthanasia of the elderly). The Holocaust has been described as an event which actualised metaphor – images of hell became real – but, as James Young says, 'it is ironic that once an event is perceived to be without precedent, without adequate analogy, it would in itself become a kind of precedent for all that follows'.[33] The question of which events or institutions are compared, for literary or political ends, to those which characterised the Nazi era, is also an ethical one. The analogies used by Hope might be offensive to survivors like Binjamin Wilkimorski who, after his 'liberation', experienced the children's and adoptive homes where he lived as extensions of the camp: 'nobody ever said right out to me, Yes, the camp was real, but now it's over. There *is* another world now, and you're allowed to live in it . . . The camp's still there – just hidden and well-disguised.'[34]

The question of adequate or appropriate literary expression is one of form as well as tone. Jacobson defends Martin Amis's *Time's Arrow* – in which the life of a Nazi doctor is narrated backwards – from its detractors because its 'grotesque conceit of reverse destruction, making a people from the weather, from thunder and lightning, with gas and shit and fire' defamiliarises and jolts the reader out of the slightly distanced reverence with which the subject is usually approached.'[35] *Time's Arrow*[36] stands at the extreme end of the scale of postmodern experimentation, separating language from the order in which we normally experience events – preserving, possibly, Lyotard's 'improper, achronological affect'. Yet there are problems with this. As Saul Friedlander puts it, 'it is precisely the "Final Solution" which allows postmodernist thinking to question the validity of any totalizing view of history, of any reference to a definable metadiscourse'.[37] For Felman, 'the cryptic forms of modern narrative and modern art always . . . partake of that historical impossibility of writing a historical narration of the Holocaust, by bearing testimony, through their very cryptic form, to the *radical historical crisis in witnessing* which the Holocaust has opened up'.[38] The Holocaust, she and Dori Laub claim, created 'an event without a witness', and Laub has described how some survivors only 'bear witness' much later, in the therapeutic situation. But Felman is claiming more than this – that the Holocaust has 'proven' the impossibility of bearing witness to any historical event, a claim that she develops as a defence of the critic Paul de Man, who wrote for Nazi journals before the war but kept silence on the matter after it. Friedlander points out the danger of this: 'the equivocation of post-modernism concerning "reality" and "truth" – that is, ultimately, its fundamental relativism – confronts any discourse about Nazism with considerable difficulties'.[39] Barbara Foley has analysed metahistorical fictions about the Holocaust in which fiction and historical fact are difficult, if not impossible to distinguish, and concludes that novels such as William Styrons's *Sophie's Choice* are characterised by 'an epistemological relativism that is philosophically akin to the subjectivist attitude towards truth characteristic of the very fascist nightmare they describe'.[40] The paradox here is that traditional literary realism, with its network of social relations and teleological plots, seems an inadequate form in which to represent an event characterised by 'denial of individuality . . . abstract bureaucracy

[and] . . . an almost indistinguishable combination of corporate and individual will and blindness to evil',[41] whilst the position summarised by E.L. Doctorow, that '[t]here is no fiction or nonfiction as we commonly understand the distinction: there is only narrative',[42] leads, ultimately, to the possibility of Holocaust denial. If the experience of the camps leaves survivors with a sense of disbelief and unreality, the task of the novelist is to communicate that unreality without distorting what is known of history.

In *Eve's Tattoo* Emily Prager makes explicit use of 'history' in her attempt to give fictional expression to the voices of the silenced: she acknowledges her debt to 'witness accounts and original source materials', and to Claudia Koontz's *Mothers in the Fatherland*. Eve has been obssessed with the history of the Third Reich for some time and uses her reading to furnish the details of the stories she tells. She identifies increasingly closely with Eva (the name she gives to the original bearer of the tattoo) as her own life falls apart. At a party she meets a young rock musician whose knowledge of history is so poor that he believes the forty-year-old Eve is actually a survivor of the camps, enabling her to tell one of Eva's possible stories as if it were her own. The text enacts in narrative form the device used in the US Holocaust Memorial Museum in Washington to encourage empathy or identification. As Philip Gourevitch describes:

> Upon admission, visitors are issued with an identity card . . . imprinted
> with the name and vital statistics of an actual Holocaust victim or survivor.
> As they pass through the three floors of the museum's permanent
> exhibition, museum-goers can push these bar-coded cards into
> computerised stations and measure their progress against the fate of their
> phantom surrogates, most of whom were murdered.[43]

This technique made Gourevitch, a first-generation American whose parents were Jewish refugees, profoundly uncomfortable: 'the political choices that I face in my life are not those of the Holocaust; nor are the crises of America shown in this museum. If . . . I should find myself in the shoes of any of these brutalised people whose stories surround me, nothing I could learn from having studied their plight would help me.'

Prager, via Eve, is determined to make these images relevant. The novel is relentlessly 'contemporary': Eve's personal crises are framed by TV coverage of the fall of the Berlin Wall and the release of Nelson Mandela, and her beloved 'uncle' Jim is dying of Aids. There is a fairly crude attempt to link these events to the Nazi past, whilst also recognising important differences: Eve tells an elderly African-American woman that 'a lot of Nazi racial programs and ideology were modeled on American ones at the time' (114), but she and Jim agree that Aids is 'a cataclysm, a disaster, a virus', but that 'Aids was not personal. The holocaust was personal' (82).

Eve says that she wants to undo the simple package – 'MAD HITLER – KILLED JEWS' (30) – which American history has made of the Holocaust, but as a result much of the novel reads like an incompletely assimilated history lesson. It attempts to explore in narrative what Claudia Koontz explores historically: the reasons why many women supported the Nazi movement when Nazi ideology enforced absolute sexual difference and, at least initially, relegated women to the home. Prager more or less reduces Koontz's complex researches into the crude observation that Hitler 'had his hands in the underpants of every German woman' (139), although she does succeed in exposing some of the contradictions in Nazi sexual ideology along the way. The novel is embarrassingly over-determined and sentimental. Any critical distance between the third-person narration and the actions and motives of Eve is hard to detect, and Eve only has to tell one of her stories for her listeners to become 'enlightened'. When Eve tells her stories, a more neutral and detached voice takes over, however, an appropriate and sometimes moving one. Eve's lover, Charlie, cannot make love to her whilst she has the tattoo, prompting her belated realisation of his hidden Jewishness. His anger turns out to be the result of the fact that his parents survived in France by working as 'catchers', handing other Jews over to the Gestapo. They are reunited when Eve ends up in hospital having been knocked down by a car and her arm (conveniently) broken in the place of the tattoo: Eve admits her own residual anti-Semitism and Charlie is able to make love for the first time without anger.

The question of identification with the victim is problematised when the 'real' Eva turns out to be a Nazi supporter whose sons had joined an anti-Nazi youth group: she turns on an SS officer with her kitchen knife when she sees them being hanged. Whilst exploring the ways in which Eve herself, as an unmarried woman who had had an abortion, might have become a victim of Nazi eugenics, the novel thus, finally, de-Judaises the Holocaust. Many of the stories Eve tells are of Christian women who contravened Nazi policy by performing abortions or protecting handicapped children. Women, not Jews, are thus constructed here as the victims. *Eve's Tattoo* signals the difficulty of preventing the Holocaust from becoming remote and apparently irrelevant 'history' without reducing its specificity and implying that we are all, and equally, potential victims.

Anne Michaels's *Fugitive Pieces* is a moving, poetic meditation upon love, loss, memory and time clearly based on extensive research in Holocaust history and survivor testimony. The preface evokes the lost stories of those who, knowing their likely fate, wrote them, buried or hid them but did not live to retrieve them. 'Other stories are concealed in memory, neither written or spoken. Still others are recovered, by circumstance alone.' Michaels thus acknowledges silence whilst also creating a voice for her

subject, the poet Jakob Beer, who also wrestles with the paradoxical demands of silence and bearing witness: 'no one could bear the responsibility
of forgiveness on behalf of the dead . . . When the one who can forgive can
no longer speak, there is only silence' (161). We are told of Jakob's death
in this preface – a random death, knocked down by a car in Athens at the
age of sixty – so that the first narrative, Jakob's memoirs, is already haunted
by this loss. He himself is haunted by the loss of his sister and parents, an
event which he did not directly witness: 'I did not witness the most
important events of my life. My deepest story must be told by a blind man,
a prisoner of sound' (17). He does – briefly – see the bodies of his parents,
but his sister Bella has simply disappeared. Later he immerses himself in the
reports and histories of the camps. The details of where the dead came
from, how they lived and how they were captured, are unimportant:
'None of that obsessed me; but – were they silent or did they speak? Were
their eyes open or closed?' (140). What concerns him is whether the
victims witnessed their own deaths – deaths which can only be followed by
their silence. 'The event is meaningful only if the coordination of time and
space is witnessed. Witnessed by those who lived near the incinerators,
within the radius of smell. By those who lived outside the camp fence, or
stood outside the chamber doors. By those who stepped a few feet to the
right on the station platform. By those who were born a generation after'
(162). Here he implicitly agrees with Primo Levi, for whom the survivors
were not the true witnesses, but who nevertheless felt the responsibility to
bear witness. It is a member of the 'generation after', his student Ben, who
finds his memoirs and thus becomes *his* witness.

The author thus builds the question of 'who bears witness for the
witness?' into the structure of her narrative. Her characters are given
the respect of distance, as if she accepts that she cannot speak for them.
Describing how prisoners were forced to dig up bodies from mass graves in
order to burn them, Jakob asks: 'How can one man take on the memories
of even one other man, let alone five or ten or a thousand or ten thousand;
how can they be sanctified each?' (52). By acknowledging the difficulty of
these questions (as Prager does not), and the power of human love and
memory, Michaels has given suffering its voice and consolation without
betraying it. The voice is clearly hers – the voices of Jakob and Ben are
almost identical – but nevertheless it is a voice which has found a way
of expressing an experience not directly hers. And the consolation offered
is only temporary: Jakob's love for Michaela heals the pain of memory
because she is able to share it, but they die before she tells him that she is
pregnant with a child who would have been called Bella if she had been a
girl: the possibility of redeeming the loss of his sister is offered but not
fulfilled.

Like Toni Morrison's *Beloved*, *Fugitive Pieces* gives form to shared memory and foregrounds the role of language and story-telling. 'Write to save yourself', Athos tells Jakob, 'and someday you'll write because you've been saved' (165). As a teenager in Canada Jakob feels that his 'life could not be stored in any language but only in silence', a silence which would echo '[t]he moment I failed to see that Bella had disappeared'. He wants to find a way of writing poems 'in code, every letter askew, so that loss would wreck the language, become the language' (111). He knows the power of language 'to destroy, to omit, to obliterate', but Athos is later able to show him 'the power of language to restore' (79).

After the deaths of his parents Jakob hides in the mud of Biskupin, an Iron Age city long buried but now being excavated by a group of archae-ologists including Athos, who finds him and takes him to the island of Zakynthos, where he lives in hiding until the end of the war. His narrat-ive evokes the pain and necessity of both forgetting and remembering: he dreams of the dead, '[t]he grotesque remains of incomplete lives, the embodied complexity of desires eternally denied' and is anguished by 'the possibility that it was as painful for them to be remembered as it was for me to remember them' (24–5). Throughout his narrative the image of double exposure recurs: the present exists as an echo of the past, the past is a shadow always just behind the present moment. Watching the candles of the Easter procession on Zakynthos

> I watched and was in my own village, winter evenings, my teacher
> lighting the wicks of our lanterns and releasing us into the street like toy
> boats bobbing down a flooded gutter . . . I . . . placed this parallel image,
> like other ghostly double exposures, carefully into orbit . . . Even now, half
> a century later, writing this on a different Greek island, I look down to
> the remote lights of the town and feel the heat of a flame spreading up
> my sleeve. (18)

Memory is thus layered, like the strata of rock which Athos analyses and which hold the memory of the earth. Events, stories, images in the present are shadowed by defining moments of his past, by what might have been, or what was, although he knew nothing of it: '[t]he shadow past is shaped by everything that never happened. This is how one becomes undone by a smell, a word, a place, the photo of a mountain of shoes' (17). 'Every moment is two moments' because of the doubleness of history and memory: 'History and memory share events; that is, they share time and space'. But the two are not identical: as a man, Jakob tries to 'bury images' under an 'avalanche of facts: train schedules, camp records, statistics, methods of execution. But at night, my mother, my father, Bella, Mones, simply rose, shook the earth from their clothes, and waited' (93). For Ben, the child of survivors who was 'born into absence', this doubleness takes the form of 'a shadow around objects, the black outline, the bruise of fermentation on things even as light clings to them . . . the aura of mortality' (204). This is the doubleness of language described by Primo Levi, in which simple words such as 'bread' or 'cold' no longer have a common referent shared by those who did and did not experience the camps.

For Jakob, the stories Athos tells him on Zakynthos provide a temporary refuge from the pain of memory. Although Athos wants him to remember his Hebrew – 'it is your future you are remembering' (21) – Jakob longs to learn Greek and 'cleanse my mouth of memory'. Athos tells him stories of exploration and discovery, of rocks and weather, of bog-people and buried cities, of 'the earth itself'. At first, 'Athos's stories gradually veered me from my past . . . Because of Athos, I spent hours in other worlds . . . [He] gave me another realm to inhabit, big as the globe and expansive as time.' Rocks hold the memory of time, and Jakob is 'transfixed by the way time buckled, met itself in pleats and folds . . . To go back a year or two was impossible, absurd. To go back millennia – ah! that was . . . nothing' (30). The 'deep stratum' evoked by Habermas here becomes the consolation of the persistence of the earth itself, but also that of love. If archaeology can uncover and even reconstruct buried cities, then perhaps the dead can be brought back to life, preserved intact like the bodies in peat-bogs: 'I fantasized the power of reversal . . . I imagined that if each owner of each pair of shoes could be named, then they would be brought back to life' (50). Athos's 'backward glance' provides Jakob with the consolation of a 'backward hope. Redemption through cataclysm; what had been transformed might be transformed again' (101). Later he writes: 'Human memory is encoded in air currents and river sediment. Eskers of ash wait to be scooped up, lives reconstituted' (53).

The idea that Jakob absorbs from Athos, of history as 'the evolution of longing', makes him realise that grief requires time, and he imagines the stars '[a]ching towards us for millennia though we are blind to their signals until it's too late, starlight only the white breath of an old cry' (53–4). These reflections offer, at times, a kind of consolation, at others an extension of grief and loss into the cosmos itself. Michaels sustains the parallel between human longing and the movements of the earth and stars in a series of poetic meditations which occasionally strike a false note. The migration of birds is compared to 'the black seam of that wailing migration from life to death' on the railways through Europe to the camps: Jakob claims that 'these passengers found their way home. Through the rivers, through the air.' This is followed by the account of prisoners digging up the bodies of the dead, where 'the dead entered them through their pores and were carried through their bloodstreams to their brains and hearts' (51–2). Although Jakob goes on to ask how one man can take on the memories of another, this elision of natural, instinctive processes with politically motivated murder is a mystification, and the suggestion of a kind of immortality strikes me as false consolation. Another false note is struck when Michaels allows Jakob's imagination (or rather, through him, her own) to enter the gas chamber: although he admits it is blasphemy, he does it because he wants to remain close to Bella, who probably died there. Is this sufficient justification for Michaels? Jakob asks: 'Forgive this blasphemy, of choosing philosophy over the brutalism of fact', but goes on to speculate on the meaning of their cries: 'At that moment of utmost degradation, in that twisted reef, is the most obscene testament of grace. For can anyone tell with absolute certainty the difference between the sounds of those who are in despair and the sounds of those who want desperately to believe? The moment when our faith in man is forced to change, anatomically – mercilessly – into faith' (168). It seems presumptuous, to say the least, to attempt to enter the frame of mind of the dying and to imagine their cries as even an 'obscene testament of grace' – although there may be resonances here which escape the non-Jewish reader. The use of 'anatomically' elides the biological with the spiritual, rational, or social – or with whatever it is we consider makes us human, rather as Athos, in recognising the impossibility of an answer to the question 'Why?' (in his researches on Nazi archaeology), 'often applied the geologic to the human, analyzing social change as he would a landscape; slow persuasion and catastrophe' (119).

These moments or ideas may strike the reader as a mystification of human and political agency, but the strength of Michaels's text is its representation and enactment of shared memory. Athos acts as witness to the first painful expression of Jakob's memories; Jakob remembers and commemorates the lives of Bella and his parents in his memoirs, which are read and shared by Ben and the reader.

Jakob and Michaela seem literally able to experience each others' memories: Michaela awakens crying for Bella having heard her story, Jakob 'cross[es] over the boundary of skin into Michaela's memories, into her childhood' (185). Through her he learns that '[m]emory dies unless its given a use', but that '[t]here's no absence, if there remains even the memory of absence' (193). Ben says that there was 'no energy of a narrative in my family, not even the fervour of an elegy' (204). He was 'born into absence', although until his parents' death it was an absence only sensed. It is their refusal, or inability to share their past – a baby son and daughter, Ben's siblings, who were killed, or did not survive – with their surviving son, which is potentially destructive. He discovers the truth in an old family photograph, but it is the fact that his mother shared this secret with Naomi, his wife, which is most painful, and causes their temporary separation. Ben goes to Greece and finds Jakob's notebooks, and it is reading

them, with their premonitive echoes of his own life – *'To remain with
the dead is to abandon them . . . One becomes undone by a photograph, by love
that closes its mouth before calling a name . . .'* (284) – that sends him back
to Canada and a possible reunion with Naomi, because he 'know[s] her
memories' (285).

'One *must*, certainly, inscribe in words, in images', writes Lyotard. 'One
cannot escape the necessity of representing . . . But it is one thing to do it
in view of saving the memory, and quite another to try to preserve the
remainder, the unforgettable forgotten, in writing.'[44] Prager, through the
crude device of Eve's tattoo, attempts to 'save the memory'; Michaels
preserves 'the unforgettable forgotten' and provides a site of memory for
those who 'come after'.

NOTES

1. George Steiner, *Language and Silence* (London: Faber, 1985), p. 22.
2. Shoshana Felman and Dori Laub, *Testimony: Crises of Witnessing in Literature, Psychoanalysis and History* (London: Routledge, 1992), p. 201.
3. Anne Michaels, *The Scotsman*, 1 February 1997, p. 15.
4. Anne Michaels, *Fugitive Pieces* (London: Bloomsbury, 1997). All further references in text.
5. Nadine Fresco, quoted by Ellen S. Fine, 'The Absent Memory', in Berel Lang, ed., *Writing and the Holocaust* (New York: Holmes and Meier, 1988), p. 42.
6. Emily Prager, *Eve's Tattoo* (London: Chatto and Windus, 1992). All references in text.
7. Christopher Hope, *Serenity House* (London: Macmillan, 1992). All references in text.
8. Quoted by Richard Evans, *In Hitler's Shadow: West German Historians and the Attempt to Escape from the Nazi Past* (London: I.B.Tauris & Co. Ltd., 1989), p. 86.
9. Jürgen Habermas, *The New Conservatism: Cultural Criticism and the Historians' Debate*, ed. and trans. Shierry Weber Nicholsen (Cambridge: Polity Press, 1989), pp. 251–2.
10. Jean-François Lyotard, *The Differend: Phrases in Dispute*, trans. Georges Van Den Abbeele (Minneapolis: University of Minnesota Press, 1988), pp. 56–7.
11. Theodor Adorno, 'Cultural Criticism and Society', in *Prisms*, trans. Samuel and Shierry Weber (London: Neville Spearman, 1967), p. 34.
12. Theodor Adorno, 'Commitment' (1962), in *The Essential Frankfurt School Reader*, ed. A. Arato and E. Gebhardt (New York: Continuum, 1982), p. 313.
13. Quoted by Alan L. Berger, *Crisis and Covenant: The Holocaust in American Jewish Fiction* (Albany: State University of New York Press, 1985), p. 33.
14. Lawrence L. Langer, *Holocaust Testimonies: The Ruins of Memory* (New Haven: Yale University Press, 1991), p. 141.

15. Helen Lewis, *A Time to Speak* (Belfast: The Blackstaff Press, 1992), p. 1.
16. Binjamin Wilkimorski, *Fragments: Memories of a Childhood, 1939–1948*, trans. Carol Brown Janeway (London: Macmillan, 1996), pp. 3–5.
17. Felman and Laub, *Testimony*, p. 57.
18. Langer, *Holocaust Testimonies*, p. 142.
19. Amos Funkenstein, 'History, Counterhistory and Narrative', in Saul Friedlander, ed., *Probing the Limits of Representation: Nazism and the 'Final Solution'* (Cambridge, Mass.: Harvard University Press, 1992), p. 77.
20. David Carroll, 'Foreword: The Memory of Devastation and the Responsibilities of Thought: "And Let's Not Talk About That"', in Jean-François Lyotard, *Heidegger and 'the jews'*, trans. Andreas Michel and Mark Roberts (Minneapolis: University of Minnesota Press, 1990), p. xiii.
21. Primo Levi, *The Drowned and the Saved*, trans. Raymond Rosenthal (London: Abacus, 1989), pp. 11–12.
22. Gillian Rose, 'The Beginnings of the Day: Fascism and Representation', in *Mourning Becomes the Law* (Cambridge: Cambridge University Press, 1996).
23. Elie Wiesel, *A Jew Today*, trans. Marion Wiesel (New York: Vintage Books, 1979), p. 234.
24. Lyotard, *Heidegger and 'the jews'*, p. 16.
25. Carroll, 'Foreword', p. xiii.
26. Saul Friedlander, 'Introduction', *Probing the Limits of Representation*, p. 17.
27. Adorno, 'Commitment', p. 313.
28. Lawrence L. Langer, *The Holocaust and the Literary Imagination* (New Haven: Yale University Press, 1975), p. 1.
29. Geoffery H. Hartmann, 'The Book of the Destruction', in Friedlander, ed., *Probing the Limits of Representation*, p. 331.
30. Wiesel, *A Jew Today*, p. 239.
31. Howard Jacobson, 'Jacobson's List', *The Independent*, 2 February 1994, p. 19.
32. Hartman in Friedlander, ed., *Probing the Limits of Representation*, p. 326.
33. James E. Young, *Writing and Rewriting the Holocaust: Narrative and the Consequences of Interpretation* (Indianapolis: Indiana University Press, 1988), p. 99.
34. Wilkimorski, *Fragments*, p. 150.
35. Jacobson, 'Jacobson's List', p. 19.
36. Martin Amis, *Time's Arrow* (Harmondsworth: Penguin, 1992).
37. Friedlander, *Probing the Limits of Representation*, p. 5.
38. Felman and Laub, *Testimony*, p. 201.
39. Friedlander, *Probing the Limits of Representation*, p. 20.
40. Barbara Foley, 'Fact, Fiction, Fascism: Testimony and Mimesis in Holocaust Narratives', *Comparative Literature* 34 (1982), p. 358.
41. Berel Lang, 'The Representation of Limits', in Friedlander, ed., *Probing the Limits of Representation*, p. 316.
42. Quoted by Foley in 'Fact, Fiction, Fascism', p. 331.
43. Philip Gourevitch, 'In the Holocaust Theme Park', *Observer Magazine*, 30 January 1994, p. 20.
44. Lyotard, *Heidegger and 'the jews'*, p. 26.

PART TWO: INTERSECTIONS

CHAPTER EIGHT

The rhizome of post-colonial discourse

Bill Ashcroft

I

The most contemporary thing about 'literature' as we move into the next century will be its increasing need to come to terms with its original construction as a vehicle for the propagation of English national culture. The profoundly imperialist operations of literary study have continued to characterise its ideology and assumptions but they have also, paradoxically, enabled post-colonial literary writing to assume a prominent place in the widespread evolution from literary studies to cultural studies. Not only do post-colonial societies provide clear demonstrations of the 'rhizomic' operation of power and its resistance, but post-colonial writing, having been deeply implicated from the start in this engagement and circulation of power and resistance, provides a very useful model for the transformation of global culture by local communities.

'Literature' in its academic guise as 'English' has been, from its inception, a particular reading practice dense with the history of cultural power in Britain, and redolent with the history of imperialism throughout the world. However much literature is held to incorporate Matthew Arnold's persuasive myth of 'the best that has been thought and said',[1] and however much we might try to define it in linguistic and evaluative terms, we are inexorably drawn to the simple conclusion that the word Literature is a key term in the construction and dissemination of imperial power in the English speaking world. Although the most far-reaching fracture of literature in contemporary times occurred with the arrival of cultural studies, a result of dissatisfaction with the marginalisation of working-class culture by the discipline, the struggle is essentially one against the ideological function of Literature in Britain and the Empire.

The discipline of English is, as we know, a surprisingly recent, if not 'contemporary' phenomenon in Britain. Although English literature was being taught in Scotland in the eighteenth century, it was Lord Macaulay's Minute to Parliament in 1835 which established Literature as the primary mode of English cultural study (indeed I would contend that it was Macaulay's Minute which first established English as cultural studies). The Minute, in which Macaulay confidently asserted that 'our language . . . abounds with works . . . which, considered as vehicles of ethical and political construction, have never been equalled',[2] can be seen as the critical moment in which the discipline of English became the principal discourse in the mission to 'civilise' and Christianise India.

Although the 'culture and civilisation' tradition had thus been present in the purposes for teaching English for some time, by the second half of the nineteenth century it found in Matthew Arnold its most influential voice. *Culture and Anarchy* was concerned with the spread of philistine culture which appeared to be accelerating with the growth of literacy and democracy. The separation of the 'cultured' classes and the masses was being eroded by the emergence of a middle class and an urban working class. Now that power could not be confined to one class Arnold was worried by the barrenness of the culture of the new masses since it must fail to equip people for the roles they would have to play in a democratic society. State sponsorship of education was the preferred mechanism by which culture could be preserved and extended to resist the driving imperatives of an increasingly mechanical and materialist civilisation.

The 'civilising' function of the study of literature which had been operating in the colonies was harnessed in earnest to preserve English national culture in Britain although the study of English Literature was not established in Oxford till 1896 and Cambridge till 1911.[3] The link between the three concepts – 'civilisation', the myth of a unitary English national culture, and the importance of antiquity – became focused in the discipline of English, in which an arbitrary and ostensively indicated set of values were held to be universal.

If political colonialism began to wane by the early decades of the twentieth century, the force of cultural imperialism did not, and there is pretty clear evidence that literature still performs its primary function of cultural imperialism rather comprehensively. By this I mean that 'Literature' invokes particular kinds of reading practices which both perpetuate the Arnoldian vocabulary of its formation, and keep its cultural connectedness at bay. They no longer do this within the English literature canon but within global culture itself. Of course this refusal to engage the broad text of culture was the very reason for the emergence of Cultural Studies out of the Leavisite watershed of English in the 1930s and 1940s.[4] But the break-away of Cultural Studies only served to confirm literature in its hege-monic rigidity. For the prestige and powerful disciplinary formation of the subject established by the Newbolt Report in 1921, in which it became the centre of the British and colonial education systems, remained intact after the arrival of Cultural Studies. Consequently, while the use of english in literary writing spread to every continent, and non-British literatures con-stitute more than three-quarters of all english literature produced, they still remain largely peripheral to the academic discipline of literary study.

The practitioners of english – readers, producers and reproducers of literature – are like people who have been carrying on an intense and protracted conversation in a tower without windows until one day we peer through a crack in the wall, to find ourselves surrounded by a vast sea of literatures in our own language, an immense cultural phenomenon which we had never really noticed. The structure of programmes in the study of english literature, even today, attests to this fact. This is the contemporary character of literature which mosts interests me – while we may be worry-ing about the 'death of the novel' and the assault upon literature by popular visual culture, we find that writing in english has become a widespread and potent tool of various projects of post-colonial identity formation. Above all, it has become manifestly *cultural* rather than *literary*. Regardless of the lingering resistance in the discipline of literary study to the cultural implica-tions of the larger text in which writing is located, such writing itself cannot avoid being a cultural product; the flourishing of post-colonial writing and its continued exclusion from the canon only confirms this fact. Post-colonial literary study will not be able to avoid the fact that it is cultural studies any more than writing can avoid being a cultural prac-tice. This is because such literary study divests the discourse of the limited and imperialistic culturalism which has historically motivated the discipline of English.

The importance of post-colonial literatures in the development of what we understand literature to be, and, subsequently, of its relationship with cultural studies will become increasingly obvious as the formative ideology of the discipline of English becomes ever more threadbare. But what-ever Literature might mean today, when we consider contemporary post-colonial reading, it is *literatures* – a recognition of the actual heterogeneity of cultures and cultural production, a heterogeneity which is first and foremost 'post-national'. J.A. Hobson's very acute description of imperial-ism in 1902 as 'the expansion of nationality' is born out by the develop-ment of English.[5] What was propagated as the epitome of the universal values of civilisation was in fact a transcendent and apparently unpolitical representation of the colonising subject – the 'Englishman' – to the colo-nised as the embodiment of those values. This characteristic of imperialism as the 'expansion of nationality', and in the case of English, as the representation of the English national subject, reveals something about imperial hegemony and its resistance which may otherwise go undetected. We are often drawn, for instance, to the structural myth in which imperialism constructs a centre and margin. In this structure London, for example, becomes the centre of Empire, the centre not only of administration and power, but also of a network of much more complex aesthetic and cultural assumptions upon which imperialism is based, what Joseph Conrad calls 'the idea': 'not a sentimental pretence of an idea; and an unselfish belief in the idea – something you can set up, and bow down before, and offer a sacrifice to'.[6]

But if we see imperialism as a *process* rather than a structure, a very different picture offers itself. To see imperialism as the extension of nationality is to see the British Empire as beginning, not with the Elizabethan sorties into the Caribbean, but even before the idea of an English nation had emerged. The inclusive dynamic which we call imperialism was already operating in Alfred the Great's proto-nationalist urging of the Saxons of South England to speak the same language in 893 as part of a strategy to keep the Vikings north of the Danelaw. Thus, taking a hugely protracted sweep of British history we see that the essentially defensive and *resistant* discourse of Alfred's consolidation of the english language, the intimation of nation, is a beginning of empire. Indeed, this *inclusive* imperial dynamic is, I would suggest, a crucial feature of all nationalisms. Not only is there no centre, but there is no beginning. Imperialism, the extension of nationality, reproduces itself endlessly in those nationalisms which rise up to oppose it. In this way the expansion of nationality becomes the transfer of nationality, that is the transfer of the idea of a nation.

The function of literature in this process should not be underestimated because those post-colonial writings which are read as a 'nation literature' are subtly made to confirm the centrality of the great national tradition of English literature. But there is a further and perhaps more far-reaching way in which the discipline itself has operated to advance an imperialist and Eurocentric view of human society: by colonising categories of resistance themselves; that is, those categories which are erected specifically to resist the hegemony of imperial and patriarchal authority.

Women's literature, migrant literature, native literature seem at first glance to embody the kind of subversive fragmentation which promises to explode the old authoritative hegemony of English Literature forever. Yet when we look more closely at the ways in which they are constituted and have been read, these sub-branches of national literatures simply reproduce the imperialist categories. Their attendant conceptual abstractions – race, ethnicity, class – when hived off into categories of literature (very often subsections of national literatures) reveal the deeply compromised nature of their formation. For the social experience to which 'woman', 'migrant', 'native' or 'ethnic' point always resides in the narrative excess, the liminal and hybrid space beyond definition.

Let us take, for example, one of these abstractions: the difficult term 'ethnicity'. Arguments about this term hinge on who can really be called 'ethnic'. But if we exclude the so-called Anglo-Saxon ethnic strand from post-colonial ethnicity and call it the dominant centre round which true 'ethnicity' revolves, we are merely reproducing the myth of centrality which keeps cultural imperialism in place. As Werner Sollors describes the situation in America, the distinction between ethnicity and American identity invokes 'the additional religious dimension of the contrast between the heathens and the chosen people'.[7]

The difficulties raised by the term 'ethnicity' are shared in the problematic discourses of migration and the field of 'migrant writing' quickly gathering strength. In Australia, the USA and Canada, for instance, the field of migrant writing proceeds as if there were some generic and shared 'migrant' or 'ethnic' experience, in nations which have been migrant societies from their inception. In this way an apparently subversive discourse uncannily reproduces the authoritative voice of the national: the unitary migrant experience and the essential experience of nation are one and the same thing. A proliferation of anthologies, studies and university courses in migrant literature show that the branch has been acknowledged, but it is still sectioned off from the whole. The discipline of English literature is brilliantly effective in this form of distraction. For whether aboriginal, migrant, native American, or woman, it is the interrogatory and interstitial space between the act of representation and the presence of the communities these terms might suggest, that the discipline of literature 'disciplines'.

But the process is wider than the discipline itself for it is one in which, as Roland Barthes might say, the 'book' disciplines the 'text'.[8] The categories isolated as discrete areas of discourse are possibly more truthfully described as new publishing markets; markets which isolate areas of textuality for the sale of *books*. The minority identity apparently represented by this new, oppositional and subversive category of literary writing is thus subtly and relentlessly brought into the centripetal structure of 'Literature'. The formation of new 'divisions' of a 'national' literature demonstrate how the imperial process reproduces itself: the tributaries of the mainstream act to confirm the primacy of the mainstream, because, we are reassured, the mainstream will always deal with the big, the universal issues of the human (meaning, of course, the European) condition. Literary study then manages to represent a situation in which categories of resistance are nicely held in check. On the political level groups who fall into these categories are provided with a rhetoric which becomes ultimately self-defeating because it reproduces the dichotomous structure of imperial control. The problem is that each of these categories of resistance is constructed as 'subtended' from the whole. They are paraded as subsections which embody a particular cultural experience. But the various minority discourses, all announcing their own peculiar and 'unique liminality', actually operate as branches which confirm the centrality of the self-instituted authorities of social experience. How, then, can we represent this restless, unpredictable 'beyond' that is the cultural subject? How can we represent the fragmentary and dissonant *process* of cultural hybridisation? I want to propose an alternative to the dichotomous tap-root of experience by which the imperial holds the marginal in place. This is the concept of the rhizome.

II THE RHIZOME OF CULTURAL POWER

Rhizome is a botanical term for a root system which spreads across the ground (as in bamboo) rather than downwards, and grows from several points rather than a single tap root. The metaphor was first popularised by Gilles Deleuze and Felix Guattari in their critiques of psychoanalysis,[9] but the image of the rhizome is sufficient in itself to provide a very different concept of social reality than the centre/margin binarism which imperialism constructs. It is important to recognise that the repressive structures of power themselves operate rhizomatically rather than monolithically. The reason we do not normally think of power operating in this way is that structures of power characterise *themselves* in terms of unities, hierarchies, binaries and centres. But it is clear that power doesn't operate in a simple vertical way from the institutions in which it appears to be constituted, it operates dynamically, laterally and intermittently.[10] There is no 'master-plan' of imperialism, neither is the advance of imperial culture necessarily violent or repressive. The greatest advancement of cultural hegemony occurs when it operates through an invisible network of filiative connections, psychological internalisations, and unconsciously implicit associations.

This is why the term 'post-colonial' is best defined as covering 'all the culture from the moment of colonisation to the present', because the complex operations of imperialism themselves problematise the existence of simple political categories of response or identification such as 'resistance' or 'minority'.[11] These positions are constantly diffracted and intersected within the rhizome of imperial contact. This intermittent and rhizomic nature is the most difficult thing to combat because it operates alongside a mythology which asserts the presence of the tap root, the canon, the standard, the patented. It is this *myth* of power which the categories of marginality are addressing, not the intermittent, overlapping and intertwining nature of its actual operation. In this way the categories which we see reproduced in critical reading – such as women, native, migrant – evolve as reproductions rather than subversions of imperial discourse.

The terms 'English' and 'englishes' may be used to indicate a difference between the authoritative language and the multitude of heterogeneous englishes actually spoken. These are not separate and distinct languages but are interconnected like the fibres of a rope. Indeed there is no simple 'language', only a welter of dialects, patois, slangs, a mesh of appropriations and variations. This rhizome helps us to see the erratic and diffuse operation of language appropriation in post-colonial societies. For instance, what Derek Bickerton has termed the 'creole continuum' suggests that the creole complex of the Caribbean region is not simply an aggregation of discrete dialect forms but an overlapping of language behaviours between which individual speakers may move with considerable ease.[12] These overlapping isolects not only contain forms from the polar lects but forms which are also functionally peculiar to themselves. But the continuum does not imply a *systematic* and structurally continuous overlapping of lects. Rather it suggests an array of language behaviours which occupy a rhizomic space within the post-colonial language culture. Individuals have available a range of entries into the network of lects which make up the social field of Caribbean language. Although not always as pronounced as the Caribbean example, this process can be used to describe all post-colonial appropriations of the dominant language.

So, too, the social experiences of marginality depicted by the rhizome overlap in ways which resist definition by those categories we raise up to define it. Just as englishes vary from the authoritative formation called English, so interweaving discourses distinguish themselves from both the tap root and its branches. If we see the ideology of imperialism as operating to cement the notion of a tap root to which all other discourses are tributaries (even in their opposition) then Literature operates in the same way. That is to say that the somewhat limited range of published expression we call Literature has the same relationship to the huge diversity of speech and narrative that the imperial tap root myth has to the rhizome.

A brilliant demonstration of the rhizomic operation of power occurs in David Malouf's *An Imaginary Life* in which an exiled Roman poet Ovid discovers a Child in the wilderness whom he attempts to teach his own language 'so that he might discover what he is'.[13] In this way, Ovid, himself exiled from the monolithic centre Rome, *reproduces* the very imperial power which has exiled him. Examples of this occasion in the civilising mission of colonialism are common; the colonised subject always needs to be *brought into* human existence by learning the language, but this is not the result of a simple 'monolithic project' of imperialism. Rather, the myth of centrality fundamental to imperialism reproduces itself in a rhizomic way through ordinary individuals to 'territorialise' or 'reterritorialise' the 'abnormal' colonised subject.[14]

Gayatri Spivak described this rhizomic process in imperialism by pointing to the example of the solitary British soldier walking across the countryside of India in the early nineteenth century:

> He is actually engaged in consolidating the self of Europe by obliging the native to cathect the space of the Other on his home ground . . . [He] is effectively and violently sliding one discourse into another.[15]

The point Spivak is making here is that the imperial project itself is heterogeneous. This 'cartographic transformation' was not only achieved by the policy-makers, but also, and more importantly, by the little people like the solitary soldier – and the thousands of colonists who follow people like him to places which are colonised by an imperial power like Britain. The discourse of mapping, even though it may proceed in a fragmentary and intermittent way, is a formal strategy for bringing colonised territory under control by *knowing it in language.*

The institutions of metropolitan 'centres' may have the *appearance* of tap roots plunging deep into the colonial earth, but this is only appearance. The *rhizomic* nature of imperialism might be likened more to a laterally spreading parasite. It is rhizomic because it has interlinked centres everywhere, but it *appears* monolithic because underlying all of these centres is a consensus about its vertical structure. The history of failures of resistance to this (apparent) imperial monolith may be traced to a general failure to recognise the *scope* of imperialistic repression. Interestingly, successful resistance arose, Deleuze and Guattari discovered, with the emergence of postcolonial consciousness, as they demonstrate in the writings of Frantz Fanon.[16] This leads to a far more interesting use of the rhizome metaphor to describe social reality, one Deleuze and Guattari base on the world of the schizophrenic. For the structures of everyday reality are ones which contest at every point the operation of a unitary and monolithic authority.

We do not need to incorporate Deleuze and Guattari's analysis to apply the full benefit of the term rhizome. For the simple botanic image of social reality conveys very well both the hidden diversity of social discourse, what Bakhtin called the heteroglossia,[17] and the intermittent, scattered, fragmentary and processural operation of imperial power. Once we understand this we see that certain ways of talking about post-colonial or resistance discourse have fallen into a very deep trap set for them. For if we see imperialism as monolithic, then its resistance becomes polarised. We then fall into all kinds of egregious binarisms, the most flagrant of which are the unspoken assumptions that all colonisers are white and all whites are colonisers, all the colonised are black and all blacks are colonised. Ultimately the concept of race reduces to this most basic of binarisms – black and white.

This limitation of post-colonial identity to race underlies a fairly important argument in post-colonial theory at the moment: the status of the former settlement colonies. The accusation seems to be that to describe the varieties of social experience within settler colonies by the term post-colonial is to advance a seamless and homogeneous definition of the word which dilutes its radical potential. But while the term 'post-colonial' is as much at risk from the danger of stereotyping and typification as any other term, the argument which excludes the settler colonies from post-coloniality performs the task of imperial control very nicely by maintaining the myth of a binary structure of power and resistance.

The process of imperial power and its resistance never operates in this binary way, and a clearer perception of the problem may be provided by the concept of the rhizome. The fact is that the 'heteroglossic' ferment of social discourse lies *beneath* the 'monoglossic' discourse of imperialism in the way Spivak described as 'slid under'. The colonised signified 'slid under' the colonising signifier might seem to imply that there are two rhizomes, the imperial and the repressed, the colonial and the post-colonial. But the multiple and heterogeneous interconnections of the post-colonial rhizome are really all part of the one rhizome of social reality. In Lacan's terms, the agency of the subject in the symbolic order of language cannot operate as a simple polarity because both power and resistance function rhizomically in the subject within language.[18] The rhizomic nature of power, even of the symbolic order, offers exactly the kinds of fractures and slippages within which strategies of post-colonial resistance may operate. The startling fact is that the authoritative and the subversive may operate in *constructing the same subject*. In other words, they may well be *connected* at various points on the rhizome. This explains the paradoxical and diffuse construction of the national subject, and demonstrates how valuable the settler colony situation might be in revealing the complex and processional interweaving of complicity and resistance in post-colonial discourse. *All* formerly colonised societies construct, in one way or another, subjects and discourses which are both colonised and colonisers. This is precisely the way the process of cultural imperialism works through subjectivity and, if we think about it, precisely the way each of us exists within our own discipline.

To assume that the word 'post-colonial' encapsulates a unified and homogeneous experience is to disregard the material consequences of colonialism upon which post-colonial discourse is constructed.[19] But to exclude some societies from the term for tawdry motives of political correctness is to ignore both the material effects of colonisation (themselves very different in different situations) and the huge diversity of ordinary and sometimes hidden responses to it throughout the world. It is to fall into a form of categorisation still controlled by imperial discourse.

Literature, in these contemporary times, then, by virtue of its disciplinary construction, its deeply problematic political and cultural status, and its appropriation by various post-colonial projects of resistance, is in a very good position to identify and reproduce the ambivalent construction of post-colonial subjectivity. The imperial pressure to colonise categories of resistance will remain strong, but the concept of the rhizome, by providing a clearer perception of the problem, may provide us with some strategy to handle the promethean nature of imperialism.

III POST-COLONIAL LITERARY CULTURES AND IMPERIALISM

The rhizomic operation of cultural power and of culture itself demands a revised conception of literary writing to apprehend it. Post-colonial writing has always seemed to occupy a different site from Literature because the division between culture as 'Art' and culture as a 'way of life' (as Raymond Williams put it)[20] becomes immediately eroded when colonised peoples appropriate cultural discourses such as literary writing. It is eroded because in these cultures such a distinction between definitions of culture becomes a deeply ontological one. For them, culture as timeless, universal and authoritative is simply unattainable, except by a process of the most parodic mimicry in which the imperial centre embodies all cultural aspirations. Post-colonial literatures, by definition, cannot be great or universal, so they become much more obviously a 'way of life'.

As well as problematising the distinction between culture as 'art' and cultures as 'ways of life', post-colonial cultural discourses of all kinds problematise the concept of culture itself. For when decolonising countries appropriate cultural discourse they must either appropriate the whole of its universalist ideology and become, for instance, 'more English than the English', or appropriate it in a way that confirms all intellectual and artistic discourse as aspects of the way of life, strands of cultural texture, intimately and inextricably connected in the textual fabric of society. Their marginalisation and exclusion from the canon has provided the ground for a much more rhizomic conception of the cultural text.

Where does post-colonial theory stand in the picture? What intellectual identity is the post-colonial critic to construct for him- or her-self? I would suggest that post-colonial studies is in a particularly strategic position to engage the increasing reality of global culture, which also operates both rhizomically and imperialistically. As Barbara Christian points out, post-colonial writers have always written theory, it just has not been recognised as such.[21] But although post-colonial theory was not an invention of the academy, it was, paradoxically, only its confirmation as an elite discourse within the academy that allowed it to achieve any sort of recognition or authority. This has had the rather ambiguous result of allowing the voice of the culturally marginalised and dispossessed to be heard, often for the first time, but often also within the frame of a theory which has leached that voice of all its materiality and political urgency. On the other hand a recurrent oppositional essentialism which would, understandably, reject Western discourse, reject English, reject literature, reject imperialism, finds itself locked into an illusory and self-congratulatory rhetoric which fails to see the protean nature of imperial power. However, I want to situate another theoretical position between these two poles: a theory which confirms the agency of the decolonising subject, while acknowledging that the protean adaptability of imperial power cannot be simply dismissed. The theory I espouse therefore, the one which most faithfully engages the actual practice of post-colonial subjects, and best negotiates the move from high culture to cultural production, is a poetics and a politics of *transformation*.

The poetics of transformation examines the ways in which writers and readers contribute constitutively to meaning, how colonised societies appropriate imperial discourses, how they interpolate their voices and concerns into dominant systems of textual production and distribution. A poetics of transformation recognises the myth of parent and child, trunk and branch, stream and tributary, by which the post-colonial is marginalised and replaces it with a perception of the rhizomic nature of discursive power and resistance. Transformation recognises that power is a critical part of our cultural life and copes with direct resistance by assuming new forms. But above all, a poetics of transformation recognises the transformative way in which post-colonial texts operate, even those which pose as simply oppositional.

The politics of transformation works constantly within existing discursive and institutional formations to change them, rather than simply to attempt to end them. By taking hold of writing itself, whether as novel, history, testimony, political discourse, or interpolating educational discourse and institutions, or transforming conceptions of place, even economics, the post-colonial subject unleashes a rapidly circulating transcultural energy.

121

Whereas 'development' acts to force the local into globally normative patterns, 'transformation' acts to adjust those patterns to the requirements of local values and needs. Ultimately a poetics and politics of transformation effects a transformation of the disciplinary field. It is this transformative energy of post-colonial textuality, the appropriations and reconstructions of cultural subjects rather than the actions of academics, which are transforming cultural discourse.

Post-colonial transformation operates in various ways in culture, but particularly in the anxious and volatile interactions of mass, folk and popular culture. Benedict Anderson once remarked in a radio interview that US popular culture is the popular culture of the world. But that is not quite true. Mass culture exists in constant tension with popular cultural forms and each is symbiotic upon the other. If folk culture, in its traditional form, largely disappears, or becomes suppressed, with the spread of modern media, the same cannot be said for popular culture which demonstrates the transformative potential of all post-colonial creative production. Popular culture represents the arena of a transformation of mass culture, in much the same way as local writing transformed the ideology and assumptions of English literature in colonised societies. The fascinating thing is that this can occur at a level much more localised than the national or transnational.

Two questions need to be asked about this. Firstly, on what basis can one make the link between the transformative energies of a specifically *post-colonial* creative production, on the one hand, and global resistance to the saturating hegemony of mass culture on the other? To this, my answer would be that the link is to be made explicitly by the fact that present-day globalism is the extension of nineteenth-century imperialism. In some ways this seems obvious, but it is remarkable how concealed it is in contemporary globalisation studies. Secondly, what is the usefulness of a post-colonial approach? A post-colonial approach is useful because the strategies of cultural transformation used in post-colonial responses to imperial discourse, such as appropriation, interpolation, and other inflected forms of resistance, become useful models for the ways in which local communities may engage the forces of globalisation. The discipline of English itself is useful as a model of cultural engagement because it shows how the deepest and most far-reaching projects of resistance are bound to strategies of transformation. Above all, post-colonial studies, by intervening at several levels in debates about culture, confirm the rhizomic nature of power, of resistance, and of culture itself.

Indeed, the concept of globalisation becomes important to post-colonial studies precisely because it demonstrates the structure of world power relations which continues in the twentieth century as a legacy of Western imperialism. In some respects globalisation, in the period of rapid decolonisation since the Second World War, demonstrates the transmutation of imperialism into the supra-national operations of economics, communications and culture. This does not mean that globalisation is a simple unidirectional movement from the powerful to the weak, from the central to the peripheral, because globalism is transcultural in the same way that imperialism itself has been. But it does demonstrate that globalisation did not simply erupt spontaneously around the world as Anthony Giddens seems to suggest,[22] but has a history embedded in the history of imperialism, in the structure of the world system of international capitalism, and in the origins of a global economy within the ideology of imperial rhetoric.

The key to the link between classical imperialism and contemporary globalisation in the twentieth century has been the role of the United States, which almost effortlessly took over the command of empire from Britain at the turn of the century. More importantly, American society during and after this early expansionist phase initiated those features of social life and social relations which today may be considered to characterise the global: mass production, mass communication and mass consumption. During this century these have spread transnationally, 'drawing upon the increasingly integrated resources of the global economy'.[23]

The interaction of culture, globalisation and post-colonial transformation hinges on the febrile and contested issue of identity, and identities are constructed in a globalised world by a continual process of transcultural interaction, appropriation and transformation. How globalism is engaged by local communities forms the focus of much recent discussion of the phenomenon, and this is where the post-colonial is useful. If globalism is not simply a result of top-down dominance but a transcultural process, a dialectic of dominant cultural forms and their appropriation, then the responses of local communities become critical. We must also recognise the tension between identity and desire, the interchange of the centripetal and centrifugal energies of globalisation which we learn from the experience of colonised societies.

By appropriating strategies of representation, organisation and social change through access to global systems, local communities and marginal interest groups can both empower themselves and influence those global systems. Although choice is always mediated by the conditions of subject formation, the *belief* that one has a choice in the processes of changing one's own life or society can indeed be empowering. In this sense the appropriation of global forms of culture may free one from local forms of dominance and oppression or at least provide the tools for a different kind of identity formation.

Ultimately, then, post-colonial studies is in a unique position to engage the subtle, heterogeneous and diffuse evolution of imperial discourse into globalisation rhetoric and global culture. Not only has its contestation with the culturalist dimension of literary study prepared the ground for this engagement, but its demonstration of the rhizomic nature of culture and of power itself articulates a resonant model for local transformations of global discourse. Far from being the perpetuation of an anachronistic cultural elitism, post-colonial literary writing provides the elements for a strategy of change in the contemporary world through which local societies may be empowered.

NOTES

1. Matthew Arnold, *Culture and Anarchy* (Cambridge: Cambridge University Press, 1948).
2. Thomas Babington Macaulay, *Speeches of Lord Macaulay with his Minute on Indian Education*, selected and introduced by G.M. Young (Oxford: Oxford University Press, 1935), p. 349.
3. See Chris Baldick, *The Social Mission of English Criticism 1848–1932* (Oxford: Oxford University Press, 1983).
4. For the importance of the work of F.R. Leavis to the development of English literary criticism, see Francis Mulhern, *The Moment of 'Scrutiny'* (London: Verso, 1981).
5. J.A. Hobson, *Imperialism: A Study* (London: James Nisbet, 1902).
6. Joseph Conrad, *Heart of Darkness* (Harmondsworth: Penguin, 1986), p. 22.
7. Werner Sollors, *Beyond Ethnicity: Consent and Descent in American Culture* (Oxford: Oxford University Press, 1986), p. ii.
8. See Roland Barthes, 'From Work to Text', in *Image Music Text*, trans. Stephen Heath (New York: Noonday Press, 1977).
9. See, particularly, Gilles Deleuze and Felix Guattari, *Anti-Oedipus: Capitalism and Schizophrenia*, trans. Robert Hurley, Mark Seem and Helen Lane (New York: Viking, 1977), and *A Thousand Plateaus: Capitalism and Schizophrenia, Volume 2*, trans. Brian Massumi (London: Athlone Press, 1988).
10. For this conception of 'power', see the formulations of Michel Foucault, *An Introduction to the History of Sexuality*, trans. Robert Hurley (Harmondsworth: Penguin, 1981), pp. 94–6.
11. Bill Ashcroft, Gareth Griffiths and Helen Tiffin, *The Empire Writes Back: Theory and Practice in Post-Colonial Literatures* (London: Routledge, 1989), p. 2.
12. Derek Bickerton, 'The Nature of a Creole Continuum', *Language* 49:3 (1973), p. 642.
13. David Malouf, *An Imaginary Life* (Sydney: Picador, 1990), p. 77.
14. 'Territoriality' is a term derived from Deleuze and Guattari's 'schizo-analysis' in *Anti-Oedipus*.
15. Gayatri Chakravorty Spivak, 'The Rani of Simur', in Francis Barker *et al.*, *Europe and its Others* (Colchester: University of Essex, 1985), p. 133.

16. For discussion of Fanon, see Deleuze and Guattari, *Anti-Oedipus*.
17. For an introduction to Mikhail Bakhtin's 'heteroglossic' theory of the novel, see Simon Dentith, *Bakhtinian Thought: An Introductory Reader* (London: Routledge, 1995).
18. For Lacan's conception of the illusory mastery of the symbolic order, see Jacques Lacan, *Ecrits*, trans. Alan Sheridan (London: Tavistock, 1977).
19. This has led, in fact, to some astonishingly selective readings of *The Empire Writes Back*. See, for instance, comments by Anne McClintock, Bob Hodge and Vijay Mishra and the editors in *Colonial Discourse and Post-Colonial Theory*, ed. Patrick Williams and Laura Chrisman (New York: Harvester, 1993). They claim, for example, that the analysis in *The Empire Writes Back* implies that post-colonialism was the same thing in a variety of cultures; this is precisely the opposite of what the book says.
20. Raymond Williams, *Culture and Society* (Harmondsworth: Penguin, 1963), p. 16.
21. Barbara Christian, 'The Race for Theory', *Cultural Critique* 6 (1987).
22. Anthony Giddens, *The Consequences of Modernity* (Cambridge: Polity, 1990).
23. Tony Spyby, *Globalization and World Society* (Cambridge: Polity, 1996), p. 3.

CHAPTER NINE
The dialectic of myth and history in the post-colonial contemporary: Soyinka's A Dance of the Forests

Mpalive Msiska

It is illustrative of the unhappy side of the post-colonial contemporary that Wole Soyinka, the 1986 Nobel laureate for literature and the pride of the African continent, should find himself forced into exile at this stage of his career. The writer has been in exile since 1994 for protesting against the refusal of the military government of General Sani Abacha to return Nigeria to civilian rule, as promised by his predecessor General Ibrahim Babangida. The regime's determination to destroy all forms of opposition could not have been more gruesomely demonstrated than in its callous execution in 1995 of another distinguished Nigerian writer, Ken Saro Wiwa. Of course, this is not the first time Soyinka has been in exile for opposing a regime in his country: he spent a few years in Britain and Ghana in the early 1970s after being released from a lengthy spell in detention, imprisoned for denouncing and obstructing the 1966–70 Nigerian civil war.

Soyinka's dissatisfaction with the post-colonial leadership began in the late 1950s while he was a student in Britain. As he recalls:

> It was a single moment at one of the earliest stages of our semi-independence when the first ministers arrived in England. I remember that a group of us went to meet them wanting to discuss issues. Within five minutes, I knew that we were in serious trouble. It was clear that they were more concerned with the mechanisms for stepping into the shoes of the departing colonial masters, enjoying the same privileges, inserting themselves in that axial position towards the rest of the community . . . That is when I began to pay very serious attention to what I saw as budding dictatorial mentality. These new leaders were alienated, that was the main theme of *A Dance of the Forests*.[1]

The play, begun in London and some portions of it read as part of Soyinka's evening at the Royal Court in 1959, was completed in Nigeria in 1960

126

and, in the same year, performed as part of the country's national independence celebrations.[2] At a time when all the nationalist rhetoric was painting a picture of a post-colonial utopia to come, Soyinka was casting doubt on its very feasibility and looking back beyond the colonial moment, in fact reducing the colonial moment to a minor episode in a long stretch of historical and mythological time, to the pre-colonial African past as well as European history, for a dynamic frame in terms of which to map out and grasp the essential contradictions and continuities within the post-colonial present and future.

Thus, Soyinka's abiding concern in *A Dance of the Forests*, eventually published in 1963, is the dramatisation of myth and history in their specific and mutual articulation with post-colonial African modernity, with the result that the problem of identity is reconceptualised as a temporal and spatial dialectic in which the post-colonial *zone*, as both time and space, is figured as both continuous and discontinuous with the spatialised past as well as future.[3] Nevertheless, Soyinka's grounding of the problematic of identity in myth has attracted severe criticism. Chidi Amuta has denounced Soyinka's use of myth as reproducing a cyclic concept of history in which the human subject is robbed of agency and presented as being wholly at the mercy of the inexorable logic of destiny. For Odun Balogun, Soyinka's use of myth exhibits the bourgeois notion of pure art. Even so, both Amuta and Balogun regard their criticism as mostly confined to the author's early work, in particular *A Dance of the Forests*, arguing that the 1967–70 Nigerian civil war marks a watershed in Soyinka's poetics. Chidi Amuta, for example, contends that in contrast with the dominance of myth in Soyinka's pre-war work, his post-war output is characterised by a more secular view of human experience and in it, 'historical consciousness intensifies and acquires a more overt political edge while his artistic philosophy and social ideology become progressively secular'.[4] Balogun expresses a similar view, seeing Soyinka as having evolved from being 'a nationalist writer espousing the bourgeois philosophy of "pure art" into a committed writer inspired by socialist ideals'.[5]

The general reconstruction of the development of Soyinka's work with regard to the problem of history and myth closely follows Frantz Fanon's model of literary historical change in the post-colony, whereby the African writer, who during the struggle for liberation from colonialism relies on the past as a way of legitimising the drive towards political autonomy, counter-identifies with the political elite who have by this time begun to reproduce an acquisitive bourgeois ideology, and instead he elaborates a new secular vision in which the focus is more on the social and class antagonism of the post-colonial condition than on the discourse and practices of colonial ideology.[6] All these, Fanon's included, are useful attempts at constructing a general linear development of the ideological content of African writing and the changing political subject position of the African writer, but ultimately, they are too neat a distinction to capture the complexity of Soyinka's engagement with myth, history and contemporary modernity. Indeed, even a critic otherwise doubtful of the efficacy of Soyinka's political solutions, such as Femi Osofisan, acknowledges the fundamental structural continuity in Soyinka's work. In his view:

> It becomes superfluous to draw a line between his 'serious' and 'lighter' plays, for all are linked by this primordial bridge of ideological ambiguity . . . there seems to be a continual, restless swing (once identified by Biodun Jeyifo as *aporia*) between on the one hand a sincere and passionate quest for modernising impulses and on the other hand a loving celebration of the exotic tropes of tradition; between a mordant censure of the destructive rituals of megalomania, and a simultaneous fascination for the masques of regal institutions and feudalist structures.[7]

His negative assessment of the nature of continuity in Soyinka notwithstanding, Osofisan draws attention to the inadequacy of simple evolutionary descriptions of Soyinka's literary development.

Above all, such an approach is itself predicated on an undialectical concept of history where contradiction is located solely between historical events rather than within the events themselves as well.[8] In addition, what we have here is a mere replication rather than the required contestation of the Western concept of time predicated on teleological and progressivist notions of historical change, a concept which, as is widely accepted now, constituted one of the validating ideologies of colonialism. Even more insidious is the underlying assumption that myth and history are diametrically opposed. This seems a rather excessive expression of loyalty to classical Marxism on the part of the African critics, since the assumption that myth and history are necessarily mutually exclusive represents a mechanistic rather than a critical deployment of the Marxist argument that in so far as myth is part of the ideological superstructure of the feudal mode of production, it is nothing more than an aspect of the means by which a ruling class reproduces and secures false consciousness. This reading of ideology has been subjected to a thorough critique by, among others, Louis Althusser, who sees ideology less as an epiphenomenon of a given mode of production and more as a concrete and material fabric through which palpable subjects are not only interpellated by a given sovereign, but recognise their subjectivity as real.[9]

Moreover, the conception of myth and history as inherently antithetical does not hold within the African taxonomies of narrative, indeed even in other predominantly oral cultures such as Homer's Greece, where history is articulated through myth and myth through history.[10] In any case, after

Roland Barthes's *Mythologies*,[11] history can no longer itself unproblematically be granted the status of an objective and autonomous discourse in the way Soyinka's Marxist opponents attempt. To the extent that both history and myth are discourses of narration, the difference between them is not so much a matter of which one is more valid than the other as a representation of the past, as a question of the specific ways in which they differentially employ strategies of narration for particular ideological effects. As Patrick Taylor has argued in his book *The Narrative of Liberation*, there is a point beyond which history and myth dissolve into each other, with myth functioning as history and history as myth and with the main determining difference being a political one: between *liberating myths* and *hegemonic myths*.[12]

Thus, in looking at Soyinka's use of myth it is less helpful to use a model that regards history as essentially progressive and myth as wholly retrogressive, for in the post-colony the most politically occluding ideologies are underpinned by this dichotomy and thus the task of demystifying such ideologies must begin by an interrogation of their founding conceptual oppositions. It is to this task, so I argue, that Soyinka's *A Dance of the Forests* is ultimately committed. In the play, he seeks to inhabit subversively history, tradition and modernity, historicising mythology and mythologising history and thus undertaking a more profound critique of available legitimating discourses of African cultural authenticity as well as of the manichean dichotomy that Abdul JanMohamed argues defines the colonial formation.[13]

That is particularly true of *A Dance of the Forests*, which both Balogun and Amuta regard as Soyinka's most quintessentially mythological play. As Balogun admits, in spite of his reservations about the play's ideological content, it offers a less than euphoric welcome to the new post-colonial social formation, contesting the romanticised view of the post-colonial future and looking back to the past, the past conceived of as both history and myth, for a measure of the difficulty of constructing a desirable post-colonial future.[14] The political relevance of the play to Nigeria's independence was not lost on the organisers of the national celebrations. As Soyinka explains in *Ibadan* (1994), having had a whiff of the play's unflattering representation of power, the organisers made certain that its production received as little material support as possible, leaving Soyinka to rely on his meagre resources for its successful presentation. Thus the play can neither be seen as a wholesale glorification of the feudal past or the mercantilist economic system through which the African feudal system came in contact via the transatlantic slave trade, nor as a validation of the post-colonial bourgeois nationalist ideology as argued by Balogun. It plumbs the depths of a variety of systems of production, particularly the feudal and the post-colonial mixed modes of production, and brings out their internal contradictions, pointing out that beyond post-coloniality as historical event and desire, there lies the realm where a dialectical interplay between the present and past, myth and history takes place, widening the frame within which the identity of the new post-colonial formation can be figured as a *multiple political ontology.*

As several critics have observed, the play remains the most ambitious of Soyinka's plays and it is difficult to offer a comprehensive summary of its complex interweaving of myth and history, time and space. It is replete with a number of what Soyinka calls 'African theatrical idioms': dance, mime, religious ritual and masquerade, to name a few. In a 1962 interview with the South African writer Ezekiel Mphahlele, Soyinka explains the importance of such devices for a radical intervention in the prevailing practices of play-writing and performance. In his view, 'They might lead, in fact, to a theatrical revolution, the moment African writers and producers become very conscious of the potentialities of these idioms'.[15] The total representational effect of such idioms is of a magnitude similar to that achieved by the German playwright Bertolt Brecht through his use of the devices of estrangement.

One of the principal means by which Soyinka re-represents the familiar is by historicising the world of the ancestral spirits, dramatising its historical time and its distinct spatial identity. The ancestors we are presented with in the play bear the stamp of their particular encounters with history and, indeed, through their physical identity provide a narrative of their respective historical times. Dead Man and Dead Woman are a far cry from the sanitised ancestors of traditional African religion who are drawn in ethereal colours and who inhabit a hazy phantasmagoric universe. This is evident from the moment they first enter the stage:

> An empty clearing in the forest. Suddenly the soil appears to be breaking and the head of Dead Woman pushes its way up. Some distance from her, another head begins to appear, that of a man. They both come up slowly. The man is fat and bloated, wears a dated warrior outfit, now mouldy. The woman is pregnant. (7)

They both inhabit the materiality of their death, its sordidness and brutality: its particular moment unmediated by the law of antecedence, of genealogy. In this, Soyinka frustrates the horizon of expectation of his audience, by dwelling on the physical form of the spirit rather than its state as a spectre produced within the conventional representational language of spectral identity. Thus he foregrounds the extent to which the identity of ancestral spirits is constructed within a language that shies away from a knowledge of the historical corporeality of their being, a discourse in which it is not only the subjectivity of the spirits that is disembodied, but also their very material moment of historical existence. Consequently, ancestors are located outside history and reified into a non-historical past, with the notion that they too were born and lived being carefully repressed. Such a view of ancestral identity turns the historical world they inhabited into an unusable imaginary past and one amenable only to a homogenising romanticisation of the Negritude type or to conservative discourses of authenticity such as advocated and practised by the former Zairian dictator Mobuto Sese Seko and Hastings Banda of Malawi. By historicising the identity of the ancestors, allowing their physical form to yield the past, Soyinka reveals that the conventional narration of myth represses the politics of both life and death and also suggests that versions of history which reduce the particularity of the existential drama of ancestral ontology to lean ciphers of the teleological progression towards the present and beyond merely cannibalise history rather than let it utter both its radical difference from as well as its very embodiment in the present.

Another way in which the world of the ancestors is brought back to life is by anthropomorphising their identity. The dead do not only have unwholesome bodies, but they also reproduce the social relations of human society, a point illustrated, for example, by the emphasis on the marital relationship between Dead Man and Dead Woman. This is given additional force by the mother–child bond that underlies Dead Woman's refusal to let her child go back to earth as an *Abiku*. Dead mothers of *Abiku* children, just like their living counterparts, cannot bring themselves to accept the fate of the gods without doing whatever they can to make their children's residence on earth or in the world of the dead a little more permanent.

There thus seems an affective similarity between the world of the dead and that of the living in addition to the similitude of social formation. There is also a striking resemblance between the human world and that of the gods, judging by the endless squabbling between Eshuoro and Ogun, confirming Soyinka's assertion that Yoruba gods embody virtues and vices of humanity, which render human foibles forgivable. The ontological similarity between the two forms of identity and location is a double-edged sword. On the one hand, the gods being similar to humans, particularly in their desire always to put their own self-interest above everything else, the human expectation that the gods and ancestral spirits will heed their principal request for earthly plenitude is misplaced. So it is not surprising that after all the drama of human entry into the realm of the gods, at the end of the play, we are left with poor Demoke lying half comatose on the ground without a sensible story to tell his fellow human beings about what the future holds for them. In this respect, it can be argued that Soyinka appropriates the logic of myth only to undermine it, by revealing its limitations as a source of usable knowledge and by returning the responsibility for the transformation of human society squarely to human agency and time. On the other hand, to the extent that the ancestors and the gods are historical forebears of the post-colonial community, their success and their failure always remain a lesson for the community, but this is true only in so far as the historicity of the ancestors and the gods is reclaimed from the ontological location in the mythical imaginary. It is in this context that Soyinka's juxtaposition of the temporality of myth and that of history in the play is less of a strategy of obfuscation and self-indulgent complexity, as his critics argue, than a rigorous attempt to insert history at the very heart of the post-colonial cultural imagination and its relation to the past and, most importantly for Soyinka, the future.

In Soyinka's view the simple versions of the African past offered by a variety of cultural and political negritudism, important as they are as vehicles of resistance during the struggle for independence, need to be sublated into a more searching view, one that fully confronts the contradictions immanent in history without, however, allowing such an understanding to sap the will to transcendence. In order to demythologise such appropriations of history, Soyinka applies the same brutal realism seen in the representation of the universe of the dead and the gods to his portrayal of the pre-colonial Kingdom of Mata Kharibu.

The inclusion of the seventeenth-century court of Mata Kharibu also provides a refreshing break from the surreal and multi-coloured world of Forest Dwellers. In contrast with the hyperbolic and colourfully fantastic world of the universe of the Forest Dwellers, the world of Mata Kharibu is presented in a realistic mode. The characters are invested with psychological complexity and here *motivation* for action seems not dissimilar to that of the present human world of Demoke and others. The warrior's anguished moment of choice between accepting Madame Tortoise's offer of her body and war, on the one hand, and rejecting her offer and risking his life and that of his family, on the other, partakes of the language of the real. Nevertheless, however life-like the historical figures appear, their identities cannot be viewed as similar to those of the living, as we have already met some of them in their dead state among the Forest Dwellers. So when the bloated ancestral spirit we encounter at the beginning of the play turns up in the historical section undeformed, he cannot escape being seen in terms of his location in the world of the dead. Thus the space of history, as anterior present, retains its distinctiveness while also being mediated through the ontic space of the dead of the Forest. This device of dual ontology in which the subjects are located both within the present and the future has the effect of demystifying what is considered the future by the inhabitants of the pre-colonial kingdom and also what lies ahead for post-colonial Nigeria in particular and Africa in general – the argument being that the future is knowable and is already here and has always been. This should not however be understood as symptomatic of Soyinka's determinism. It is, rather, an attempt to call attention to the extent to which the future, the present and the past are mutually imbricated even as they constitute themselves as discrete time and spatial zones.

Nevertheless, if Mata Kharibu's kingdom is the paradigm of the post-colonial future, then one must welcome the new dawn with a great deal of caution. Significantly, the version of the past the play proffers is not the glorious African past of Negritude, of maidens singing great warriors into battle to choruses of forest birds in idyllic green pastures. Mata Kharibu's kingdom is full of tyranny, greed, pettiness, machination and opportunism. Above all, it is a world dominated by a deep-seated cynicism as regards the possibility of human progress. Matters are made much worse by the fact that when the inhabitants of the kingdom examine historical antecedent, there is no consolation whatsoever, as what is revealed is a culture of violence similar to their own, which leads the learned historian of Mata Kharibu's court to the conclusion that:

> War is the only consistency that past ages afford us. It is the legacy which
> new nations seek to perpetuate. Patriots are grateful for wars. Soldiers have
> never questioned bloodshed. The cause is always the accident your
> Majesty, and war is the Destiny. (51)

This condition is not particular to Africa, as the court historian's research amply shows. He notes that the citadel of civilisation itself, Greece, was founded on grisly acts of violence. When the military leader who has been cautioning the king not to go to war protests at the historian's insinuation that his refusal to fight shows that he is a traitor, the historian puts him in his place by recounting the Trojan war:

> Be quiet soldier! I have here the whole history of Troy. If you were not
> the swillage of pigs and could read the writings of wiser men, I would
> show you the magnificence of the destruction of a beautiful city. I would
> reveal to you the attainments of men which lifted mankind to the ranks of
> gods and demi-gods. And who was the inspiration of this divine carnage?
> Helen of Troy, a woman whose honour became as rare a conception as
> her beauty. Would Troy, if it were standing today, lay claim to
> preservation in the annals of history if a thousand valiant Greeks had not
> been slaughtered before its gates, and a hundred thousand Trojans within
> her walls? (51)

Evidently, Soyinka presents history as malleable and as determined by the particular ideology of the agency of interpretation, including institutionally approved producers of knowledge such as the court historian whose seemingly objective interpretation of history is in fact sponsored by the sovereign and determined by the politics of patronage. The subordination of intellectual labour to political authority seen in the historian's rereading of history in terms of the king's interests is characteristic of other intellectuals we encounter in Soyinka's later plays, in particular the professor in *A Play of Giants* (1984) who provides intellectual legitimacy to dictatorship, as well as Professor Bagbapo in *Opera Wonyosi* (1977) who decides to acquire some much-needed transferable skills from a band of criminals during his sabbatical leave. In this regard, Soyinka seems to suggest that knowledge is not intrinsically emancipatory and that its capacity as a means of interrogating and counter-identifying with dominant ideology can only be fully activated through the independence of thought and practice exemplified by the military leader who embodies the redemptive qualities of Soyinka's adopted deity, Ogun, rather than through the court historian's immense knowledge of the past. The military leader's life is in the end destroyed, but, seen from the perspective of the future, his death has a greater social and political significance than that of the historian and many others that Kharibu's philosophy of living by the sword has contributed to the population of the Forest Dwellers and also of the present inhabitants of the Town. Significantly, the former court historian reappears in the post-colonial formation as Adenebi, the council orator and book keeper, a role that enables him to continue his pre-colonial habit of using knowledge solely in order to advance his own personal interests. Besides, he is still the agent of death: after taking a bribe, he changes the capacity of a lorry from forty to seventy and when it overturns all but five are killed.

In this context, then, the warrior's view of life as fundamentally driven by a logic of an endless and repetitive triumph of evil is merely an identification of the essential ontological character of his world, but, as he has shown in his resistance to Mata Kharibu, such a conclusion need not by itself lead to apathy and acceptance of fate, but is in fact the necessary ground that must be traversed before possible action. Moreover, his argument that human beings are inherently cannibals subtly inserts a radical alterity within the ideology of human self-destruction, as conceivably it is not only dictators who have a monopoly on eating others: they may eat others, but they may be eaten too, thus suggesting an almost eternal struggle between the forces of good and evil, a struggle which those with a humane vision for humanity may not always win, as in the case of the military leader, but which nevertheless brings out the nobler qualities of humanity which serve as an example of the possibility of politics as ethics. In this regard, Soyinka would appear to accord a greater role to individual redemptive agency than perhaps ordinarily allowed for in other socialist ideologies. Even so, it needs to be recognised that the military commander's refusal to fight is not an isolated gesture of resistance; it becomes the means by which an individual's exceptional leadership engenders mass resistance to oppressive power, since his troops remain loyal to him, suggesting that by personalising the hostility to his regime, the king has failed to grasp the national significance of the commander's dissidence.

The king's blindness to the reality of the situation is presented through the frame of Greek tragedy. The rebellion of his once trusted commander is one of the many signs that are meant to make him realise that all is not well in his kingdom. The king is too hubristic to heed even the advice of his soothsayer, who sees clearly that he has embarked on a course of self-destruction. Thus the king is a typical figure of classical tragedy, displaying all the errors of judgement that precede the downfall of a tragic protagonist. However, unlike the fate of the familiar Greek tragic hero, such as Sophocles' Oedipus and Creon, Mata Kharibu is never taken to the moment of recognition of his error, which punishment would have served to rehabilitate him. In this respect, he can be viewed as a tragic hero who is so beyond the pale that he forfeits the saving grace of redemptive suffering, which fits in well with Soyinka's overall uncompromising views on African dictators. More pertinently, the pre-colonial dictator is a sign of an iterative negative genealogy that co-exists with the transforming Ogunian will of the rebel warrior – a sort of Lacanian killjoy without whom there would be no need nor desire for change.

Furthermore, the master's awareness of the slave's new political identity leads him not so much to a thorough examination of the root cause of the transformation in the attitude of his once loyal soldier, as to an obsessive preoccupation with his standing in the eyes of posterity; and it is this desire to inscribe himself positively in the future that makes him miss the opportunity to redeem himself or to be saved by the logic of the structure of tragedy which demands that the tragic protagonist take full responsibility for his part in his own downfall even while accepting the role of fate. It is as if, given that his success has so far depended on the constant surveillance of the possibility of failure, he can only be at peace with himself when he no longer needs to fear failure, when he has put himself beyond all possibility of failure by willingly failing. For Soyinka, this is the essence of unredeeming tragedy, and one which in his most pessimistic moments he regards as underpinning the post-colonial dispensation in Africa. It is also worth noting that this insight is enabled by the transcendence of the dichotomy between Africa and the West, confirming the author's view that ultimately what is useful for Africa is not the specification of superficial Afrocentricity, but the use of diverse forms of knowledge for a deeper understanding of the continent.

As a study of the multiple ontology of being, the play's representation of the subjectivity of the dead and the living is yet another innovative engagement with the nature of being and identity. The world of the living and the dead mirror each other, as the living see themselves reflected in the dead and the dead in the living. The living see themselves in the dead as both history and present where, along the diachronic as well as synchronic time, the two operate as both absolute difference and similarity. The dead are the historical possibility of the present living community and as such share the attributes of the living, but they are a part of a different historical space, a different ontology, as it were. As the dwellers of the Forest, geographically separate, but temporally co-existent with the living, the dead occupy the same macro-time of the post-colonial, but inhabit it in the modality of non-historical time. But Soyinka's rewriting of Yoruba cosmology is dedicated to the re-inscription of history in ontology, rendering history the means by which both life and death are mediated, configuring both universes as timeless, but mutually dependent and determining spaces which are nevertheless separately modified by the differential iteration of history. Thus Soyinka validates the mythological world, but in a way that defamiliarises the experience of living as well as that of being dead. In this memorably phantasmagoric dance of image, dance, mime and myth, Soyinka expands post-colonial space to include the environment, earth and sky, and it is this that gives the play a certain epic dimension. It traverses a broad range of ontological levels and forms. In the end the only difference between the living and the dead is the difference in the modality of being and its relation to the past.

The use of multiple ontology is additionally at work in the duality of subject formation. The living have a trace or identity from the past, a model of identity similar in some ways to Jacques Lacan's idea of decentred subjectivity, but one which clearly is based on the Yoruba belief in reincarnation, particularly as elaborated through the endless birth and rebirth of *Abiku* children. For Soyinka, the essential ontological duality of subjectivity is ample justification for a play celebrating post-colonial liberty to reflect on the future by simultaneously inhabiting both the past and the present. Thus post-colonial desire encounters its specular alterity which is both the promise and interdiction of its full plenitude. Indeed, it is human vanity and greed that precipitate conflict in the play between the living and the dead. The invitation to the ancestors is produced within an anthropocentric value system in which ancestors are conceived of as specimens of perfection and wholesomeness, and where the possibility of ancestral blemish is denied. Here Soyinka highlights the extent to which the human conception of the spirit world is in fact a projection of human desire, an imaginary construction that dehistoricises and dematerialises both the subjectivity and universe of the spirit world, ultimately making myth an instrument of narrow social human interests. However, as *A Dance of the Forests* demonstrates, myth can also serve as a bearer of a vision of justice, especially when it is assigned a radical political role within African traditional cosmology, continuing to function as a point of reference for a people's sense of ontological location in relation to their past and the supernatural, but also providing a source of the history of the present social and political contradictions as well as of the ever-present possibility of their reproducibility in the future.

In the grotesque figures that roam the stage during the duration of the play, Soyinka deftly interrogates traditional African religion as well as Christianity, post-colonial triumph as well as the Western values of linear progression and the idea of the past as the golden age. Most important of all, in the play, conventional notions of history and myth, modernity and tradition, ontology and metaphysics are defamiliarised, resulting in an imaginative retrieval of African myth from the domain of a static ontology to that of a non-essentialist and dynamic *multiple political ontology*. In this way, the universe of myth functions both as a paradigm and critique of the post-colonial moment, enabling a greater understanding of the underlying tensions of the new society and political culture. Moreover, since indigenous beliefs constitute a significant part of the social imaginary of contemporary Africa, the foregrounding of the similarity of social contradiction in myth and the contemporary serves as a counter-hegemonic intervention within the contemporary ideological formation, resisting appropriations of the past which insist on its homogeneity and its plenitude. All the same, Soyinka does not reduce the past to the present or vice versa, as he is always conscious of its radical difference from the present and only uses such difference as a unique resource for replenishing contemporary models of self and social formation which he regards as massively impoverished, but nevertheless potentially redeemable.

NOTES

This essay was initially presented at a conference on cultural identity in Africa at the University of Leeds, September 1997. I wish to thank Professor Richard Werbner of Manchester University for his thoughtful and stimulating comments on the paper, and Birkbeck College for a conference grant.

1. Biyi Bendele-Thomas, 'Wole Soyinka Interviewed', in Adewale Maja-Pearce, ed., *Wole Soyinka: An Appraisal* (London: Heinemann, 1994), pp. 144–5.
2. For more biographical detail, see James Gibbs, *Wole Soyinka* (London: Macmillan, 1986) and Mpalive-Hangson Msiska, *Wole Soyinka* (Plymouth: Northcote House in association with the British Council, 1998).

137

3. *A Dance in the Forest*, in *Collected Plays I* (Oxford: Oxford University Press, 1973). All references in text.
4. Chidi Amuta, 'From Myth to Ideology: The Socio-Political Content of Soyinka's War Writings', *Journal of Commonwealth Literature* 23:1 (1988), p. 117.
5. F. Odun Balogun, 'Wole Soyinka and the Literary Aesthetic of African Socialism', *Black American Literature Forum* 22:3 (Fall 1998), p. 517.
6. Frantz Fanon, *The Wretched of the Earth* (London: Penguin, 1967), pp. 166–89.
7. Femi Osofisan, 'Wole Soyinka as a Living Dramatist', in Maja-Pearce, ed., *Wole Soyinka: An Appraisal*, p. 53.
8. See Mpalive Msiska and Paul Hyland, eds, *Writing and Africa* (London: Longmans, 1997), pp. 62–3.
9. Louis Althusser, 'Ideology and Ideological State Apparatuses', in *Lenin and Philosophy and Other Essays* (London: Verso, 1971), pp. 160–6.
10. See Robin Law, 'Oral Tradition', in Msiska and Hyland, eds, *Writing and Africa*.
11. Roland Barthes, *Mythologies*, trans. Annette Lavers (London: Paladin, 1973).
12. Patrick Taylor, *The Narrative of Liberation: Perspectives on Afro-Caribbean Literature, Popular Culture and Politics* (Ithaca: Cornell University Press, 1989).
13. Abdul JanMohamed, *Manichean Aesthetics: The Politics of Writing in Africa* (Amherst: University of Massachusetts Press, 1983).
14. Balogun, 'Wole Soyinka', p. 506.
15. Ezekiel Mphahlele, interview with Wole Soyinka, in Dennis Duerden and Cosmo Pietersen, *African Writers Talking* (New York: Africana Publishing Corporation, 1972), p. 170.

The gender differential, again and not yet

Caroline Rooney

I

It has become an established practice to invite post-colonial critics to address questions of gender and to invite feminist critics to address questions of race.[1] While such invitations are to be welcomed, it remains necessary to consider the historical provenance of such requests or demands so as not merely to recite exercises in a liberal political correctness. It might be assumed that the double invitation referred to above presupposes a general dis-articulation of 'gender' and 'race', one that requires mutual readjustment; if so, this assumed generality and this mutuality need to be contested. In the West, the centrality of gender may be claimed to have displaced questions of race and class that are then reintroduced into a certain middle-class Western feminism as its blind spots, prompting current attempts to take into account what is often termed 'the other'. The work of Gayatri Spivak has for some years served to stimulate a vigilance against the universalist assumptions of Western feminism. About a decade ago, Spivak argued:

> My historical caveat is, in sum, that feminism within the social relations and institutions of the metropolis has something like a relationship with the fight for individualism in the upwardly class-mobile bourgeois cultural politics of the European nineteenth century. Thus, even as we feminist critics discover the troping error of the masculist truth-claim to universality or academic objectivity, we perform the lie of constituting a truth of global sisterhood where the mesmerizing model remains male and female sparring partners of generalizable or universalizable sexuality who are the chief protagonists in that European contest.[2]

From the standpoint of this formulation of such an inheritance, I, amongst others, would argue that the blind spots of Western feminism cannot simply be addressed through a will to 'include' other women in its discourses, for these discourses have first to recognise their historical and institutional limits, albeit limits which enable them. What also requires recognition is that Western feminism is not the only feminism and that this heading is not the only heading of 'feminism'.[3] For example, in a number of African countries, feminist movements have consolidated themselves as part of national liberation struggles. For but one example of this, Khadijia Naib, writing of the National Union of Eritrean Women, states: 'N.E.U.W.'s main activity during the revolutionary years was to involve as many women as possible in the Liberation Front and to encourage them to fight side by side with the men'.[4] While the post-Independent nation then often regresses from or betrays a commitment to the struggles and rights of women, the revolutionary years remain nonetheless crucial: 'We cannot forget that Eritrean women achieved a great measure of social and political power during the liberation struggle through the conscious efforts of the E.P.L.F. and the Women's Union, during the years of struggle'.[5] I will not consider the specificities of the formation and development of women's movements in Africa, but instead will begin a limited exploration of the colonial and anti-colonial legacies of feminisms from different nations.

In the first part of this essay, I will look at an instance of the English nineteenth-century provenance of gender imperialism, by making an example of Dickens's *Bleak House*. I will then go on to consider the deferral and upsettings of an imperative of gender in an African literary setting through a reading of Ama Ata Aidoo's *Our Sister Killjoy*.

Anita Levy, in her book *Other Women*, examines how in the nineteenth century the gender differential is systematically privileged in order to eclipse and transcend other possible differentials. She writes: 'It would appear that the human sciences depended on the notion of the gendered individual. As a feature suitable for application to a large group of people regardless of regional, generational or genealogical ties, gender made the individual universal or generic.'[6] While 'gender' may be thus used to universalise the individual, this operation at the same time serves to universalise the 'law of gender'. Levy goes on to talk of 'gender as a strategy by which the modern middle classes legitimized a culture- and class-specific set of norms as nothing less than the stuff of human nature itself'.[7]

Levy looks at the deployment of gender in the discourses of sociology, anthropology, psychology, sexology, and aligns literary texts with these discourses – problematically, I think. The assumption here seems to be that literature can be read as a universalising, objectifying discourse, complicit with other discourses in the production or reproduction of regulating norms and their 'abnormalities'. While it is not always possible (in terms of strategic agendas) to spend time on the vagaries of literature, there needs be some recognition of, some hesitation over, the specificity of 'literature' and the singularity of the writing of a text as well as the renewable occasions and chances of its readings. Anita Levy chooses Emily Brontë's *Wuthering Heights* as an illustration of the progressive dominion of 'gender rules' over the supposed chronological span of the novel. However, *Wuthering Heights* is notoriously un-straightforward, and I think of it as a text that reserves itself for future occasions, as I hope to indicate briefly later.

I warned that the text I would make an example of is *Bleak House*. I can make an excuse for treating *Bleak House* as an open and shut case, by pointing out that the novel is permeated by an anxiety or phobia of what looks like being interminable.[8] The pervasive obsession of the novel (an obsession within it, and of it, about itself, uncontainably then) is that of the interminability of legal cases – an endless deferral of the law, its sentencing. The long novel ends with an incomplete sentence: '– even supposing –'.[9] It would thus seem not to complete itself, but this suspension (also) comes across as a plea for the reader to finish it off (a sort of 'mercy-killing'). That is, the reader of the text is asked to complete the sentence, and the reader has been schooled by the text as to what an appropriate formulation might be: '– even supposing – that my beauty had been restored to me. Full stop.' For example, or approximately. However, I appear to be dawdling with words. I will sum up my case, pass sentence.

Firstly, *Bleak House* makes a case of a character called Mrs Jellyby, a character into – as the chapter title has it – 'Telescopic Philanthropy'. This refers to Mrs Jellyby's 'African project', one of, we are told, 'cultivating coffee and educating the natives of Borrioboola-Gha, on the left bank of the Niger' (34). She is exposed to us through a visit made by Esther, the novel's main female character, and what Esther cannot help but notice is what a mess and muddle the Jellyby household is in – since Mrs Jellyby's 'African duties' leave her no time for domestic duties. Many microscopic details of household filth and neglect are shoved under our noses, and the household inhabitants are depicted, via simile and metaphor, as having 'gone native' (the husband is 'silent as a native'; the daughter completely blackened with ink from correspondence over Africa). Briefly, the message seems to be: philanthropy or charity should begin at home, and, perhaps, remain at home. Seeping fog-like into the text of *Bleak House* (that house of fiction) are contemporaneous debates over the abolition of slavery. Catherine Callagher, in *The Industrial Reformation of English Fiction*, shows how the rhetoric and arguments of debates concerning 'colonial slavery' were both redeployed in and yoked with controversial discussions concerning the conditions of labour and the working class in Britain. For instance, the pro-slavery writer and critic of industrial capitalism, William Cobbett, wrote an open letter to the leader of the Anti-Slavery Movement, William Wilberforce, in which he says:

Wilberforce,

> I have you before me in a canting pamphlet . . . At present I shall use it
> only thus: to ask you what need there was in spending your time writing
> and publishing, 'An Appeal to the religion, justice and humanity of the
> Inhabitants of the British Empire, on behalf of the Negro slaves in the
> West Indies'; to ask you what propriety, what sense, what sincerity,
> there could be in your putting forth this thing in the present state of
> this country?[10]

Cobbett goes on to insinuate that British labourers are far worse off than
Black slaves: 'you never attempt to tell us . . . that the Blacks perish or even
suffer for want of food. But it is notorious that great numbers of your free
British labourers have actually died from starvation.' It could be said that it
is 'telescopic philanthropy' that is the target, and that what is advocated is
the substitution of a concern over the 'domestic conditions' for a concern
over 'colonial slavery'.

As far as Mrs Jellyby is concerned, it could be said that the novel is
sceptical of her 'civilising mission'. However, the critique in *Bleak House* is
not angled in this direction. That is, the novel does not go into the details
of Mrs Jellyby's project (which is but a fleeting, superficially treated topic),
while it does go on to focus on the conditions of the poor in England, that
neglected domestic area of domestic neglect. When we are introduced to
Jo, a child of the slums, he is apparently casually, but with calculated
narrative irony, eating his breakfast on the doorstep of the Society for the
Propagation of the Gospel in Foreign Parts ('foreign parts' being the point
of contention [203]). And, in the chapter that stages Jo's death scene we
are told: 'He is not one of Mrs Pardiggle's Tockahoopo Indians; he is not
one of Mrs Jellyby's lambs; being wholly unconnected with Barrioboola-
Gha; he is not softened by distance and familiarity; he is not a genuine
foreign-grown savage; he is the ordinary home-made article' (588).

Thus, while class upstages race, the national-domestic theatre taking preced-
ence over the theatre of imperialism, class issues are, in turn, put to one side
in the novel. That is, having bracketed off the national-domestic sphere from
the international, this national-domestic sphere is further split into civic state
versus domestic household, where it is gender that makes all the difference.

One of the major problems posed by the poor in *Bleak House* is that
they spread disease (and crime) because they are not properly housed. The
novel's female protagonist, the kindly Esther, is called out of her house one
night to attend to the sick Jo, and she, as a consequence, catches his disease
which ruins her looks. One message is that feminine philanthropy outside
of the literal home is also a folly (never mind 'telescopic philanthropy').
Esther's main talent is that of 'housekeeping', which needless to say keeps
her home and is her keep, and she is eventually rewarded with a house
of her own and a husband. While the husband blends career and social

paternalism, his wife's role is to set up a model home. Such a home serves both as a refuge, a regenerating haven, from the ravages of the so-called outside world, and as an example to society of what a home should be – hygienic, well-run, well-regulated – an example to all classes (even, perhaps, races). Beyond this, it is also an example of ideal social relations: a family practice of caring for your own kind, endlessly 'practising', in the sense of rehearsing, keeping yourself diligently employed day-by-day, slaving away. At one point Esther says: 'when at last I lay down to sleep, my thought was how could I ever be busy enough?' (556). Esther's freedom from poverty and homelessness is a debt to be interminably repaid by her agreeing to police, enslave, colonise herself as a housewife. Tellingly, the last we hear of Mrs Jellyby is that her African project collapsed in farcical failure: 'but she has taken up with the rights of women to sit in Parliament' (806). I will not tease out the substitution here, but point out the way two 'genders' (genres) of the same gender are closed in on: the housewifely Esther versus the feminist Mrs Jellyby.

Bleak House is about a house called 'Bleak House', but it is also the title of the novel. What sort of a house is a novel? In certain respects, there is an analogy to be made between the ideology of the Victorian household and that of the cultural institution of literature in the nineteenth century. That is, in brief, just as the home was to serve as a serene refuge from the rapacious outer world, and idealised as the locus of the good example, literature and literary criticism were set up as areas to be reserved from the contaminations of immediate class interests and political causes. Matthew Arnold is often pointed to in this respect. Edward Said writes: 'Arnold believed that culture palliates . . . the ravages of a modern, aggressive, mercantile, and brutalizing urban existence'.[11] And Ruskin wrote: 'This is the true nature of home – it is the place of Peace. . . . so far as the anxieties of the outer life penetrate into it, and the inconsistently-minded, unknown, unloved, or hostile society of the outer world is allowed by either husband or wife to cross the threshold, it ceases to be home'.[12]

> And now where was she? How did she get there?
> What strings, pulled by whom . . .[13]

And now where am I? How did I get here? Where I am yet to talk about the problematic of gender in an African setting? What was all that about *Bleak House*, that busy show of blowing the dust off the pages, as if to prepare for something when it was perhaps just a forestalling of more urgent business. 'Maybe in some other life I'll just be a woman cooking food and having babies, but just now Shylock is demanding his pound of flesh. I have to attend the trial.'[14] How, then, do I get from *Bleak House* to *Our Sister Killjoy*? The point may well be that there is no transition at all, although I too am pulling some strings, exerting some influence. The phrase 'what strings, pulled by whom' occurs in *Our Sister Killjoy* when the protagonist, Sissie, wakes up to an awareness of her bizarre historical situation. What for Sissie seems to be so strange is how it is, after the violent, racist histories of colonialism in Africa and Nazism in Germany, that a German (woman) can desperately come to be kissing an African (woman), as if all were oddly forgotten. I will return to this scene. First, there is more scene-setting to do.

There is a moment in *Our Sister Killjoy* in which Sissie, in a crowd of white people, is pointed out as: **'das Schwartze Mädchen'** (emphasis in text, 12). She looks around, asking herself: 'Black girl? Black girl?' (and this could arguably be read as 'black person'? but not as 'girl'). In this moment of interpellation, in which she is 'raced', rather than sexed, it is the *setting* that confers an identity on her from without, and this very moment of identification is simultaneously one of self-dispossession and self-doubt. Who, me?

Now I find myself in something of a preposterous situation, one of both farce and sadness. When writing of gender in an African setting, I can but (be made to) notice the colour of my skin. White. Impolitely white, comically white, alarmingly white. It appears as something I must be responsible for – whose skin if not mine? – and as something that is beyond my control, a leakage 'I' cannot cover or contain. That me? Who me?

Who was Marija Sommer?
And Our Sister? (48)

I cannot simply go on to say 'now I will tell you about your? our? gender'. Even if I were to venture a 'you tell me', instead of an 'I'll tell you', the question of sources of authority would still have to be addressed. In *Our Sister Killjoy*, the request or demand for knowledge from the West is described as the 'Most merciless/Most formalised . . ./Spy system' (86). The novel parodies it: 'Tell us about/Your people . . .', and one could add, in the same tone: 'Tell us about African women'. Beyond this being a question of the extraction of knowledge that could be powerfully made use of, it is a demand that the addressees of the question produce themselves in terms of the questioner's discourse, here one which insists on gender, as that which is to be understood. So, it becomes a matter of: confess, give up, surrender 'your' otherness in order to make the intelligibility of gender 'your' concern as it is 'our concern'; let our concerns be yours. Tell us about African woman? Tell whom, my sister, and not just what but why do they want to know?

It is sometimes maintained of women from the Third World that there is a reticence when it comes to talking of sexual matters and that this reticence is due to an enforced modesty, or oppressive moral strictures or taboos imposed on them by their cultures. There may sometimes be truth in that and there sometimes may not be, but there are other things to consider also. Not only should there be a consideration of wise suspicions, or a defence against intrusiveness and manipulation, but a consideration of the compulsive necessity to talk of sex. For whom, and under what circumstances, is this sex-consciousness so compelling?

Furthermore, there are also other forums and other forms for a talking about sex that may be carefully constructed so as to exclude certain eavesdroppers. A 'resistance' to talking about sex need not be only, if at all, cultural or psychological, but may be political. Such issues are introduced by *Our Sister Killjoy* and also Bessie Head's *A Question of Power*. In both texts, the obscenity or disrespect of what can be glossed as the compulsoriness, or, at least, compulsiveness of discourses of power-knowledge is spoken of or dramatised, and there is a concomitant preoccupation with the imperatives of privacy. A few citations from *A Question of Power* can be offered:

> What was this? Did it mean she had no privacy left? (48)

> The elegant pathway of private thought . . . had been entirely disrupted. The steady peace and stability of soul had been blasted away and replaced by a torrent of filth. (148)

> The elegant pathway of private thought stretched ahead of her . . . undisturbed . . . (206)

And, in *Our Sister Killjoy*, it is said: 'all that I was saying about language is that I wish you and I could share our hopes, our fears and our fantasies, without feeling inhibited because we suspect someone is listening. As it is . . . we are sure they are listening, listening, listening' (115). It is also said: 'They pretend they are not interested in our carryings-on. But really, you would think that is all they do . . . Trying to find out how we dance, how we make love, how we reason' (116).

In *Our Sister Killjoy*, Sissie, object of curiosity in Germany, is subjected to much questioning. At the same time another questioning, and answering, takes place in a voice which haunts the text from both the past and the future. This haunted and haunting voice (which is less silent in its word-music than the words supposed to be spoken aloud, and yet which is not 'heard aloud' anywhere, is heard only spectrally, by an inner ear, disturbing any sense of homeliness and composure) is both intimate correspondence, a love letter (poetry), and political critique. But how to name this loving, ironic voice that itself knows? Self-knowingly, it names itself, Killjoy, and Our (not 'my', 'your', 'their') Sister. How do you decline this self-naming? 'This is Our Sister – it is our sister', for there she is, right there on the threshold of life. Or, does the text announce itself as follows: 'I am Our Sister', 'I belong to us', 'I am *ours*'? Or, 'This is, she is Our Sister Killjoy', as a brother would say. And, if it is said as a brother would say it, then it becomes hard to tell the difference between the sister and/or the brother.

At the end of the story of the travels, we are given this approach of a brother: 'I know everyone calls you Sissie, but what is your name?' (131). The text leaves this hanging, suspended in mid-air, as we turn the page to find, in a kind of postscript, Sissie on a plane descending, rousing herself from what she has been writing, shedding herself from her text, the text casting itself off. '[B]ut what is your name?' End of story as it is about to name or sign itself. Indeed, this text teases us with the desire to know the true name. This is delightfully played out in an exchange with Marija:

'Mary . . . Mary . . . Mary. Did you say in school zey call you Mary?'
'Yes.'
'Like me?'
'Yes.'
'Vai?'
'I come from a Christian family. It is the name they gave me when they baptised me. It is also good for school and work and being a lady.'
'Mary, Mary . . . and you an African?'
'Yes'.
'But that is a German name!' said Marija. (24)

I would like to stay with this extract and what follows on from it, but I appear to be stalling.

II

The subtitle of *Our Sister Killjoy* is *Reflections of a Black-Eyed Squint*. This might read as an invitation to read the text in terms of a slanted or an askew mirroring, and it would be possible to use *Our Sister Killjoy* to mirror a text like *Bleak House*. As pointed out, *Bleak House* may be read as ending with an appeal that a looking glass be held up to it to fulfil the wish of an Esther with the miraculous restoration of her face to flawlessness, the scars of the past erased. In *Our Sister Killjoy*, Sissie is given an ambassadorial travel grant to visit Europe so that she might take in the cultural sights and 'sing of the wonders of Europe' (9) despite the scars of the past, 'the face of reality that is more tangible than the massive walls of the slave forts standing along our beaches' (6). The novel registers but does not comply with the appeal to see and show Europe as it would see itself – that is, in its post-Arnoldian, self-flattering 'best lights'. Edward Said writes: 'Most professional humanists . . . are unable to make the connection between the prolonged and sordid cruelty of such practices as slavery, colonialist and racial oppression, and imperial subjection on the one hand, and the poetry, fiction, and philosophy of the society that engages in these practices on the other'.[15] In *Our Sister Killjoy*, it is said of African humanist apologies: 'The academic-pseudo-intellectual version is even more dangerous, who in the face of reality that is more tangible than the massive walls of the slave forts standing along our beaches still talks of universal truth, universal art, universal literature and the Gross National Product' (6).

If I labour the point, it would be possible to say, in terms of this essay, that our sister killjoy and *Our Sister Killjoy* refuse to satisfy a demand that may be phrased as: 'despite the ugliness of imperialism, the scars inflicted by colonialism, will you not affirm through replication, the kindness and beauty of our civilisation?' One singular instance, rather than allegory, of this appeal is to be found in the encounter that takes place between Sissie and Marija, the German housewife who befriends her. The appeal, demand or desire of Marija, who seems actively to court the company of non-Europeans, could be paraphrased as a certain: approve of me, reassure me, recognise me, love me. Through Sissie, the seductiveness of that appeal is acknowledged in terms of both the flattery it affords and the power. Moreover, there is 'the great romanticism in the setting' (41). This is a matter of Bavarian-Europe's dream of itself, a romance of boy-meets-girl gendered hetero-normality: 'A game in which one day, she became so absorbed, she forgot who she was, and the fact that she was a woman. In her imagination, she was one of those black boys in one of these involvements with white girls in Europe' (61). Meanwhile, Sissie is jolted out of this somnambulism when the reality of this imaginary scenario, with its narcissistic complementariness, strikes her. This happens on a visit to Marija's home, that hearth of lightness, heart of whiteness. When invited into the inner sanctum of this sanctuary, the marital bedroom, Sissie notices its white walls, white bed and 'funereal elegance', this being reminiscent of Conrad's phrase in *Heart of Darkness* for European womanhood, 'whited sepulchre'. It is a dis-homing moment, a distorted echo of 'the horror, the horror'. I would suggest that what is revealed to Sissie, or, via her to us, is the heartless heart, the generator, the gender-motor of Western culture.

In the text, this bedroom scene (a certain primal scene, the room described as a 'primaeval cave') is linked with the vast theatres of imperialism and colonialism in a revelatory flash: 'Suddenly Sissie knew. She saw it once and was never to forget it . . . And so this was it?' (65). It is possible to hear the tones of both discovery and anticlimax: so this was it? In the text, this 'this . . . it?' is elaborated or condensed as

L
O
N
E
L
I
N
E
S
S

Where am I?

It would be important to consider simply the effects of the type-setting – the ghostly 'concrete poetry' of a tear-drop, the dis-locating drop away of the text from itself, the chasm produced by the vertical bar, and so on. However, I will simply gesture towards the marking of the discovery of a source – 'this . . . it' – as an emptiness, the homelessness of the home. Apparently, it is this that drives Western man (and woman). It would be crude to dignify this in terms of a thrilling uncanniness or an ontological homelessness, for this would be to ignore the banality of it, the, *in turn*, routine homeliness of the unhomeliness.

I am working towards a reading that would take place between *Bleak House* and *Our Sister Killjoy*, rather than in the texts, in order to see the gulf 'between' them, but also to attempt a cross-eyes reading, cross-focused. Or, with one hand 'Esther' will be manipulated as a puppet again, while with the other, 'Killjoy strings' will be pulled. Esther, then, keeps house so compulsively not because she is a woman; rather, it is keeping house that produces her as a woman. It is an interminable labour for genderhood cannot be securely attained, only constantly maintained, and it is because there is no end to it that gender keeps going (and cannot be surpassed) and at the same time that gender imperatives keep everything going, in a maximum performativity.[16]

What a good little worker she is
What a fine example
What an 'excellent' system

So this is it? How captive maidens weave the world? I am thinking of a painting by Remedios Varo that pictures this and that is described in Pynchon's *The Crying of Lot 49* as viewed by the novel's heroine house-wife, Oedipa.[17] It is enough to make Oedipa feel very sad.

'This is weri sad, Sissie.' (73)

Marija was crying silently. (65)

... Sissie knew that she had to stop herself from crying. Why weep for them? the entire world has had to pay so much and is still paying so much for some folks' 'unhappiness'. (66)

There it was. Still falling. (66)

All this zeal, to what end? There is no end to it. There is then an unmet need for approval and recognition, for someone to impress with the home and home culture ('So this was it . . . bring the world to the heathen hoards' [65]). Marija, after the houseproud exhibit of her bedroom to Sissie, urges Sissie to visit Munich. While the haunting voice of the text has already spoken of the bedroom as 'a holy place' (63), it goes on to decline Marija's appeal in the following:

Marija,
There is nowhere in the
Western world is a
Must –

No city is sacred.
No spot is holy.

The 'geist' of Marija is addressed by or in another spirit, a political spirit that says: No, sadly and sadly, no.

While gender may be phantasmatic in its production and in its enactments, gender is not spooky, not at all. What would be perhaps spooky rather is gender loss and what is lost by gender in its institution.

'This is weri sad, Sissie.'
So it was. The sadness was not in her words but in her voice . . .
A sudden gust of air blew across from the river as though a ghost had passed. (73)

Now, in *Bleak House* there is a ghost. It is *not* Esther. However, one could fancy holding up a murky mirror to Esther to reveal there the flawless beauty of her dead mother. At any rate, this mother, Lady Dedlock, has in the text been haunted by or in search of a ghost:

In search of what? of any hand that is no more, of any hand that never was, of any touch that might have magically changed her life? Or does she listen to the Ghost's Walk, and think what step does it most resemble? A man's? A woman's? . . . Some melancholy influence is upon her; or why should so proud a lady close the doors, and *sit alone upon the hearth so desolate*? (my emphasis, 367)

Indeed, ladyhood is a melancholy state, haunted by this sexually undecidable ghost. Earlier in the novel it is explained to us that the ghost of Ghost's Walk is that of a former Lady Dedlock who opposed her Royalist husband in favour of her renegade brother, and: 'After her favourite brother . . . was killed in the civil wars . . . her feeling was so violent *she hated the race into*

which she had married' (my emphasis, 83). This is what Victorian womanhood occludes, a certain political brother–sister alliance against the master-
house, husband-father race (this is also the story of *Wuthering Heights*, the
haunting brother–sister relationship of Heathcliff–Catherine that opposes
the world of gendered hetero-normality). In *Bleak House*, the Victorian
Lady Dedlock mourns, without knowing it, the phantom 'brother'.

But then again, who or what is Esther? Flaubert is noted for saying,
'Madame Bovary, c'est moi'. So finally holding up another mirror to *Bleak
House*, to Esther, we might see a Dickens in drag, a man imagining himself
as a woman: 'Charles' her? Is that you?'. Gender is not a ghost but a drag,
although in its loneliness spectres gust past. What, if anything, has this to
do with African womanhood? 'Sometimes when they are hotly debating
the virtues of the African female, I ask myself: "But who am I? Where did
I come from?"' (117).

The above is from an imaginary dialogue Sissie writes (but does not
send) to a 'brother', a 'lover'. She continues: 'No, My Darling: it seems as
if so much of the softness and meekness you and all the brothers expect of
me and all the sisters is that which is really western. Some kind of hashed-
up Victorian notions, hm?' It might seem that in quoting this, in the context of what has gone before, my purpose is to reiterate, all too obviously,
the inapplicability of gender norms with their Victorian provenance. But
that is not it exactly. As Sissie says, differently, things are a whole lot more
complicated. While the non-applicability of 'hashed-up Victorian notions'
could be a conclusion to be reached, that has been but the starting point of
all this all along. Here there may be a conclusion of sorts.

Without further ado then, we are stuck with gender, yes, but we are
stuck with it insofar as it will not stick, insofar as its condition is one of a
certain congenital inapplicability. Or, 'gender cannot be made to adhere',
and it is this non-transmissibility that is the condition of its transmission.
That is, we have to start again and again with gender, and it is this beginning again with nothing gained, nothing secured, that keeps the issue(s) of
gender going. Caught up in constant re-applications of gender, in that
production line, you/we can but ask: what makes us/them do it? This can
be said with a certain camped-up helplessness: what makes me do it? Said
in such a way, this would indicate a tacit acknowledgment of pleasure in
playing-out-gender, an enjoyment in its absurdity: 'That was a game. A
game in which one day she became so absorbed, she forgot who she was,
and the fact that she was a woman' (61). Here, being absorbed by (the
game of) gender is also to forget your sex – even if you are a girl playing
a girl. So, it is important to remember 'the fact' of your sex, as addressed
obliquely in *Our Sister Killjoy*. In the novel the thought of being an African
man involved with a European woman gives rise to the thought of 'Lost

Black Minds' and 'Beautiful Black Bodies/Changed into elephant-grey corpses . . . Their penises cut' (62). If a rationalisation were to be forced on this, it might be to suggest the dangers of a game in which, in terms of political and material realities, the players are not equal. Or, turning to another page in *Our Sister Killjoy*, it is said: 'Being a woman/Has not/Is not/Cannot/Never will be a/Child's game' (51). This fact of being a woman is to be distinguished from the 'Child's game' of somnambulistic gender identifications. This consideration points in the direction of analyses which explore both the relationships and non-relationships between culturally distinct or differing gender productions and the oppression of women in different cultural circumstances. Where am I? Still struggling with, within, with the locations of a certain repetition compulsion of gender. You or 'I' do not 'possess' a repetition compulsion; it is something we are 'possessed by'. But some are more possessed than others, and it is still necessary to enquire, Killjoy-wise, from where do such 'possessions' or imperatives come.

Now I wish to move beyond these interminable cautions and to risk saying something about gender in an African setting. To cite again: 'No, my Darling: it seems as if so much of the softness and meekness you and all the brothers expect of me and all the sisters is that which is really western. Some kind of hashed-up Victorian notions, hm?' (117). What holds my attention in this passage is not really the terms 'really western' or 'hashed-up Victorian notions'. In reading the novel, a reader interested in finding out 'what African women say they are really like' might think the moment of testimony has come. The text bypasses such an expectation, that is, if you/we were expecting to hear: 'As an African woman I am not like this, I am, instead'. We do not get the 'I am, instead this and this'. But there is something, perhaps, understood. In the passage just cited, the emphasis may be heard as follows: 'My Darling . . . you and all the brothers . . . me and all the sisters'. The addressee of Sissie, of our sister, is a beloved brother. Now this brother, although a fictional character, is not a phantom. He is not of the same order as the forgotten ghostly political favourite brother of the Dedlock family history in *Bleak House*. Put otherwise, the brother–sister relation in Aidoo's text is still a living one, although it is under threat due to Western (gender) notions (among other things) that the brothers are adopting. As yet, in the time of the text, it is a threatened but still living political kinship, and point of identification.

In *Our Sister Killjoy*, there is also what may be termed an imaginary sister–brother identification. Sissie is not only interpellated into a Western gender theatre in a male role, but she also imagines herself in terms of a masculine version of herself. She is this imaginary twin, but she is also, in the fiction, in fact a twin. When Marija asks Sissie her birth date the latter replies, while the other-haunting-voice remembers: 'They had been twins'

(68). No more is said of this twin in the text, a twin who must have died: 'had been twins'. From this brief yet passing reference to a twin, I can very tentatively draw attention to a poem by Ama Ata Aidoo entitled 'To Him Who Said No to the Glare of The Open Day' and dedicated as follows: 'In memory of my twin-brother whom I never knew because he had been still-born'.[18] It is not my intention to raise biographical questions but rather, very hesitantly, to ask the question of a link between the absent other of writing, of poetry (the intimate unknown one you co-respond with when you write) and a certain political kinship. Other poems of Ama Ata Aidoo mourn lost brothers, as in *Our Sister Killjoy*, and in 'Of Love and Commitment',[19] an elegiac political love poem, it is said:

> Kwame Ata should not have died.
> For where shall I
> carry
> a double soul
> doubly restless, and an incestuous desire for
> my brothers?

This 'incest' is not literal obviously, but politico-poetic (and if the psychogenesis of this were to be speculated on it would be necessary to take into account the creative imagination).

As I have indicated, a section of *Our Sister Killjoy*, 'A Love Letter', is addressed to a brother-lover. If I continue to risk drawing this string of tentative connections, the brother-lover is, in a sense in the sense of a transference, a certain Africa. While certain 'brothers' talk of 'Mother Africa', in *Our Sister Killjoy* the countries of Africa are spoken of, in the text's poetry, as 'offspring' (52); the brother–sister countries of a continent. So, it could be said: Africa is a place of brother and sister (and sister, for let us not forget 'me and all the sisters'), and the place of brother and sister is Africa. When Sissie does not send the letter to The Beloved, she addresses instead and in his place, first Africa and then herself (133). My brother, my lover, my Africa, my twin, twin-self. There are further connections to be made, but I will merely add that a brother–sister Africa (one sometimes of Pan-Africanism, at other times of anticolonial or anti-neo-colonial struggle), as opposed to the Mother Africa of cultural nationalism, is to be remarked in the works of other African writers, not least the work of Bessie Head.[20]

There is a passage in *Our Sister Killjoy* which includes succinctly some of the things I have been suggesting, in particular the unconscious search of Marija for a brother she never had (before Sissie there were two Indian male friends), and what might reach us in the English language, get through to us in the West, concerning something of gender in an African setting. I will end by quoting the passage in full.

'I like to be your friend, yes?' asked Marija wistfully.

'Yes.'

'And I call you Sissie, . . . please?'

'Sure.'

'Zo vas is zis name, "Sissie"?'

'Oh, it is just a beautiful way they call "Sister" by people who like you very much. Especially if there are not many girl babies in the family . . . one of the very few ways where an original concept from our old ways has been given expression successfully in English.'

'Yes?'

'Yes . . . Though even here, they had to beat in the English word, somehow.'

'Your people, they see many small things about people, yes?'

'Yes. Because a long time ago, people was all people had.'

'Ah zo. And you have many brothers and no sisters?'

'No. I mean, it is not like that for me. They call me Sissie because of something else. Some other reason . . . to do with school and being with many boys who treated me like their sister . . .'

'Oh yes?'

'Yes.'

'I really liked zose Indians. I sink of zem weri much when you speak English.'

POSTSCRIPT

In the prefatory note to her novel *Changes*, Ama Ata Aidoo, intending the slippage, writes: 'Several years ago when I was a little *older* than I am now' (my emphasis), and this statement could lead us to place *Our Sister Killjoy* (1977) as coming after *Changes* (1989). *In Spectres of Marx* (1993), Derrida writes: 'But what is one to think today of the imperturbable thoughtlessness that consists in singing the triumph of capitalism or of economic and political liberalism'.[21] In its opening pages, and beyond, *Our Sister Killjoy* denounced then (in the present of the past), denounces now (in the past of the present), and again now (present of the future), this 'singing the triumph of capitalism', refusing to recognise its universal boast. Aidoo's novel-poem is also a radical critique of the contradictions between the self-advertisements of so-called European democracies (and of the posturings of African neo-colonial governments) and the wretchedness of those who these systems conspicuously fail to address, account for, attend to, again and again. And so, the novel-poem-critique is also a work of mourning (the non-forgetting of the traumas of history; the mourning of impossible friendships; the mourning for lost brothers; the mourning with and for the mothers who mourn . . .) and it is also an appeal for justice. This appeal concerns the chance of a future for Africa, for the non-elite of Africa, for the women of this non-elite. In both *Our Sister Killjoy* and *Changes* this opening is signalled as the texts 'end' with elliptical dots, and if there is any injunction here it is in the direction of an affirmation of an uncertain yet hoped-for future. There is both a letting go and a letting come. 'Below was home was its unavoidable warmth and even after these thousands of years, its uncertainties. "Oh Africa. Crazy old continent . . ."' (ellipsis in text).

Reaching the end of the novel, a reader realises that Sissie, having just finished writing the story of her travel stories in a letter, is preparing to land. Then it strikes you – this whole text-letter has been written in the night, in the self-absorption of a night flight, spinning itself out of itself, and now a landing is about to take place; that is, a return to life. The text is here poised on the brink of a return and a resurrection. We have both reached the place where it begins, its point of departure (towards the end of a flight), and the moment when it is just about to burst into ordinary miraculous life.[22] And so, I cannot be done with *Our Sister Killjoy*, this old-young text that keeps arriving, so youthful today, with its patient urgency that stays urgent. From which groove or line in the text to begin again? Black girl?

> Black girl?
> She looked around her, really well this time.

NOTES

1. This essay is a slightly revised version of a paper that I gave at the Centre for Commonwealth Studies, University of Stirling, that appeared in *Images of African Women: The Gender Problematic*, Occasional Paper Number 3 (Centre of Commonwealth Studies, University of Stirling, 1995), pp. 85–107. I am very grateful to Stephanie Newell and Angela Smith for the invitation to speak at the Centre and to the Centre for agreeing to the publication of this revised version.
2. Gayatri Spivak, 'Imperialism and Sexual Difference', *Oxford Literary Review* 8:1–2 (1986), p. 226.
3. See Jacques Derrida, *The Other Heading*, trans. Pascale-Anne Brault and Michael B. Naas (Bloomington: Indiana University Press, 1992).
4. Khadija Naib, 'Women's Rights and their Challenging Struggle', in *Images of African Women: The Gender Problematic*, p. 79.
5. Naib, 'Women's Rights', p. 84.
6. Anita Levy, *Other Women: The Writing of Race, Class and Gender* (Englewood: Princeton University Press, 1991), p. 8.

7. Levy, *Other Women*, p. 12.
8. For a discussion of this, see D.A. Miller, *The Novel and the Police* (California: University of California Press, 1988).
9. Charles Dickens, *Bleak House* (London: Dent, 1972). All references in text.
10. Catherine Gallagher, *The Industrial Reformation of English Fiction: Social Discourse and Narrative Form, 1832–1867* (Chicago: University of Chicago Press, 1985). The sources are given by Gallagher as follows: 'To William Wilberforce, on the State of the Cotton Factory Labourers, and on the Speech of Andrew Ryding, Who Cut Horrocks with a Cleaver', *Political Register*, 27 August 1823. Reprinted in *Selections from Cobbett's Political Works*, ed. John M. Cobbett and James P. Cobbett (London, not dated).
11. Edward W. Said, *Culture and Imperialism* (London: Vintage, 1994), p. xiii.
12. John Ruskin, *Sesame and Lilies* (London: Dent, 1907), p. 59.
13. Ama Ata Aidoo, *Our Sister Killjoy: Reflections of a Black-Eyed Squint* (London: Longman, 1977), p. 64. All further references in text.
14. Bessie Head, *A Question of Power* (London: Heinemann, 1974), p. 192. All further references in text.
15. Said, *Culture and Imperialism*, p. xiv.
16. For an analysis of the repetitive performance of gender, see Judith Butler, *Gender Trouble: Feminism and the Subversion of Identity* (London: Routledge, 1990).
17. See Thomas Pynchon's *The Crying of Lot 49* (London: Picador, 1979). See, also, Janet A. Kaplan, *Unexpected Journeys: The Art and Life of Remedios Varo* (London: Virago, 1988), Plate 13, p. 21.
18. Ama Ata Aidoo, 'To Him Who Said No to the Glare of the Open Day', in *Someone Talking to Sometime* (Harare: College Press, 1985), p. 68.
19. Ama Ata Aidoo, 'Of Love and Commitment', in *Someone Talking to Sometime*, p. 12.
20. I have given further consideration to this issue in the following two articles: 'RePossessions: Inheritance and Independence in Chenjerai Hove's *Bones* and Tsitsi Dangarembga's *Nervous Conditions*', in Abdulrazak Gurnah, ed., *Essays on African Writing*, vol. 11 (London: Heinemann, 1995) and 'Post-Colonial Antigones', *Oxford Literary Review* 19 (forthcoming). See, also, Lyn Innes and Caroline Rooney, 'African Writing and Gender', in Mpalive Hangson Msiska and Paul Hyland, eds, *Crosscurrents: Africa and Writing* (London: Longman, 1997).
21. Jacques Derrida, *Spectres of Marx*, trans. Peggy Kamuf (London: Routledge, 1994), p. 64.
22. The observations that I make here touch on Derrida's 'A Silkworm of One's Own', trans. Geoffrey Bennington, in *Oxford Literary Review* 18 (1997).

CHAPTER ELEVEN

Back to the future: revisiting Kristeva's 'Women's Time'

Carol Watts

> Our Toil and Labour's daily so extreme
> That we have hardly ever *Time to Dream*
>
> Mary Collier (1739)[1]

If there is one issue that occupies current debates in the media, and which is shaping British society in the last years of the century, it is the nature of time. This is arguably less to do at present with millennial fever than with the transformations in working practices which have, for the first time since the war, brought women into the workforce in greater numbers than men.[2] If the dream was once of a future where increasing leisure would be the norm, that future now appears oddly anachronistic: like the Lost Planet of the B movie, with the monster of flexible accumulation breaking through the perimeter fence. Anxieties about work have intensified for those without employment and those attempting to hold it down; work is, as the Blairite puritanism has it, what gives us self-worth; and it is women's work, in particular, which is serving as a litmus test for fundamental changes in the way that we live, a measure of our modernity. 'Working mothers', writes the journalist Melissa Benn, 'are forever talking about time. Their need for more of it is a craving akin to hunger or the wish for sleep'.[3] Time has been rendered visible today in ways that would have appeared almost unimaginable even a decade ago. It is continually monitored, tracked, and traded. Its disciplinary rhythms are now internalised as a form of regulative virtue.

It is feminism which is often credited with the widespread 'success' of women, outperforming in schools, dominating the workforce. Ironically, not just because this is seen as part of the reason for its demise, having achieved its purpose, but because feminism has had a lot to say about why it should be women, and indeed certain women, who come to the fore in a part-time, low-wage economy, and why their acceptance of 'flexible' working conditions makes them a model for the future. Paradoxically the possibility arises in Britain at least for a renewal of a feminist politics which last emerged in the activism of the 1970s, a politics able to explain why it is that the growing 'success' of women is accompanied by old and unresolved problems: those stemming from the real conditions of labour subsumed by the ideological notion of success, including that work carried out in the domestic sphere which remains largely invisible and devalued. Given the density of these contradictions and their denial in contemporary society, it is unsurprising that the 'craving' for time is felt so intensely.

Yet the feminism invoked in these millennial times appears to take what we might call a post-political form. What is noticeable about its manifestations in the British media as a cultural discourse – beyond the wearying assurances about the wearing of lipstick – is that it often serves to *explain* the emergence of those 'feminised' practices of the late capitalist economy (flexible labour markets, radical transformations in the relation between public and private, post-Fordist production, consumption as citizenship), even as it smoothes away class and ethnic differences and systemic contradictions. Girlpower is selling much more than slickly packaged CDs. Feminisation and feminism have become indistinguishable to some in the culture at large, to the point where women are the ideological focus of the hegemonic battles of the moment: as scapegoats, the limits of regulation (unremittingly in the guise of the single mother); as instruments of change, promulgators of those caring values which will underpin those 'hard choices' of the future. The dominance of feminine values is thus said to lie behind the 'compassion with a hard edge' which brings so many women MPs – 'Blair's babes' – to vote to deprive single women of welfare and anoint them with the work ethic;[4] behind a number of perceived crises in masculinity, not least the shocking levels of suicide amongst young men; behind the swell of (inter)national feeling at the death of Diana, a woman hailed by some in the media (and by certain Professors of English) as a 'feminist icon' who was both modern mother and Marilyn Monroe all in one, for whom men wept unashamedly in the streets.

This chimeric form of cultural feminism, ubiquitous, powerful, and yet at an end, confronts us with paradoxes. It continues to point to a sexual difference which, as Julia Kristeva puts it, 'feminism has had the enormous merit of rendering painful, that is, productive of surprises and symbolic life in a civilization which, outside the stock exchange and wars, is bored to death'.[5] Yet if feminism remains potently productive of our symbolic life, as the backlash against it attests, it is also an index of a contemporary sense of modernity, of transformations in ways of living and expectations of a future which are readily given a sexual political key. The continual reiteration of its 'end' might thus not simply – or only – point to a flight from the political, but to the fact that modernities change through time. Is it possible to think the relationship between these two conditions of contemporary experience – feminism as symbolic form, feminism as an index of modernity – in terms offered by a feminist critique? That is, an approach that might recognise the ideological movement of feminism's symbolic form(s), while attempting to articulate their relation to the desire for social change such a term implies? One way of negotiating this might be to imagine the stakes for a feminist politics of time, in which the times of the late capitalist world and those shaping women's lives are thought together. In what way has the time of modernity become a 'women's time'?

I FUTURE PERFECT

The relation between feminist struggle and the concept of time was classically articulated in Julia Kristeva's essay 'Women's Time' in 1979. In what follows I want to explore in what sense these turn-of-the-century years are the future anticipated in that essay, and to test out what her account has to offer as a diagnosis of the present. This might after so long appear a rather perverse return, particularly given the anti-feminism of her work which has been well documented by feminist critics. Ann Rosalind Jones, for example, detailed Kristeva's rejection of collective politics in an article in *Feminist Review* in 1984, suggesting her work was nonetheless significant for its opening up of a 'feminine position in culture' and negatively as a measure of 'post-political tendencies'.[6] In her partial response to Jones, 'Kristeva – Take Two', Jacqueline Rose agreed that feminism 'has never been the place from which she has chosen to speak', but argued for Kristeva's use of psychoanalysis as a fundamental attempt to understand the social and political in terms of psychic identity, a rich terrain that Rose has continued to explore in *States of Fantasy*.[7] Gayatri Spivak's pathbreaking essay 'French Feminism in an International Frame' saw Kristeva's anti-feminism specifically in terms of its location within the 'individualistic critical avant-garde' in France, shaped by its disillusion with the Left following 1968; pointing out both the ethnocentricity of her work and nonetheless the political potential of French feminism's symptomatic readings.[8] And the formulation of Kristeva's 'feminine position in culture' has recently been challenged on both philosophical and psychoanalytical grounds by Judith Butler in her

Bodies That Matter, which engages in a certain exclusionary logic in identity politics that Kristeva's work also identifies, but that the latter might be seen to buy into (I am thinking here of the homophobic dimensions of her analysis).[9] My purpose here is not to explore what resonances might be discovered between Kristeva's work from the late 1970s and that of feminist critics writing today, however. Rather, it is to risk a certain repetition, and to return to the 'Women's Time' essay as a posited past that might be seen, in Homi Bhabha's terms, 'to define the prerogative of my present'.[10]

Back in 1981, in the introduction to her English translation of Kristeva's essay, Alice Jardine asked, 'what will have to have happened before she can be read?' She was responding as an American critic in part to the cultural specificity of the text, embedded as it was in a European arena informed by the concerns of French cultural-political life. The question also arose because of a particular temporal modality of the text, 'a complex stratification of predictions and regressions' which seemed best summed up in the notion of a 'future perfect': *what will have happened.*[11] This tense has often been associated with the temporality of the postmodern, as in Jean-François Lyotard's 'What is Postmodernism?', published in the same year as 'Women's Time', where Lyotard discusses the paradox of the future anterior in which the writer works 'without rules in order to formulate the rules of what *will have been done'.*[12] Both works might be seen to share a certain future-oriented tone, and what lies behind the invocation of the future perfect in the rhetorical staging of each is a suspicion of the grand narratives of history, enacted by this curiously deterministic temporality-without-formation – a suspicion that manifests itself in very different ways. Kristeva's essay is located in the shadow of that 'field of horror' fought over in the Second World War, and her next work on Céline, *Powers of Horror*, takes as its object the psychodynamics of fascism. 'Women's Time' undoubtedly shares the view of feminism as 'the last of the power-seeking ideologies', as she puts it in that subsequent work.[13] For an essay which possesses the status of a manifesto, it stages the drama of the political for reasons other than the cause of feminism as collective struggle. In her view, feminism, like all political discourse, risks a totalitarianism in which it becomes our 'modern religion: the final explanation'.[14] Despite this anti-feminist stance, however, Kristeva's drama of the three 'phases' of feminism not only addresses the relationship between feminism's 'symbolic life' and the desire for social transformation with which I began, but it also poses the question of how that relationship is to be temporally conceived: both as a historical process and as anticipating a possible, transformed future. My aim in constituting my present in terms of the essay as past might thus be to challenge the inevitable futurity of Kristeva's essay, and thus its 'post' political logic.

It is interesting to examine briefly in this context how far Kristeva's essay is prepared to recognise a utopian impulse within its temporal strategies, given its suspicion of 'the political interpretations of our century'. Fleetingly, perhaps, is the answer, and then only as a moment of enunciation ('if the preceding can be *said* – the question whether all this is *true* belongs to a different register' [209]). Her discursive strategy appears to anticipate the figure of the 'contemporary interpreter' elaborated in 'Psychoanalysis and the Polis', one who follows a 'post-hermeneutic and perhaps even post-interpretative' path:

> the new interpreter no longer interprets: he speaks, he 'associates', because there is no longer an object to interpret; there is instead the setting off of semantic, logical, phantasmatic and indeterminable sequences. As a result, a fiction, an uncentred discourse, a subjective polytopia come about, cancelling the metalinguistic status of the discourses currently governing the post-analytic fate of interpretation.[15]

This associative drive shapes that 'complex stratifications of predictions and regressions' which Jardine terms the modality of the future perfect in 'Women's Time'.[16] There is a performative element here in which the essay's utopian impulse resides: its tilt at the future constituted through the subjunctivisation of a speech act – 'if the preceding can be said'. The 'polytopia' she refers to here might be seen, then, as the generative limit of the future perfect, one which 'will have' changed the very form of its determination: a utopian truth become montage.

Yet the logic of Kristeva's future perfect suggests rather a configuration of modernity than Lyotard's postmodern, which might make us read her polytopic hope rather differently. It is as if the essay's enunciative gesture depends after all upon the interpretation of a truth – the truth of desires which are temporalised within political discourse – if only to attempt to leave it behind. In other words, 'Women's Time' as manifesto depends on a form of historical reflexivity that is both its rhetorical form and its object; on the elaboration of a process of a coming to consciousness that is as yet unfinished, even as it anticipates moving beyond such a temporal scene. The concept of modernity, as Peter Osborne discusses in *The Politics of Time*, is marked by a 'paradoxical doubling', a dialectical contradiction whereby 'it designates the contemporaneity of an epoch to the time of its classification; yet it registers this contemporaneity in terms of a qualitatively new, self-transcending temporality which has the simultaneous effect of distancing the present from even that most recent past with which it is thus identified'.[17] It is this doubling – a spatialisation of the temporal that is a form of historical totalisation – which I will argue is present in 'Women's Time', and which shapes Kristeva's famous location of three 'generations' of feminism in Europe in terms of a 'problematic of time'. The difficulty of assessing that 'complex stratification of predictions and regressions' derives from the need to think this condition, which as I will argue is both invoked and disavowed by Kristeva's text. It is a doubling articulated in the very term 'generation', a 'phase' which is less understood by Kristeva as a chronological stage – as in first or second wave feminism – than as a *'signifying space'* (209), which suggests a distinct, though not exclusive, praxis of women's time. As the essay progresses, however, it is clear that while each phase is seen to occupy synchronically the *same* historical moment, 'in parallel' or 'intertwined', a periodising movement kicks into effect, and a third 'generation' begins to separate itself off from the two 'preceding' it. As if by some latent dialectic, it also suggests a transformation of their concerns, and the future possibility of feminism's 'end'. What makes Kristeva's analysis even more abstract is that the three phases of feminism are mapped against a temporal topography which offers a number of different landscapes for the thinking of this paradoxical condition: on one level, the differential time of the nation; on another, the times of production and reproduction; and finally, that of a fundamental psycho-symbolic logic which brings the social into being, what we might see as an encounter with the originary timelessness of the unconscious.

II TEMPORAL ENCOUNTERS

The 'strange temporality' of the future perfect is not just part of the rhetorical method of 'Women's Time', but located rather more specifically in the essay as a modality produced by the waning of the nation-state, or rather, as Kristeva has put it more recently, its status as a 'transitional object'.[18] Following the Second World War, she argues, the nation as a homogeneous entity becomes no more than a powerful ideological illusion, transformed by the pressures of globalisation, and by the emergence of latent symbolic determinants of cultural and religious memory, which suggest other affiliations beyond its geographical confines, and thus broader 'socio-cultural ensembles' (of which Europe might be one). The nation thus becomes another signifying space, a social imaginary, whose borders as Homi Bhabha explains 'are constantly faced with a double temporality: the process of identity constituted by historical sedimentation (the pedagogical); and the loss of identity in the signifying process of cultural identification (the performative)'.[19] In Bhabha's view it is one of the strengths of Kristeva's account that she attempts, like Fanon, to redefine the way in which the process of psychic investment in such collectivities as the nation might be understood. However this 'double temporality' is expressed in 'Women's Time' in the first instance by a disjunctive encounter between two discrete temporal dimensions which appears to be more limited than that presaged in Bhabha's account: in which the time of production – 'a logical and sociological distribution of the most modern type' – is shaped by memories 'of the most deeply repressed past', the time of reproduction (189). The times of capital, of political life, of historical change – all characterised in terms of a single form of linear time narrowly equated with history – thus encounter a monumental temporality associated with the body and the life and death of the species, which is the object of anthropology. Such an encounter is figured less in terms of a fracturing disjuncture that might open up the temporal process of formation and loss in terms of the contingencies of history, than as a return of the repressed, in which the time of reproduction – as the unconscious – is located outside the time of history.

Kristeva suggests that the three phases of feminism are determined by this temporal topography. The first phase situates itself within the confines of the socio-politics of the nation, seeking to insert itself in historical time and identifying 'with the logical and ontological values of a rationality dominant in the nation-state'. Its struggle is for equality (she lists the battles over abortion, contraception, equal pay, professional recognition) which 'have already had, or will soon have effects even more important than those of the Industrial Revolution'. Her conclusion is clearly that the demand of this generation has been met to the extent that the principle of women's inclusion has been accepted, though it continues to be fought for. The second phase, dating from 1968, links radical separatist concerns and a rejection of the political process to aesthetic experimentation. This feminism demands recognition of women's 'irreducible' identity, attempting 'to give a language to the intrasubjective and corporeal experiences left mute by culture in the past' (194). In part Kristeva associates these moves with the feminist critique of a socialism wedded to an economistic model of production; what is evident is that its valorisation of the time of reproduction reveals supranational connections between women, across continents and cultures. Both phases invoke a universal subject, Woman, but where the former globalises the problems of women in terms of a progressivist model of historical change, the second reconnects with a traditional and archaic account of female subjectivity, verging on the eternal and spatialised time of myth. Yet even as the essay sets out its schema, it invokes a third 'generation' – 'I am not speaking of a new group of young women (though its importance should not be underestimated) or of another "mass feminist movement"' but of a 'third attitude, which I strongly advocate – which I imagine?' – which constitutes the contemporaneity of all three' (209).

III   THE THIRD PHASE

If it is possible to trace a logic of modernity as part of the rhetorical momentum of Kristeva's text as manifesto – in contradiction to what it theoretically avows – it also interacts with another conceptual movement in 'Women's Time' that ultimately comes to define such a logic as its symptomatic truth. Kristeva's future perfect is undoubtedly informed by a *psychoanalytical* account of time in which the future is approached retroactively, as in the Freudian concept of *Nachträglichkeit* or afterwardsness.[20] In this way it might be seen to reveal a different kind of 'historical decision', as Jean-François Lyotard describes in an elaboration of that concept, whereby 'the decision to analyze, to write, to historicize' takes place in terms of an encounter with 'the time of unconscious affect': 'in order to give it form, a place in space, a moment in temporal succession, . . . representation on the scene of various imaginaries'.[21] The historical totalisation promised by one model of modernity thus meets a different spatial logic of time, another scene, with which it engages in what Kristeva terms in 'About Chinese Women' an 'impossible dialectic':

> A constant alternation between time and its 'truth', identity and its loss, history and that which produces it: that which remains extra-phenomenal, outside the sign, beyond time. An impossible dialectic of two terms, a permanent alteration, never one without the other. It is not certain that anyone here and now is capable of this. An analyst conscious of history and politics? A politician tuned into the unconscious? Or, perhaps, a woman . . .[22]

The rendering contemporaneous essential to the political logic of modernity can thus also be read in terms of a psychic movement of identity in which, as Lacan describes, 'past contingencies' are given 'the meaning of necessities to come, such that the little bit of freedom through which the subject makes them present constitutes them'.[23] Each generation of feminism might thus possess its 'little bit of freedom' to reconfigure time and thus its own contemporaneity. If the first and second 'phases' assert that freedom through a logic of identification and counter-identification with the social order, the third attempts to understand the nature of the psycho-symbolic contract which founds both that order and their freedom. At the centre of 'Women's Time' – I am tempted to say, according to Freud's archeological topography, at its bedrock – is a psychoanalytic account of the social code which is at once the most generatively productive insight of the essay and its limit. Productive, because Kristeva locates the social in terms of psychic formation. As Jacqueline Rose has suggested, Kristeva's engagement with psychoanalysis has, far from necessarily entailing a retreat from political commitment, often been a means of exploring 'the pre-condition of any effectivity in the social'.[24] Limited, because while it demystifies what Kristeva calls the 'symbolic bond', her psychoanalytical model produces an overwhelmingly phallocentric theorisation of power, and a formalistic account of what might be seen as 'women's time' that locates women *outside* the time of history (and modernity). It is in this paradoxical space that feminism's third phase recasts its struggle in symbolic terms.

Any attempt to think the connection between feminism and 'a problematic of time' must engage with the issue of power at some level. What limits the first and second generations of feminism in Kristeva's account is the extent to which they define themselves in terms of the power of the dominant and patriarchal symbolic order, either by wanting to assume the mantle of its 'executive, industrial and cultural' forms, or by producing a counter-society which is a fetishised 'simulacrum' of its dominant other (201–2). Kristeva's famous example of women's terrorism emerges here as an example of the way the brutal exclusion of women's affective life from the socio-symbolic order is counterinvested as violent struggle against the state. It is not that it is possible to step outside the dynamics of such an economy, for Kristeva, since power is what constitutes the very possibility of agency. To borrow the terms of her 'Psychoanalysis and the Polis', it is rather that these might be seen as choices defined by a political logic 'which does not lead its subjects to an elucidation of their own (and its own) truth'.[25] Contrastingly, this elucidation is the starting point for a third generation, which recasts the concerns of the first two by asking according to an analytic dynamic: '*what can be our place in the symbolic contract?*' Drawing together the Lacanian concept of the symbolic order with Freud's formulation of the castration complex, Kristeva defines the constitution of the social, of language, of meaning, in terms of the privileged signifier of the phallus, and the violent separation – from the imaginary plenitude of the mother – brought about through the paternal function. This is the 'common destiny of the two sexes' (199). The aim of such an elucidation is in part to grapple with the truth of a contradiction in which 'power is both external to the subject and the very venue of the subject', as Judith Butler puts it in *The Psychic Life of Power*, a double bind which is at the heart of Kristeva's thinking of the complicity of feminist agency.[26] If this is the truth that the third generation of feminism is working to comprehend, it is also seen to be the particular role of women and the 'new feminist ideology' to voice its sacrificial effects: 'they find no affect there, no more than they find the fluid and infinitesimal significations of their relations with the nature of their own bodies, that of the child, another woman or a man' (199). With knowledge, emerges the possibility of what Kristeva calls a 'redoubling' of the social contract. The terrain of this struggle is cultural – the realm of 'aesthetic practices' – which through its contact with 'an otherwise repressed, nocturnal, secret and unconscious universe' might provide the means to trouble the terms of that symbolic economy.

If the third generation anticipated here constitutes its contemporaneity according to the logic I have described, then its 'making present' resembles an analytic scene in which the subject 'is lead to the economy of his own speaking'.[27] But what is this economy, and why is it women who speak it? In earlier essays, such as 'Woman can never be defined', an interview given in *Tel Quel* in 1974, Kristeva had positioned women in terms of a textual negativity:

> we must use 'we are women' as an advertisement or slogan for our demands. On a deeper level, however, a woman cannot 'be'; it is something which does not even belong to the order of being. It follows that a feminist practice can only be negative, at odds with what already exists so that we may say 'that's not it', and 'that's still not it'. In 'woman', I see something above and beyond nomenclatures and ideologies. There are certain 'men' who are familiar with this phenomenon; it is what some modern texts never stop signifying.[28]

If Kristeva does not locate herself in terms of feminism, though recognising its political subjecthood here, she clearly identifies with the subversive possibilities of this practice of negative inscription. It is such a negativity that feeds into the ethical attitude advocated at the end of 'Women's Time', one which promises to produce in Homi Bhabha's terms 'a dissidence, and a distanciation, within the symbolic bond itself'.[29] In Kristeva's political writings it is figured in terms of female exile, the view, in *Strangers to Ourselves*, that women were the 'first foreigners to emerge at the dawn of our civilization'.[30] Such a negativity produces a kind of translatable alterity, expressed in *Tales of Love* by the view that 'we are all E.T.s', in which universality is rethought in terms of difference.[31]

Such a figuring of negativity also suggests a spatialisation of relations in which it becomes difficult to sustain a notion of 'women's time' as such. 'Women', Kristeva states expansively in 'What of Tomorrow's Nation' in 1993, 'have the luck and responsibility of being boundary-subjects: body and thought, biology and language, personal identity and dissemination during childhood, origin and judgment, nation and world – more dramatically so than men are.' It is not just that women, as 'boundary-subjects', might be seen to mediate the differential times of the nation, as Kristeva argues in this later essay, as Hegel's 'everlasting irony of the community'.[32] Nor even that they are located simultaneously within the times of production and reproduction more 'dramatically' than men, whatever that might mean. It is that the woman as a boundary-subject – as 'something maternal' – is *spatially* located at the very constitution of the social, at the meeting place of the imaginary and the symbolic. In this way the 'economy of her own speaking' suggests both the limits of what the symbolic order is prepared to recognise of itself, and yet that which brings it into being: what Judith Butler, following Ernesto Laclau, might call its 'constitutive outside'. [33] Kristeva's exploration of what it means to articulate negativity in the social brings her to an elaboration of abjection in the work following 'Women's Time'. What might this incription of identity in terms of negativity mean for the *temporal* dynamics of the essay? One way of approaching this is to consider Kristeva's construction of the figure of the mother.

IV MOTHER TIME

Kristeva argues that the figure of the mother will prove central to the concerns of the third phase of feminism, which might, with its understanding of the symbolic contract, be able to explore why it is that women desire to bring children into the world. As she suggests, in Freud's view such a desire corresponds to the desire for a penis – a substitute for 'phallic and symbolic domination' in Kristeva's words – which locates women's desires once again in terms of that privileged signifier. It is a view the essay is only 'partially' willing to acknowledge, in favour of an attempt to imagine a transformation of that phallic economy. The experience of maternity is seen as a border condition in 'Women's Time', 'a radical ordeal of the splitting of the subject', 'a separation and coexistence of the self and of the other'. The pregnant woman undergoes a transition from a state of narcissistic plenitude – that monumental realm of the eternal mother which appears as a 'socialized, natural psychosis' – to the experience of separation from the child in which she is brought to an understanding of love for an other (206). Kristeva's notion of women as 'boundary-subjects' is in part a rejoinder to those who might want to valorise one or other side of the border; in particular the imaginary 'maternal' space of the semiotic which is the focus of the revolutionary poetics of her early work. Her privileging of the maternal has often risked becoming implicated in the symbolic dynamics of the feminine she analyses, perhaps because, as Spivak argues, her project has been in some sense against the deconstructive grain: its aim 'has been, not to *deconstruct* the origin, but rather to *recuperate*, archaeologically and formulaically, what she locates as the potential originary space *before* the sign'.[34] Rose points out that an idealisation of this space dangerously constitutes the feminine as 'the excluded instance of all culture', and ignores the psychic pain and violence which characterises the early relation between mother and child.[35] It is an idealisation that is explicitly countered in 'Women's Time' in both psychoanalytic and political terms, though as I will argue the prospect of feminine exclusion returns in the essay as fundamental to its thinking of time.

What impact does this figuring of the maternal as a 'border' condition have on the temporal logic of 'Women's Time'? Superficially it might appear to confirm the way that the essay has often been read as a kind of shorthand for stages of feminist thought and practice. This was certainly my experience of it, coming to it in a feminist reading group for students in the early 1980s. The first phase of feminism thus identifies with a notion of linear 'historical' time (hence battles for equality, the demands of socialist feminism); the second eschews the political, valorising the time of reproduction, 'all encompassing and infinite like imaginary space' (191), and falling in to a bad essentialism in the process (radical feminism, certain forms of *écriture féminine*); and the third – the ethical turn – promises the acknowledgement of difference, having internalised the critique of the ethnocentricity of the previous generations' universal concept of Woman. The third phase raises the prospect at least of the encounter of heterogeneous, perhaps incommensurable or fractured temporalities, in keeping with a vision of 'the singularity of each person and, even, more, along with the multiplicity of every person's possible identifications . . . the relativity of his/her symbolic as well as biological existence' which the essay will finally imagine (210). The ethical argument advanced in the final section is predicated on the radical splitting Kristeva associates with the maternal, a relation between self and other which refuses both conformity to the law of the symbolic and absolute difference from it (like the first and second generations respectively). What the third phase of feminism anticipates is, she argues, a fundamental challenge to identity, inaugurating

> the demassification of the problem of difference, which would imply, in
> the first phase, an apparent de-dramatization of the the 'fight to the death'
> between rival groups and thus between the sexes. And this not in the
> name of some final reconciliation . . . but in order that the struggle, the
> implacable difference, the violence be conceived in the very place where it
> operates with the maximum intransigence, in other words, in personal and
> sexual identity itself, so as to make it disintegrate in its very nucleus. (209)

Yet the difficulty of the essay in the last section is I think symptomatic of a number of conceptual moves that the argument to some extent disavows, making it easier to consume the three-stage model of feminist generations without realising quite what is given away. Most immediately, the issue of women's time itself seems to disappear or become rerouted in a way that requires explanation. It may be that just as the prospect of such ethical transformation entails the end of feminism – 'as but a moment in the thought of that anthropomorphic identity which currently blocks the horizon of the discursive and scientific adventure of our species' (211) – it also might be seen to render redundant the need to theorise a time specific to women's experience. Yet this is premature even in the essay's terms, when it is clear that the phases of feminism are still to be read (as in that doubling of modernity I discussed earlier) as occupying the *same* historical moment, and that their interrelation is assumed, if untheorised.

I argued earlier that the third phase of feminism constitutes the contemporaneity of all three, to the extent that it recasts their concerns in terms of its own symbolic knowledge. The issue of women's time – its complex determinations already constrained within closed and homogeneous temporal categories denoting 'history' and 'reproduction' – is thus repositioned wholly within that psychoanalytic logic in which the 'little bit of freedom' of each generation to constitute itself in time is revisioned in terms of the *freedom of the mother*. Since the phallic economy of the symbolic order makes it difficult to imagine political desires as other than forms of identification or counter-identification, the temporal praxes of the first and second phases can only seem irredeemably collusive or impossibly utopian. The political desire for transformation thus gives way to an ethical spatialisation of relations figured by the maternal as negativity. This, for a moment, returns us to that 'originary space before the sign', in order to understand what the mother's freedom might mean.

In a reading of Kristeva's account of primary identification drawn from her later work *Tales of Love*, Peter Osborne addresses the painful process of separation of the child from the mother that takes place as a precondition of psychic formation, which is also a 'process of the formation and deformation of meaning': signification. The mother's desire establishes the phallus not simply as the object of identification, but also the privileged signifier, which will 'ground' the child's later access to the symbolic order and mirror phase. The child experiences the loss of the mother's desire as an emptiness which it attempts to recover, by identifying with the object of that desire, what Freud calls 'the father of personal prehistory', Kristeva terms 'the Imaginary Father', and Osborne, reacting to the phallocentrism of the model, names 'the Imaginary Other'. As Osborne describes:

in identifying with the Imaginary Other the child may be said actually (unconsciously) to be identifying with the mother. The independence of the Imaginary Other from the child, the 'gap' which identification covers over, stands in for the independence of the mother, the independence which threatens the child with 'emptiness'. We may trace the origin of 'death' within this framework back to *this* fundamental mapping or substitution.

What is significant about Kristeva's account is the centrality of the freedom of the mother, as both a 'threat to [the child's] existence and the condition of its identity'.[36] It is clear from this why the maternal is such a crucial concept for her work in general. On one level it is the freedom of the mother, her independence as a fundamental negativity, which guarantees the child's later entry into the symbolic order. It is also that border place – the mediating term of that 'impossible dialectic' – where the relation with the other is negotiated, hence its centrality to the ethical position outlined in 'Women's Time', a point of view shared with the earlier essay 'Stabat Mater', where she calls for 'an herethical ethics separated from morality, a herethics', which 'is perhaps no more than that which in life makes bonds, thoughts, and therefore the thought of death, bearable'.[37] Hence the social responsibility anticipated in 'Women's Time' – via an account of maternal love – for those negotiating the violence and 'threats of death' associated with the acknowledgement of difference at its very 'nucleus'.

Osborne's discussion of the freedom of the mother goes further, in a complex argument that I have only begun to sketch, to suggest that 'it is the freedom of the (m)other . . . in the possibility of the refusal of recognition, which brings death (and hence *time*) into the world of the child'.[38] This realisation is I think illuminating of the temporal structure that shapes Kristeva's 'Women's Time'. The 'little bit of freedom' with which each generation constitutes its own contemporaneity as I argued earlier becomes via the psychoanalytic account of the freedom of the (m)other that which sets in motion the movement of temporalisation *per se*. 'Women's time' in this sense names an originary spatialisation of relations – a disjunctive border encounter with the other – that brings time into the world. The conceptualisation of time within the essay is thus inscribed within a psychoanalytical logic in which we shift our categories of reference, brought out, as it were, on the other side of a Möbius strip. And at the moment when the double bind takes place, it is possible to see both the constitutive moment of the psychic as social and what we might see as the symbolic site of its post-political stance. For if the maternal is one way of posing the possibility of the refiguring of the sacrifical logic of the symbolic order, it is also essentially outside time.

V   MODERNITY REVISITED

At the outset of my argument I suggested that a feminist politics of time might offer the means to think the relations between two related conditions of contemporary experience: feminism as a symbolic form, and feminism as an index of modernity. Kristeva's essay makes it possible to explore a particular constellation of the two, setting in motion its 'impossible dialectic' of political and psychoanalytic logics. On one hand, it makes a powerful case as to why feminism as a cultural form might prove so potent, identifying the struggle and violence which constitute the social bond. On the other hand, and relatedly, it suggests how feminism might then become an index of those transformations taking place in the social, to the extent that a feminine ethics might bring about a wholly new regulation of its economy. Yet what is the relation posed in the essay between 'women's time' and that movement of modernity? On one level it might appear to name the split that Bhabha terms the 'time-lag', making possible 'a transvaluation of the symbolic structure of the cultural sign' and thus the constitution of modernity as such: 'Modernity as a sign of the present emerges in that process of splitting, that lag, that gives the practice of everyday life its consistency as being contemporary.' The interrogative stance that Bhabha associates with modernity – 'what do I belong to in this present? In what terms do I identify with the "we", the intersubjective realm of society?'[39] – is similar to the question posed by Kristeva's third phase of feminism: '*what can be our place in the symbolic contract?*'. In its privileging of the 'problematic of space', 'women's time' is elevated in this third phase to the very generative disjuncture that makes social time possible.

Yet in this enunciative gesture much is lost.[40] By sloughing off space from time in this way Kristeva structurally locates women outside history – which we remember in her schema is that 'linear' obsessional time shaped by the actions of men. The sphere of reproduction disappears from history in a way that reinforces current ideological conditions. Given the overweening phallocentrism of her model, it appears impossible for her to conceive of the symbolic repercussions of the long history of women's political and economic struggles, or even the retroactive significance for her phases of the insight that the symbolic order might be resignifiable, a hegemonic imaginary, as Judith Butler's work explores.[41] In other words, it is difficult to think of the politics of time here in terms of the *social practices* that might make sense, for example, of the continued coexistence of three phases she outlines. The logic of modernity that I have identified as shaping 'Women's Time' is thus oddly formalistic, its enunciation of contemporaneity ultimately an exercise in forgetting. This is essential to its post-political stance. It has no way of acknowledging the heterogeneity of times corralled within its categories, nor their historicity, nor their complex interactions. Women's time spatially conceived may mark a generative foundation of disjuncture – that principle of dissidence – but it isn't a social form of temporality thought in terms of the disjunctural times of modernity. Why would we want it to be?

VI FEMINISM/FEMINISATION: MARY COLLIER'S 'THE WOMAN'S LABOUR'

What might it mean to return to Kristeva's essay in order to interrogate this moment in all its contemporaneity? In what sense have the determinations of its future perfect already imagined it? There are significant reasons for thinking they have, in a political culture seemingly marked by feminism's continuing end, in which the ethical demand has superseded political desire. Books on 'new motherhood' abound, and calls for responsibility, for a gentler management of change in this stakeholding society, are the norm. This is only a parody of 'Women's Time' in certain ways. Yet if the essay identifies a certain symbolic economy that 'women's time' makes present, it is unable to get to the ideological crux of why it is an index of the moment. For the flexible times of the late capitalist world are more than equal to the fluid subjectivities and the polytopic spaces of Kristeva's enunciated future; indeed they would seem to require them. To put it another way, rather than providing the terms through which an interrogation of the equation between feminism and feminisation might be possible – that space in which the current hegemony is being fought out – Kristeva's account dovetails with just such an equation. If women's time, and particularly that of working mothers, is the index of contradictions, it is also the locus of a great deal of ideological work, a systemic requirement. Women's time in this sense is a temporality that incorporates, interpellates, in conditions which are not of women's choosing.

I want at this late hour to consider an alternative manifesto to women's time, one that provides the opportunity to read the Kristeva essay, and the contemporary moment, against the grain. In 1739 Mary Collier, a washer-woman from Hampshire, had printed a poem called 'The Woman's Labour'. It was a response to a much-lauded poem by another farm labourer, Stephen Duck, whose work, 'The Thresher's Labour', had brought him considerable recognition and a pension from Queen Caroline. Collier's poem had been formed orally and committed to memory, until its transcription and circulation by the husband of an employer encouraged her to have it printed. In a preface to a later edition of her poems, 'remarks of the Author's Life, drawn by herself', an elderly Collier recalled how she had committed Duck's poems to memory: 'fancying he had been too Severe on the Female Sex in his Thresher's Labour brought me to a Strong propensity to call an Army of Amazons to vindicate the injured Sex. Therefore I answer'd him to please my own humour, little thinking to make it Public . . .'.[42]

Collier's poem is an important document, exposing as it does an acute consciousness of the role of women's labour as underpinning an economy based on the male breadwinner. Where, as she argues, Duck's poem renders women's work invisible ('our hapless Sex in Silence lie/ Forgotten, and in dark Oblivion die') or in their seeming leisure and gossip a foil for the labour of men ('on our abject State you throw your Scorn,/And Women wrong, your Verses to adorn'), Collier's response is to detail the continuous cycle of work in which poor women are trapped.[43] It was, Edward Thompson wrote in his essay 'Time, Work-Discipline and Industrial Capitalism', the rural labourer's wife who experienced the 'most arduous and prolonged work of all',[44] and it is this collective figure – the working mother – who Collier ventriloquates in her poem, bringing her children from the hearth to the field and back again, making meals and clothes for her family, waiting to be let in to the House to start charring, sleepy and 'Oppress'd with cold' (20), washing, polishing, brewing and mending by candlelight. In characteristic eighteenth-century fashion Collier imagines women's present state as a kind of Fall from grace – from a golden age when sexual difference presented no antagonism but rather reciprocity, in which men had been brought to recognise 'as from us their Being they derive,/They back again should all due homage give' (16). Her poem resembles a manifesto because it acknowledges that women's reproductive role – their domestic labour – continues to produce the 'Being' of men even as they work alongside them in the fields:

We must make haste, for when we Home are come,
Alas! we find our Work but just begun;
So many things for our Attendance call,
Had we ten hands, we could employ them all.
Our Children put to bed, with greatest care,
We all things for your coming Home prepare:
You sup, and go to bed without delay,
And rest yourselves till the ensuing Day,
While we, alas! but little Sleep can have,
Because our froward Children cry and rave.
Yet without fail, soon as Daylight doth spring,
We in the field again our Work begin. (19)

Mary Collier's work, like that of other labourer poets of the period, intervenes in a long tradition of country estate poetry, and powerful in its refusal of an aesthetic pastoralism that surfaces even in Duck's 'The Thresher's Labour'. If the men are caught in a Sisyphean cycle of work, Collier suggests, then in this infernal economy, in a mythic reference fit for a washerwoman, the women resemble Danaus's daughters, endlessly pouring water into a holed jar (their crime, we remember, having been the murder of their bridegrooms on their wedding night). Like Kristeva, for whom the Danaids are notably the first foreigners, Collier senses a violence at the heart of the social bond, and her response is no less a work of cultural politics than the aesthetic practices described in 'Women's Time'. Collier's aesthetic intervention is distinctively articulated in terms of a sexual politics which goes beyond the 'battle of the sexes' rhetoric that was widely used, following Pope, by many rhyming coupleteers of the period. Her poem might equally be titled 'Women's Time', for it is the sexual politics of time that appears to produce the political consciousness of the text. The cyclical patterns of life – diurnal, seasonal – are cut into, against the grain, by the necessities of labour of all kinds. Time is no longer passed, but as Thompson describes it, is rather increasingly subject to a disciplinary logic: spent, measured, husbanded, costed, squandered, saved, expropriated. The feeling that 'lack of time is reaching crisis proportions' is not exclusive to the late 1990s. In Collier's case it is experienced as a continual and inexorable pressure: ''tis often known,/Not only Sweat but Blood runs trickling down/ Our wrists and fingers: still our Work demands/The constant action of our lab'ring hands.' The cyclical times of day and night, of the harvest, are incorporated into the grind of work to produce an impossible rhythm in which there is never enough time. Collier's women labourers 'fear the time runs on too fast', 'piecing' 'the Summer's day with Candle-light', in a phrase that picks up simultaneously on the domestic metaphor for assembling, or adding on to, and the notion of piece-rated wages (22). The effect of this in the poem is to disorder and render more urgent the sense of time: women often begin their work in the evening, getting up at midnight and working on several tasks simultaneously, while juggling domestic responsibilites to home and hearth. Such is the intensity of labour that, at times, there is no respite to be had: 'Our Toil and Labour's daily so extreme/That we have hardly ever *Time to Dream*' (20).

No time to dream: such is the disciplinary penetration of time into women's mental space, that, if we might read the phrase in its strongest sense, there is no utopian potential for imagining that things might be otherwise. What we witness in this text, emerging in a world increasingly shaped by the not so hidden hand of capital, is the space of what Henri Lefebvre calls 'the everyday': in modern existence marked by a crushing of the cyclical patterns of reproduction by the instrumental repetitiveness of work. It is women, Lefebvre argues, 'who are sentenced to everyday life'.[45] This suggests an already more complex set of temporal relations between the realm of production and reproduction than that offered by the Kristeva essay, and a historical and social specificity to the spatial positioning of women. The 'women's time' of the woman labourer is not the same as that of the woman she serves, who is nonetheless subject – as a consumer – to the rapidly changing times of new fashions ('Fashions which our Forefathers never knew') and no less aware that time is money (20).

In Thompson's account of the transition to industrial capitalism, he suggests that the hours of work detailed in 'The Woman's Labour'

> were only endurable because one part of the work, with the children and in the home, disclosed itself as necessary and inevitable, rather than as an external imposition. This remains true to this day, and, despite school times and television times, the rhythms of women's work in the home are not wholly attuned to the measurement of the clock. The mother of young children has an imperfect sense of time and attends to other human tides. She has not yet altogether moved out of the conventions of 'pre-industrial' society.[46]

Yet though Thompson goes on to question the easy categorisation of historical change in terms like 'pre-industrial', the complexity of Collier's text also demands closer consideration of the the way women's experience is understood in historical terms, then as now. For the sense of oppression – of 'external imposition' – in her poem is palpable, and the 'slavery' she describes takes place as much in the home as elsewhere. While Thompson's account identifies the problem of the naturalised 'necessity' of domestic labour, part of the force of Collier's argument is to situate that necessity within the wider world of work increasingly marked by 'the measurement of the clock'. It is not just that women's labour is rendered visible, but that it is framed temporally in a number of ways. What emerges from her poem, then, rather than an 'imperfect sense of time' in Thompson's terms (once again the time of 'reproduction' proving outside the reach of history), is an acute and practiced awareness of it: as a series of differentials simultaneously and multiply lived in everyday life (at the workplace and home, and in the home *as* workplace); marked by the passage of the days and the seasons; according to the task, the employer, the technological means available; as representing various degrees of autonomy and imposition (that is, the extent to which it suggests agency and subjection, coercion and leisure, often simultaneously); as ideological, to the extent that the 'time' of reproduction and the home might appear to be no time at all, marked by other rhythms, 'other human tides'; and differently experienced by men and women. For Collier it is the labouring mother who evidently expresses the contradictions of women's experience of time in the extreme, contradictions which, Thompson suggests, remain 'true to this day'.

VII AND NOW

If 'The Woman's Labour' is a manifesto for the politics of 'Women's Time' *circa* 1739, it continues to suggest the complexities of abstracting out such a concept as we approach the twenty-first century. It does so not least because it registers in sexual political terms the disciplinary pressures of another form of modernity – the time of capital – as it attempts to regulate the relations between the public and private worlds of women's work, between the cyclical times of reproduction (of the seasons, of childbearing, of the body), and the husbanded times of production. The significance of the figure of the working mother, the saturation of work and its supposed conferring of worth, the invisibility of domestic labour, the internalisation of temporal constraints: all strike a deeply familiar chord. It is not surprising perhaps that parallels are to be found between two 'transitional' moments of capitalist change – the shift into industrial capitalism, the flexible regimes of late capitalism – requiring new forms of time-discipline, new kinds of subject. But if, as Walter Benjamin puts it, 'the past can be seen only as an image which flashes up at the instant when it can be recognized', what might made of this moment of recognition?[47]

The formalistic movement of modernity in Kristeva's essay makes it impossible to think the contemporary as a 'now' in the fullest historical sense of the term, one able to forge alternative forms of possibility – despite its naming of difference – and to think through the manifestations of feminist discourse and their relation to the real contradictions of women's lives. If one of the insights of her remarkable work is the painful psychic process of investment in the social, might it not be possible to acknowledge the memory of *desire* that 'Women's Time' represses in its suspicion of political truths? To open up a desire for futurity not contained within the what 'will have happened'? A desire uncompromisingly present in the Collier text, which has its own account of the anger and violence of the experience of women's time, and which reminds us of the constitution of another time of modernity – that of capital – which now appears like an eternal and global condition of everyday life. If feminism is in part a practice of negativity, as Kristeva suggests, it may continue to set limits to the way we think modernity, here by saying 'not yet' to the post-political stance anticipated in her essay. In these circumstances the *'Time to Dream'*, in Collier's terms, continues to be a political imperative.

NOTES

I would like to thank Mike Baron, Catherine Boyle, Roger Luckhurst and Lynne Segal for useful discussions, and in particular John and Harry Kraniauskas for bringing home what 'women's time' might mean in the richest terms.

1. Mary Collier, 'The Woman's Labour', in her *Poems on Several Occasions* (London, 1762), p. 20.
2. As Sheila Rowbotham reports, the Office for National Statistics registered women's outnumbering of men in the workforce in September 1997, and 'men have been creeping back up since then'. See her 'Girl power: all work and no say', in *The Guardian*, 3 January 1998, p. 5.
3. Melissa Benn, 'The New Motherhood', *The Guardian*, 31 December 1997, G2, p. 4.
4. These phrases – 'hard choices', 'compassion with a hard edge' – are part of the rhetoric of the current Labour government. Though they are part of the New Labour lexicon, they indicate the ethical discourse that is couching a programme of welfare reform which is not exclusive to Britain, already being tested in in the United States. Thus Clinton's government might look to the 'soccer mums' for a litmus test of current values, while attacking the rights of poor single mothers on welfare.
5. Julia Kristeva, 'Women's Time', trans. Alice Jardine and Harry Blake, *The Kristeva Reader*, ed. Toril Moi (Oxford: Blackwell, 1986), p. 193. All further references in text.
6. Ann Rosalind Jones, 'Julia Kristeva on Femininity: The Limits of a Semiotic Politics', *Feminist Review* 18 (1984).
7. Jacqueline Rose, 'Julia Kristeva – Take Two', in her *Sexuality in the Field of Vision* (London: Verso, 1986), p. 157. Rose's point is that Kristeva nonetheless locates her position in terms of what it means to speak as a woman within the symbolic economy, understood in terms of a fundamental negativity.
8. Gayatri Spivak, 'French Feminism in an International Frame', in *In Other Worlds: Essays in Cultural Politics* (London: Methuen, 1987).
9. Judith Butler, *Bodies That Matter: On the Discursive Limits of 'Sex'* (London: Routledge, 1993).
10. Homi K. Bhabha, *The Location of Culture* (London: Routledge, 1994), p. 247.
11. Alice Jardine, 'Introduction to Julia Kristeva's "Women's Time"', *Signs: Journal of Women in Culture and Society* 7:1 (1981), p. 5.
12. Jean-François Lyotard, *The Postmodern Condition: A Report on Knowledge*, trans. Geoff Bennington and Brian Massumi (Manchester: Manchester University Press, 1984), p. 81.

13. Julia Kristeva, *Powers of Horror: An Essay on Abjection*, trans. Leon S. Roudiez (New York: Columbia University Press, 1982), p. 208.
14. Julia Kristeva, 'Psychoanalysis and the Polis', in *The Kristeva Reader*, p. 304.
15. Kristeva, 'Psychoanalysis and the Polis', p. 306.
16. Jardine, 'Introduction', p. 5.
17. Peter Osborne, *The Politics of Time: Modernity and the Avant Garde* (London: Verso, 1995), pp. 13–14. I am indebted to this remarkable philosophical analysis of the politics of time for providing me with the space to think through the Kristeva essay.
18. Julia Kristeva, *Nations Without Nationalism*, trans. Leon S. Roudiez (New York: Columbia University Press, 1993), p. 41.
19. Bhabha, *The Location of Culture*, p. 153.
20. The term 'afterwardsness' is favoured as a translation of Freud's term by the philosopher and psychoanalyst Jean Laplanche, who transforms the concept using a model of translation. See his 'Notes on Afterwardsness', trans. Martin Stanton, in *Jean Laplanche: Seduction, Translation and the Drives*, ed. John Fletcher and Martin Stanton (London: ICA, 1992).
21. Jean-François Lyotard, *Heidegger and 'the jews'*, trans. Andreas Michel and Mark Roberts (Minneapolis: University of Minnesota Press, 1990), pp. 16, 17.
22. Julia Kristeva, 'About Chinese Women', trans. Seán Hand, in *The Kristeva Reader*, p. 156.
23. Jacques Lacan, 'Function and Field in Speech and Language', in *Ecrits*, trans. Alan Sheridan (London: Tavistock, 1977), p. 48. This wording is taken from John Forrester's version of the passage in his *The Seductions of Psychoanalysis: Freud, Lacan, Derrida* (Cambridge: Cambridge University Press, 1991), p. 206. Lacan uses the category of the future anterior to describe the tense in which the subject identifies 'himself' in language: 'What is realized in my history is not the past definite of what was, since it is no more, or even the present perfect of what has been in what I am, but the future anterior of what I shall have been for what I am in the process of becoming.' *Ecrits*, p. 86.
24. Rose, 'Kristeva – Take Two', p. 147.
25. Kristeva, 'Psychoanalysis and the Polis', p. 313.
26. Judith Butler, *The Psychic Life of Power: Theories in Subjection* (Stanford: Stanford University Press, 1997), p. 15.
27. Butler, *The Psychic Life of Power*, p. 15.
28. Julia Kristeva, 'Woman can never be defined', in Elaine Marks and Isabelle de Courtivron, eds, *New French Feminism* (Brighton: Harvester, 1981), p. 137.
29. Bhabha, *The Location of Culture*, p. 155.
30. Julia Kristeva, *Strangers to Ourselves*, trans. Leon S. Roudiez (London: Harvester Wheatsheaf, 1991), p. 42.
31. Julia Kristeva, *Tales of Love*, trans. Leon S. Roudiez (New York: Columbia University Press, 1987), p. 383. As such Kristeva's work – and her imagining of a 'paradoxical community' in which all are strangers to ourselves – can be seen to participate in a current debate in France arising from a crisis in republicanism and its concept of a universal subject, in which the social bond has to acknowledge the rights of different subjects. See Etienne Balibar, 'Ambiguous Universality', *differences* 7:1 (1995), and Joan W. Scott's interesting article on the parity movement in France: '"La Querelle des femmes" in the Late Twentieth Century', *New Left Review* 226 (1997).
32. Kristeva, *Nations Without Nationalism*, p. 35.

33. 'The constitutive outside means that identity always requires that which it cannot abide.' See Judith Butler's use of this concept in the context of her discussion of categories of identity in psychoanalytical and political thought and the nature of abjection in *Bodies That Matter*. The quote is taken from p. 188.

34. Spivak, 'French Feminism in an International Frame', p. 146.

35. Rose, 'Kristeva – Take Two', p. 154.

36. Osborne, *The Politics of Time*, pp. 94, 96, 97.

37. Julia Kristeva, 'Stabat Mater', trans. Leon S. Roudiez, in *The Kristeva Reader*, p. 185.

38. Osborne, *The Politics of Time*, p. 102.

39. Bhabha, *The Location of Culture*, pp. 242 and 245.

40. For a useful discussion of the limitations of Bhabha's account of hybridity in this regard, see John Kraniauskas, 'Hybridity in a Transnational Frame: LatinAmericanist and Postcolonial Perspectives on Cultural Studies', in Avtar Brah and Annie E. Coombes, eds, *From Miscegenation to Hybridity? Rethinking the Syncretic, the Cross-Cultural and the Cosmopolitan in Culture, Science and Politics* (London: Routledge, forthcoming).

41. For a discussion of the notion of the 'hegemonic imaginary' in the context of Butler's work see 'Gender as Performance', *A Critical Sense: Interviews with Intellectuals*, ed. Peter Osborne (London: Routledge, 1996).

42. Mary Collier, 'Some Remarks of the Author's Life drawn by herself', in *Poems on Several Occasions*, p. iv. I would like to thank John Goodridge for a very interesting talk about Collier in a seminar held at Birkbeck College, which first set me thinking about her work. See his *Rural Life in Eighteenth-Century English Poetry* (Cambridge: Cambridge University Press, 1995). See also Sheila Rowbotham, *Hidden from History* (Harmondsworth: Penguin, 1974) and Morag Shiach, *Discourse on Popular Culture: Class, Gender and History in Cultural Analysis, 1730 to the Present* (Cambridge: Cambridge University Press, 1989), for further key discussions of Collier.

43. Mary Collier, 'A Woman's Labour', p. 16. All further references will be included as page references in parentheses.

44. E.P. Thompson, 'Time, Work-Discipline and Industrial Capitalism', in *Customs in Common* (Harmondsworth: Penguin Books, 1993), p. 381.

45. Henri Lefebvre, 'The Everyday and Everydayness', *Yale French Studies* 73 (1987), p. 10.

46. Thompson, 'Time, Work-Discipline and Industrial Capitalism', pp. 381–2.

47. Walter Benjamin, *Illuminations*, trans. Harry Zohn (London: Fontana, 1973), p. 257.

CHAPTER TWELVE

Crossing the present: narrative, alterity and gender in postmodern fiction

Andrew Gibson

I NARRATIVE, ETHICS AND ALTERITY

The concept of the encounter with alterity is crucial to the philosophy of Emmanuel Levinas. The Other whom I encounter is always radically in excess of what my ego, cognitive powers, consciousness or intuitions would make of her or him. The Other always overflows the frame in which I would seek to enclose the Other. But that means that the frame itself is broken or disintegrates. Levinas often writes of the delusion of the possibility of possession of the Other. As I fail to 'capture' or 'possess' the Other, so the mechanisms by which I have sought possession come into question. The more or less stable structure of my frames for the world appears as a function of my will to identity, of my will to persist in my being or, in a phrase of Pascal's that Levinas employs repeatedly, my conviction of my right to a place in the sun. My self-assertiveness is an imposition of force and, as such, unethical. What lies outside me neither asks for, requires or justifies such an imposition. As I fail to 'capture' the Other, the ego is deposed, gives up its drive to sovereignty and enters into ethics, into social relationship, dialogue, disinterestedness. Ethics is constituted as what Levinas refers to as an 'incessant disenchantment of the Same intoxicated with itself'.[1] But what concerns him is not a disenchantment with a world that fails to correspond to the subject's expectations, but a disenchantment of the self that seeks to contain the world within its perspectives; in effect, a disenchantment of subjectivity.

Narration might seem principally to be a mode of activity in which a subject takes another, others, the world as the object or objects of knowledge, and claims possession of them. But since there are large and significant differences in the degree to which those claims are exercised, Levinas provides us with a precise and compelling sense of the ethics at issue in the act of narration itself. The important formal distinctions between narratives or modes of narrative are not merely formalist. Nor do they consider narrative form as simply a reflection or embodiment of an ethics primarily found elsewhere in the narrative text. Rather, in the context of Levinas's ethics, where ethical questions and epistemological questions are often inseparable, distinctions between modes of narration are also the crucial ethical distinctions. Thus ethical distinctions would be involved, for example, in the distinction between an 'omniscient' third-person narrator, and one who professes only a limited or partial knowledge of the world he or she narrates; between a third-person narrator-character who is absent from the world narrated and a narrator-character who is very much a character in the story he or she tells; and so on. For Levinas, each of these distinctions would have an ethical dimension. The relevant distinction would ultimately express the ethics of a given text.

It should be clear, too, that the narrative ethics in question may often involve and be inflected by questions of gender, though in different ways and to different degrees from narrative to narrative. Indeed, narrative ethics may well turn out to *be* an ethics of gender. We might take as examples Willa Cather's *My Ántonia* and *A Lost Lady*, in which the narrator-character is male whilst the most important character in his story is female. Jim's and Niel's narratives are respectively presented to us as different modes of knowledge. On the one hand, for all his romantic admiration for Ántonia, Jim's narrative is a means by which he wholly converts her into meaning or symbolic depth. This much is evident in the concluding passage to the first section of the last book of the novel, where Jim 'rounds off' his portrait of Ántonia as 'a rich mine of life, like the founders of early races'.[2] *My Ántonia*: Jim's narrative is the means by which he arrives at a comprehensive possession of the heroine. In *A Lost Lady*, by contrast, Marian Forrester insistently escapes Niel's frames of reference. This is particularly the case with her sexual and passional life, which the novel indicates is beyond Niel's powers of representation and comprehension. We are repeatedly given a sense of the drastic limitations to Niel's cognitive horizons. They are the limitations to his narratorial 'possession' of a world, and, as they break down, so Niel finds himself opting for a different mode of possession of the object, one that aspires to superiority but is in implication a confession of drastic weakness: moralism. ' "Lilies that fester," he muttered, "*lilies that fester smell far worse than weeds.*" '[3]

II THE ZWISCHEN

The mode of ethical reading I have briefly exemplified here has the advantage of not needing to resort to any account of Cather's supposed intentions or 'attitudes' to make its point. It does not need to show the existence or non-existence of moral irony in Cather's text. We may be tempted to read Cather's handling of much of Niel's later conduct and later discourse in *A Lost Lady* as ironical. But the more one looks at the moments when irony seems to be at stake, the less one can be sure that Cather absolutely does not 'mean what Niel says'. Not so with the epistemological issue in Cather's novel, however, nor with the ethical question that is inseparable from it. Yet the model for reading that I have deployed here may nonetheless seem limited, not least because, whilst it actually problematises the subject–object relation, it does not see it disappear. This might appear to be a problem with Levinas's thought. The ethical encounter with alterity takes place as the subject–object relation founders, but in a situation, nonetheless, in which a subject confronts what it seeks to take as an object.

There is, however, another, less familiar strand to Levinas's ethical thought which states the ethical encounter in slightly but significantly different terms. In the end, too, the difference necessarily involves questions of gender. In his essay on Lévy-Bruhl, Levinas suggests the following:

> Since the primary experience of being is situated at the level of emotion, exterior being is deprived of the form which assured thought of a familiarity with it. The subject thus finds itself confronting an exteriority over to which it is delivered, for that exteriority is absolutely foreign, that is to say, unforeseeable and, by that token, singular. The unique character of situations and instants, belonging to no type, their naked existence, is thus the moderns' great theme. For its part, the I, delivered over to being in this fashion, is ejected from its home within itself and into the realms of an eternal exile, loses its mastery over itself, is overflowed by its own very being. It is a prey to events which have already determined it from the start.[4]

Here Levinas suggests that the primary experience of exteriority is affective. Affective experience – rather than the breakdown of the movement of cognition – appears to be the key to the ethical encounter itself. It is in the affections that we experience the world in its strange, unforeseeable singularity. Furthermore, the ethical encounter is not 'structured', but is understood as an *event*. Yet Levinas is still writing in terms of a subject deemed to exist prior to events. In another passage in the same essay, however, Levinas takes a rather different direction, deploying a lengthy quotation from Lévy-Bruhl:

It is not necessary to take it for granted that 'beings are *given* first, and then enter into participations. For them to be given, for them to exist, there must already be participations. A participation is not only a mysterious and inexplicable fusion of beings who, at one and the same time, conserve and lose their identity . . . Without participation, they would not be *given* in their experience, they would not exist . . .' For the individual, participation 'is a condition of his existence . . .'[5]

Here, precisely, as an event, the ethical encounter is a 'participation' *before* it can be construed in terms of entities – subject/object, man/woman – that may be deemed subsequently to emerge from it. The event itself has priority. So, too, in Levinas's essay on Buber. But here, 'participation' becomes what Buber calls the concept of the *Zwischen* (Between). Buber sees the self as existing only in relation: 'It can only exist as an I concerning itself with a You or as an I grasping a *That*'.[6] There is no more fundamental ontology than that encounter: 'The "between-the-two", the interval between the I and the You, the *Zwischen*, is the site where the work of being takes place'.[7] It is precisely in this concept of the *Zwischen* that we must abandon 'the notion of a being as content, of a realized being' and – most significantly, in this context – of a 'narrated being'.[8]

By and large, narrative theory has been unable to think the 'entre-les-deux', the median ground, the event of narration as a self–other relation.[9] Yet narration can be thought of in terms of an encounter that is a 'participation' before it is construed into entities. Insofar as those entities are describable as male and female, the issue at stake is not just the boundary between narratological categories but between genders as well. If narrative may be thought of in terms of 'participations' rather than strata, gender differences are radically problematised if not destabilised. In narrative, in a sense, men regularly do become women and speak with women's voices, and vice versa. In what is, for me, the most memorable passage in *Gender Trouble*, Judith Butler writes of gender in terms of the 'illimitable *et cetera*':

> The theories of feminist identity that elaborate predicates of color, sexuality, ethnicity, class, and able-bodiedness invariably close with an embarrassed 'etc.' at the end of the list. Through this horizontal trajectory of adjectives, these positions strive to encompass a situated subject, but invariably fail to be complete. This failure, however, is instructive: what political impetus is to be derived from the exasperated 'etc.' that so often occurs at the end of such lines? . . . It is the *supplement*, the excess that necessarily accompanies any effort to posit identity once and for all. This illimitable *et cetera*, however, offers itself as a new departure for feminist political theorizing.[10]

The point is made in the context of an eminently Levinasian discussion of 'the language of appropriation, instrumentality and distanciation germane to the epistemological mode' as belonging 'to a strategy of domination that pits the "I" against the "Other" and, once that separation is effected, creates an artificial set of questions about the knowability and recoverability of that Other'.[11] Butler's 'illimitable *et cetera*', however, might seem to point towards what she calls 'new departures' in the future as they may be produced by the feminist imagination. But suppose we reflect a little further on the contingency of the epistemological mode and the 'artificial' separations that it institutes. Suppose we try to think about narrative outside a 'language of appropriation, instrumentality and distanciation' which sets an author at a distance from a narrator, a narrator at a distance from a character, and then presents the first as appropriating the second, or using the second for certain ends. Might not the 'illimitable *et cetera*', the actual, endless fluidity of gender identities be much more in play and at stake in narrative than we have thus far tended to acknowledge? Might we not find ourselves concerned with the *Zwischen*, after all?

III EXCENDANCE

To some extent, a destabilisation of narratological and gender categories is evident in Cather's novels, or those of Henry James. It was of course more radically accomplished in certain properly modernist texts, of which Virginia Woolf's *Orlando* is the most obvious example. But it has also been a conspicuous feature of a range of postmodern texts. In contemporary fiction, sexual and gender difference has repeatedly been consciously set at issue precisely in the activity of narration itself. In such novels, we are no longer concerned with gender as median condition or with 'ambiguities in gender' but precisely with something more like the full implications of Butler's 'illimitable *et cetera*'. In postmodern fiction, gender is increasingly emerging, not just as a more or less ambivalent state, but as an activity, a performance, or a site where identities may intersect, proliferate and undo one another. In Butler's terms, gender emerges as an insistent repetition within which there are always potentially productive differences, an 'instability' which 'is the deconstituting possibility in the very process of repetition'.[12] The activity or process in question is irreducible to the terms of a singular present or presence. There are always breaks and discontinuities in it, what Butler calls 'gaps and fissures'. The present of sexuality and gender is incessantly traversed or 'crossed'. In other words, gender is never contemporary with itself. The postmodern novels in question can be characterised in terms of what Levinas calls *excendance* or 'crossing', in Butler's sense of the term. But the question of 'crossing', here, is also a question of narrative. Indeed, narrative, that eminently temporal form of art, is a singularly appropriate mode for the deconstitution of identity. Certainly narrative today is precisely where we are likely to encounter a 'crossing' of identities and, perhaps above all, of gendered identities.

Butler understands the 'illimitable *et cetera*' as 'the excess that necessarily accompanies any effort to posit identity once and for all'. The excess in question bears a close relation to that designated by Levinas's concept of *excendance*. The term appears in Levinas's first philosophical text, *De l'Evasion*.[13] *De l'Evasion* is concerned with the movement or process that *precedes* the encounter with the other. In fact, Levinas articulated this movement or process before he articulated the encounter with alterity itself. As Marie-Anne Lescourret indicates, *De l'Evasion* expresses the imperative of escape, but is not as yet clear as to the means.[14] But escape from what, exactly? According to Levinas, from the idea of being. The revolt against being, he says, has long been well-established in Western tradition. But it has invariably been construed in terms of a conflict between human liberty and being as brute reality or stifling fact. The subject is conceived of as emerging into full subjecthood in opposition to being, a construction invariably flattering to the subject and his will to power. According to *De l'Evasion*, this conception of subjecthood takes shape on an axis at the other end of which is an exterior world in which things simply *are*, in which identity and being are the absolute and definitive character of things.

Levinas, however, turns this structure round. Being is not a quality of the exterior world to which we are opposed as full subjects, but is rather the principle of our own self-sameness or self-insistence. As such, it is a limitation from which we immediately seek an escape (hence the term 'evasion', one of whose meanings is escape, in French). *Excendance* designates precisely this drive to escape being as the principle of selfhood:

> Thus, to the need for escape, being would not only appear as the obstacle that free thought would have to surmount, nor as the rigidity that, luring one into routine, demands an effort of originality, but as a state of imprisonment from which it is a question of emerging.[15]

Excendance is the spontaneous and immediate desire to escape from the absurdly narrow limits of the self. It is thus a principle of unease within and inseparable from the self. *Excendance* is a response to nausea, a nausea which serves, for Levinas, as a figure for an upheaval within the self. It is nausea at one's self-enclosure. For Levinas, evasion is what he will eventually take to be the ethical impulse towards or openness to the other that effects a release from the confines of the self. *Excendance* is therefore kinetic. For 'the fact of being ill at ease is essentially dynamic'.[16] This dynamism is ethical: it turns us incessantly elsewhere, outside – towards the other.

If *excendance* is the condition of what we call the subject, then it is also always anachronic.[17] Thought in relation to the subject, the contemporary therefore has its origin in a situation which cannot exactly be understood as of the moment. The present is not exactly a circumstance we inhabit, but one into which we continually cross. In that respect, subjecthood can be conceived of, not merely as incomplete, but as intrinsically a projection towards the future. In a fine passage in 'Philosophie et Transcendance', Levinas gives an account of this non-intentional consciousness which is also precisely a description of the movement of *excendance* itself:

> Duration as pure duration, as non-intervention, as being-as-insistence, as being on-the-tip-of-one's-toes, as being without daring to be; instance of the instant without insistence of the I and already a lapse, 'leaving as it enters'! . . . Without name, titles or place in the world. A presence which fears presence, which fears the insistence of the identical I and is naked of all attributes.[18]

Consciousness is fissured precisely in that the 'instance' of consciousness 'leaves' even as it 'enters' and 'the contemporary' is thereby divided. By the same token, the ethical relation, it would seem, is implicit in the very structure of temporality itself.

This intractable fissure in the instance of consciousness makes impossible any categorisation of the latter in terms of full being. This includes any categorisation in terms of gender. In Levinas's terms, to trust gender categories is to retreat into a reassertion of the principle of self-sameness. From the start, we are irretrievably caught up in the movement of *excendance* and the indeterminacy of categories that it generates. In that respect, we will simply never know our gender, and it is with that recognition that an ethics of gender may begin. As Judith Butler and other gender and queer theorists have reminded us, to insist on gender categories is precisely to ensure and even to intensify a continuing confusion about them. For Alan Sinfield, for example:

> Feminine and masculine are cultural constructs, obviously with the primary function of sustaining the current pattern of heterosexual relations. Of course, very many heterosexuals are not respectively masculine and feminine, or not in certain respects, or not all of the time. As usual, ideological categories fail to contain the confusions that they must release in the attempt to achieve control.[19]

And yet: hasn't most gender and queer theory quite rightly been less concerned with a philosophical interrogation of the concept of gender than with a political critique of power relations? Does not Butler insist, for instance, on the need for the identity categories I have called in question, even whilst aware of their risks?[20] In fact, theorists like Butler and Sinfield are caught in an intellectual dilemma that has increasingly troubled gender, queer and feminist theorists. On the one hand, the identity principle is crucial to their work as political practice. On the other, that work would not have been possible if there had not been fierce opposition, not just to the categories of identity produced by the dominant culture, but to the practice of identification itself. From this derive all the debates around the relative value of what J.K. Gibson-Graham rather awkwardly calls 'strategic essentialism' and 'strategic non-essentialism' as exemplified in feminist, gay and lesbian identity politics, on the one hand, and deconstruction and deconstructive ethics, on the other. Gibson-Graham argues the continuing need for both practices.[21] Certainly, if the second is no more than a utopian trace, then it at least needs to be maintained as such. In Levinas's work ethics is always utopian. Dealing as it does in an 'ought' rather than an 'is', ethics holds open a breach in the present in that it is the principle of a future knowledge which cannot be produced in itself, but may be speculatively anticipated. At the same time, and for that reason, a postmodern ethics is likely to have a particular interest in instances produced by current gender theory of a destabilisation of the identity principle. Transexualism, hermaphroditism and evidence of cultures that, historically, have not thought gender in binary terms would all be examples of this.[22]

For my purposes, however, the two most significant such instances are bisexual theory and drag. Some of the emphases in bisexual theory correspond helpfully with my case. Clare Hemmings, for example, has set out to theorise bisexuality as precisely what gets left out of the current hetero/ homo divide. For bisexuality is not only what challenges the traditional boundaries of both, but what disputes the very existence of the boundary. Bisexuality is the recalcitrant offender *par excellence*.[23] In fact, bisexuality is a sexuality irreducible to the static category which throws into question the epistemological habits ('knowing what one is') that are crucial to heterosexism and queer theory alike. Bisexuality cannot be definitively understood within the heterosexual matrix. But it cannot be exactly understood as resistance to it, either. It rather insists that sex difference is not real or essential or an aspect of original being itself. Bisexuality is not really an identity at all. It is rather a process in which the I re-emerges in different terms, is constantly re-created and re-situated. Here, sexuality is always and only a dynamic, *excendance* in a concrete mode whereby sexuality constantly escapes both the terms of being and the structuration of sexuality in the binary terms of either/or.[24]

The bisexual's emphasis is close to Butler's discussions of 'drag' and 'crossing'. For Butler, the woman in drag blurs and destabilises the terms of 'a prevailing truth-regime of "sex"'. Gender is revealed as neither 'a purely psychic truth, conceived as "internal" and "hidden"', nor as 'reducible to a surface appearance; on the contrary, its undecidability is to be traced as the play *between* psyche and appearance'.[25] Like bisexuality, drag is distinguished by 'play', by a movement towards the other, by a practice of reversal in which the 'inside' and its supposed unity and stability are precisely what are fled from ('evaded'). Indeed, drag is the instant in which the present of gender is doubled up and divided from itself, in which the contemporaneousness of gender is fissured. By that token, drag is also an ethical representation of the 'truth' of gender. If, in Butler's phrase, drag and bisexuality are 'abjected by heterosexist logic',[26] it is because they contest, not only the categories produced within that logic, but also the logic itself, and its dependence on static, unitary formulations, on the determination of identities in a singular temporality.

IV   CROSSING THE PRESENT

In drag and bisexuality, then, the present is 'crossed', in more senses than one. The chimerical character of gender is openly displayed. Drag and bisexuality expose that 'resistance to identity' that lies 'at the very heart of psychic life', in Jacqueline Rose's well-known phrase.[27] But my emphasis is different to Rose's. Rose insists that the resistance to identity requires the resumption of difference into identity.[28] But this is also a resumption of *excendance* into time as being. If, however, as Joseph Bristow suggests, there is only a 'precarious break between "homo" and "hetero"' that the dominant culture strives to keep as distinct as possible,[29] that break may be precisely as precarious and uncertain as that between the structure of repetition and the play of difference.

A perception of gender as precarious and uncertain in this specific respect is being articulated in contemporary fiction in various ways. On the one hand, there is the attempt to produce narrative from within an intermediate position that I earlier described in terms of the *Zwischen*. In the contemporary novel, however, that position is likely to be interpreted in performative terms or converted into drag. Take Gordon Burn's *Alma Cogan*.[30] Before the novel begins, we are told that Cogan died in 1966. Yet by the time we've reached the end of the second chapter, we have encountered a Cogan alive, for instance, in 1976. Part of the novel, then, is told by an Alma Cogan artificially revived, ventriloquised, made to live on after her death by an implied male author. But is this narrative indeterminacy really an integral part of the novel's effect? Lest we should doubt it, the novel provides analogies for its narration in the male figures who are, in a sense, responsible for 'keeping Alma alive': the 'tender of the flame' and 'hoarder of my life', 'biografiend' and 'fetishizer' Francis McLaren, who is indeed precisely like Burn himself in being a 'stasher and storer' and 'considerer of trifles' (175); Cogan's transvestite ex-cleaning 'woman', Ricci Howe, who does an act in which he is billed as 'Mr Ricci Howe appearing in the gowns of Miss Alma Cogan' (169). The drag act, like the use of Peter Blake's painting of Cogan as resembling 'a woman imitating a man imitating a woman', like all the other references to drag (Trevor as Big Rita, Gerard, Cary Grant in women's underwear) seems to underscore how far the narrative itself is a mode of drag in which the relationship between language and narrative progression and gender is radically destabilised. In effect, *Alma Cogan* denies us the possibility of assuming that a particular instance or mode of the use of narrative language can be identified with a particular gender at all.

Burn's novel is extremely conscious of itself as an act of ventriloquism. But ventriloquism, like drag, puts gender categories at risk in that it exposes their inessentiality, their existence through and as performance. The most revealing moment in *Alma Cogan* is a walk-on appearance by Tony Hancock, who pokes 'his head into an empty room', sees one of Alma's dresses 'standing on its own', and finds it 'as disturbing as the occasion he glimpsed Peter Brough's dummy, "Archie Andrews", hanging on a hook behind a door' (171). Alma Cogan is a name that deserves the inverted commas as much as does that of Archie Andrews. What Hancock properly sees is Alma Cogan and her gender as prop and accessory, a sign without a body. In Butler's terms, gender exists only as repetition. Its tokens can be re-played indefinitely and it can be ceaselessly confirmed, but only artificially, in a manner that severs any bond with a 'nature', and therefore paradoxically deprives the confirmation of all force. Yet gender is repetition in that, as performance, it can be appropriated by another. The novel is about Alma Cogan as a system and apparatus: the system and apparatus of her stardom; the system and apparatus of Cogan as archive, after her death; and the system and apparatus of Alma's gender. The latter can be mimed out again in a different time and place by a male performer or even, after death, by a male author.

Burn's novel thus loosens the supposed fixity of gender positions in a process that one might describe as gender equivocation. But it does not convey any sense of gender as activity or becoming. It does not engage us in the temporal dimension of the production of gender, in *excendance*, in the contemporary as the moment of 'crossing'. As examples of the latter, I want to look at three novels that hinge on a moment of what I shall call 'gender shock': Ackroyd's *Dan Leno and the Limehouse Golem*, Banks's *The*

Wasp Factory and Duncker's *Hallucinating Foucault*. Ackroyd's novel[31] works by asking us to sympathise with the woman accused of murder, Elizabeth Cree, at the expense of the man deemed to be her victim, her husband John, because we gather from John's diary that he has been that far more notorious and extreme murderer, the Limehouse Golem. The shock comes when we find that Elizabeth is in fact responsible for all the murders and has impersonated her husband as diarist. Like *Alma Cogan*, then, *Dan Leno* provokes its reader into asking awkward questions about the assumptions according to which s/he has understood a particular discourse as gendered, as free from any troubling taint of alterity. A particular discourse opens itself up to the possibility of gender reversal, of being 'read both ways'. As in *Alma Cogan*, gender is a role that can be repeated with a more or less subversive difference but that has no authentic, inner life. The reader encounters a world in which gender instability is a constitutive principle, from the scene at the beginning of the novel in which the prison governor Stephens dresses up in Elizabeth Cree's gown, to the central position in the novel of Leno the female impersonator himself. The characters are caught up in a play of *excendance* in which identity is always likely to be disturbed by movement, transformation, a flowing out towards the very other it appears to exclude. In that respect, Ackroyd's novel gestures towards a conception of gender as 'monypolylogue' (150), as exemplified in Elizabeth's stage act:

> The 'Older Brother' had become a great draw, and within a very short time I had taught him how to be cocky and yet naive, knowing yet innocent. Everyone knew that I was also 'Little Victor's Daughter', but that was the joy of it. I could be girl and boy, man and woman, without any shame. (152–3)

The point about the act is that it is not just a stage act, that Elizabeth can take it 'out into the streets of London' to 'see the other world' (153). The music hall and its shifting 'medleys' are not merely an image of the outside world (177). They make explicit the 'medleys' of that world. Hence, for all Ackroyd's (rather banal) insistence, here as elsewhere in his work, on a bleak, insurmountable fixity to nature, insofar as its concern is gender, *Dan Leno* actually works in the opposite direction.

It is important to stress that, in both *Alma Cogan* and *Dan Leno*, a destabilisation of gender categories is inseparable from a destabilisation of narrational categories. In *Alma Cogan*, the boundary in question is that between male implied author and female narrator-character. In *Dan Leno*, the boundary set at risk is the gendered distinction between narrating and observing subject and narrated and observed object. Narrative veers towards and threatens to incorporate the other which it narrates, as though it could only have set out to narrate the other in the first place because the other was always part of it from the start. The same cannot exactly be said of Banks's *The Wasp Factory*,[32] where we are solely concerned with a single narrator-character, and where the moment of gender shock or crisis might appear to be comparatively crude:

> Part of me still wants to believe it's just [my father's] latest lie, but really I know it's the truth. I'm a woman. Scarred thighs, outer labia a bit chewed up, and I'll never be attractive, but according to Dad a normal female . . . (181–2)

Banks's novel might appear ultimately to prise masculinity and violence apart, to transfer responsibility for murder and mayhem to the feminine. But it can equally well be read as suggesting that all the violence has resulted from the absence or repression of the very female element which finally intrudes into the novel. 'My greatest enemies are Women and the Sea', says murderous Frank, at the beginning of the third chapter:

> These things I hate. Women because they are weak and stupid and live in the shadow of men and are nothing compared to them, and the Sea because it has always frustrated me, destroying what I have built, washing away what I have left, wiping clean the marks I have made. (43)

The important point, however, would seem to be, not just that Frank must admit the feminine, but also that he must think masculine and feminine together. What he has built is not exactly destroyed. He does not lose all sense of the reality of the performance: 'But I *am* still me; I *am* the same person, with the same memories and the same deeds done, the same (small) achievements, the same (appalling) crimes to *my* name' (182). There has been a crucial shift, however, from the Frank who began by saying 'I'm me and I'm here and that's all there is to it' (13). It is precisely the fact that Frank can finally think identity and non-identity together that makes for the possibility of ethical transformation at the end of *The Wasp Factory*. At the beginning of the novel, the Frank who has carefully avoided reading Gore Vidal's *Myra Breckinridge* has also idealised the single, self-intent male body: 'I saw myself, Frank L. Cauldhame, and saw myself as I might have been: a tall slim man, strong and determined and making his way in the world, assured and purposeful' (48). This Frank has cast himself as 'the unchallenged lord of the island' (139). But his interior world is finally invaded by those catalysts – unease, self-disquiet, self-antagonism, nausea – that, for Levinas, are the beginning of ethics, but which trauma has nullified, in Frank's case. It is thus appropriate that the book should end with a Levinasian celebration of openness to alterity and the event:

> Each of us, in our own personal Factory, may believe we have stumbled down one corridor, and that our fate is sealed and certain (dream or

nightmare, humdrum or bizarre, good or bad), but a word, a glance, a slip – anything can change that, alter it entirely, and our marble hall becomes a gutter, or our rat-maze a golden path. (183–4)

Hallucinating Foucault[33] is a powerful, feminist novel about the necessary queering of the contemporary bourgeois, *soi-disant* heterosexual and, above all, English intellectual. It is important to note that Duncker does not situate the protagonist's homosexual love as part of a 'learning experience'. If anything, as a feminist novel about masculinity and male experience, *Hallucinating Foucault* is an inverted *Bildungsroman*, concerned less with *Bildung* than *Entbildung*, not formation but the breaking down of what has been formed. It is very important that Duncker's novel is indifferent to the question of whether the protagonist has 'finally turned out to be gay' or whether his love for Paul Michel has been a stage in his (basically heterosexual) development. Duncker's novel makes both notions seem equally banal. *Hallucinating Foucault* is not about the more or less triumphant or anguished discovery or confirmation of identity. It is rather about the crumbling of identity and the possibility of transformation together. It is about 'evasion', rather than the arrival at a destination. One of Paul Michel's novels is called *L'Évadé*, a title which could easily be made to apply both to Duncker's protagonist and her own novel. *L'Évadé* pleads the cause of a 'contempt' which is close in implication to what Levinas means by nausea, insisting as it does 'that the only escape is through the absolute destruction of everything you have ever known, loved, cared for, believed in, even the shell of yourself must be discarded with contempt' (16–17). Significantly, Michel is 'defiantly against nature', believing that 'we are not born comme ça' (29). *Hallucinating Foucault* is about the becoming of sexuality, sexuality as an event that continually threatens to escape any categorical identification. Hence the closing emphasis on indeterminacy in the figure of the protagonist's dream. Indeed, *Hallucinating Foucault* might appear to be trying to satisfy the demands Paul Michel makes of 'fictional texts . . . that they should be open-ended, carry within them the possibility of being and of changing whoever it is they encounter'. (111). Certainly, like Michel himself, it embraces what he calls 'the hostility of difference' (114).

All the same, *Hallucinating Foucault* arguably hinges not so much on a moment of what I have called gender shock as a transformation in the protagonist's sexuality: 'I had a terrible sensation of urgency . . . I ceased to understand anything except his hands upon my body. Then I lost all control of myself. I fell headlong down a tunnel that had no end' (144). But there is another, subtler moment, too, which comes near the end of the novel, when Paul Michel tells the protagonist of the boy who was his first love. It emerges, of course, that the 'boy' was in fact an 'ambiguous' girl in whose sex – but nothing else – Paul Michel was 'deceived' (161).

'She', of course, was the lover who sent the protagonist in search of Michel. The protagonist is confounded in the recognition that the girl who was Michel's boy has made of him the boy who 'became Michel's girl'. Furthermore, as Michel himself says, they have become interchangeable. '"Well, you've been through it, I see"', she says, briskly, when she arrives from England. 'But she didn't specify what it was that I had so unsuccessfully traversed', he adds (167). Traversal or crossing is very much what Duncker's riveting novel is finally about. The protagonist has indeed been double-crossed.

After such knowledge, what forgiveness, if not a Junior Research Fellowship and a job 'at one of the London colleges' (176)? Not surprisingly, the protagonist ends by defining himself as a doing ('I simply work on the texts', [176]), rather than a being. In that respect, *Hallucinating Foucault* promotes an ethics of loss: grief, confusion, emptiness and recovery through praxis which is also a surrender to the other. On the one hand, then, *Alma Cogan* proceeds by simulation, the production of the narrating space as an intermediate or performative one; by what I have called gender equivocation. On the other hand, *Dan Leno*, *The Wasp Factory* and *Hallucinating Foucault* all adopt a tactic of 'gender shock'. By contrast, Martin Amis's *Other People*[34] operates according to a kind of gender irony. On a simple level, an ethics of loss similar to that in *Hallucinating Foucault* underlies Amis's novel. Mary, the heroine, wants to be good, which, in the novel's terms, means a loss of identity. Mary operates on an 'uncertainty principle' in questions of identity. Such a loss of identity necessarily involves a loss of gender categories, not only as they determine Mary, but also in themselves. For Mary, there are actually 'six kinds of people', and the distinctions at issue overlap with gender categories in crazy and illogical ways (16). For the ethical Mary, being good is not knowing how to play the 'memory game' (11), and a fleeting return to a past self and identity instigates a 'nausea' in which she 'can't get rid of enough of herself' (73).

But the structure of *Other People* is actually the reverse of the structure of *Hallucinating Foucault*. *Other People* is an ironic fable of the loss of ethics in the resumption of gender and full identity. Mary must learn how not to be 'multiform, instantaneous and random, like the present itself' (53). She must learn that 'Everybody's something' (26), and that process of socialisation — and the gendering that is crucial to it — is one that Amis's novel duly and sardonically enacts. It is clear from the conclusion to Mary's relationship with Jamie, for instance, that learning to 'be something' involves learning how to suffer and inflict suffering. The 'laws of life' that Mary has to 'divine' are precisely to do with identity and violence. Identification involves a progressive clarification and determination of gender: on the one hand, ethical Mary can scarcely tell the difference between men and women of a certain age (86) and knows that 'some men turn into women too' (143). On the other hand, Mary is involved in a process of formation and steadily registers and accumulates the signs of gender:

> Like the woman in black, Mary held her cup in both hands. She thought, I'm a girl, so I drink hot drinks with both hands. Girls always do that for some reason. Why? George uses only one. Men use only one hand, although their hands aren't nearly so steady as ours. (94)

This, *Other People* tells us, is how to become a good bourgeois subject with a house in a 'remote arcadia' and a policeman as partner. But the price of safety is complicity, and the loss of the impulse to the good with which the novel began.

I have noted three distinctive features of the treatment of gender in contemporary writing: gender equivocation, gender shock and gender irony. A fourth, the utopian writing of gender, is exemplified in the work of Jeanette Winterson. Winterson has edged towards such a writing in successive texts, but it is only in *Written on the Body* that questions of gender and of narrative are altogether fused. In *Sexing the Cherry*,[35] the novel's Rabelaisian mode allows Winterson a free masculinisation of the feminine in the figure of the Dog Woman, whilst the Menippean and fairy-tale elements equally make possible a feminisation of the masculine, in Jordan's case. The novel is clearly concerned to interrogate, cross and obscure the 'great division' between heroes and home-makers. It is much concerned with grafting, the production of 'unrealistic' or 'unnatural' or 'monstrous' composites which may nonetheless be taken for nature, in the long run (78–9). What Winterson cannot find, at this stage, is an appropriately composite or equivocal form of narrative, which means that the 'great division' disappears only incessantly to reappear again, as though the graft obstinately keeps refusing to take. She had actually come closer to a successful graft in the earlier novel *The Passion*.[36] Here, as in *Sexing the Cherry*, the novel had been structured around male and female narrators, male and female principles: Henri and Villanelle, Napoleon and Venice, linearity and the labyrinth, the will to conquer and 'the unpredictable, the out of control' (71). But it also works precisely to resist and break down that polarising structure of oppositions. At two key moments – when Henri deserts from Napoleon's army and abandons the militaristic principle (71), and when he is taken to San Servolo as a lunatic (142) – his narrative is invaded by Villanelle's, as though to underscore what appears to be a crucial confounding of gender identity at these points in the text.

Yet ultimately Henri remains inside San Servolo and Villanelle remains outside. In a sense, the 'great division' could not be reasserted more emphatically. 'In this enchanted city', says Villanelle of Venice, 'all things seem possible . . . The laws of the real world are suspended' (76). But, in the context of the novel's ending, that claim can only be seen as ironical. In *Written on the Body*,[37] however, this has changed, notably with regard to its ungendered, bisexual narrator. This aspect of the novel has provoked controversy, and critics have tended to retreat from its full implications. Valerie Miner has argued that Winterson's way of raising 'identity questions' in *Written on the Body* seldom takes her 'beyond the gimmick'.[38] But what Miner sees as a 'gimmick' is surely an exacting practice which looks trivial only if we seek to turn it into a 'content'. Cath Stowers has suggested that 'although Winterson's narrator is not simply portrayed as a lesbian, s/he nonetheless fulfils the aims of a lesbian aesthetic'.[39] But this surely hardly means that, whilst *Written on the Body* deconstructs lesbianism as 'essentialist being', it also reconstructs it as a 'subject position'. Here, for all her praise of Winterson's efforts to release us 'from the stultifying binary of heterosexual authoring and narrative', Stowers has merely replaced the latter with a lesbian binary. She rightly wants 'to correct any tendency that would elevate the meaning of Winterson's texts to a realm supposedly separable from sexual politics'.[40] The trouble is that she can only equate sexual politics with identity politics. But *Written on the Body* is deconstructive *rather than* reconstructive, and as such, it is utopian and ethical. Indeed, Stowers herself is well aware of the utopian thrust to Winterson's work, quoting her as saying that she is 'striving to create an "enchanted place" . . . which "doesn't exist" and "never did"'.[41] What Stowers does not see is that, in *Written on the Body*, the 'enchanted place' is one in which identity no longer counts and is no longer an appropriate category.

What sets *Written on the Body* apart from the novels I looked at earlier is that it insistently proceeds by a kind of 'narrative crossing'. Not only are we always unsure of the gender of the narrator, we are also likely to be led into narrative identifications that are not only conflicting but multiple, since questions of sexuality as well as gender are in play. In *Written on the Body*, narrative surfaces no longer serve as indications of identities beneath them. Rather, narrative generates a host of moments in which identifications cross, when the narrative present is divided from itself. In Winterson's text, the repetition intrinsic to narration is an index only of an indeterminate source or origin. Winterson not only institutes a consistently aporetic mode of narrative, but transfers it to the issue of gender. In *Written on the Body*, gender is only performance or drag. At the same time, and as a result of Winterson's narrative practice, an acute sense of the historical and cultural contingency of the gendering of discourse emerges. This is surely the point to the deliberate, tawdry, contemporary banality of much of the discourse in *Written on the Body*. It circulates in the novel as a kind of sedulous mimicry of the trivialities that our culture is willing to take for tokens of 'natures'.

Yet this is true only on one level of reading. On another, *Written on the Body* is precisely concerned with gender and sexuality as irreducible to categorical description. It is concerned with what Winterson calls the movement to the 'uncharted and unseen' place (80), a movement she identifies with love and saintliness but, in the novel's terms, also breaks the boundaries of gender. For Winterson, this is a creative principle, too: Stowers quotes her as saying that 'It's all on the move. I don't like to do the same thing again. So now that people think they know what I'm about, I'm on the move.'[42] This insistent movement away from subjectification and objectification is the ethical movement of *excendance*. It is the movement out and towards alterity which, in *Written on the Body*, is the movement in which gender itself is caught up. No practice or activity, here, can ultimately be identified as gender-specific, and to identify a gender is quickly to have one's identification thrown into question by a contradictory set of signs. The appropriate figure for such narration is not so much the graft as elaborated in *Sexing the Cherry*, as the knot as discussed in *Written on the Body*: the knot, with its 'formal complexity', whose challenge lies 'in the rules of its surprises' (87). In *Written on the Body*, both narration and gender are formally complex knots that cannot be undone. Alterity has always intruded from the start. This is reflected in the novel's fascination with a range and diversity of sexual tastes and practices. The implication is that, in that world, there are no monolithic, generalised sexualities at all. It is the world of Butler's 'illimitable *et cetera*'. Here again, in spite of Stowers, however much Winterson's is a lesbian aesthetic, I wonder how far *Written on the Body* is finally any more reducible to the categories of lesbian theory than to those of heterosexist logic.

In the postmodern novel, then, not only are the categories of gender identity being interrogated. The habit and practice of gender identification itself is increasingly being put into question or set at risk. In one way or another, contemporary novelists are exploring what we might call the limits of the narrativisation of gender. Set alongside modernist experiments in the novel, of course, none of the contemporary texts I have considered may seem to be formally very adventurous and, insofar as they are, might seem parasitic on modernist experiment itself. Equally, set alongside the tradition of 'sexual dissidence' in modernist writing as articulated by Jonathan Dollimore, the novels I have discussed might seem to be nothing more than a domestication or cheap popularisation of the latter. For Dollimore, Wilde, Genet and Orton, in particular, all subvert the 'depth model of identity'.[43] Surely the texts I have been looking at are, in comparison, lame and minor pastiche? This kind of view of postmodernist fiction as comparatively tame, conservative, self-consciously derivative is by now familiar. In the case of the texts I have been looking at, however, it seems to me to be unhelpful. If these novels dismantle certain narrative forms as kinds of epistemological apparatus; if what is deconstructed in the process is gender as a mode of knowledge; if narrative becomes a play or movement in which the categories of gender are opened up to the alterity they appeared to exclude, in which gender has no distinct, determinate or final form; then it is possible to read these texts as finally injecting what Dollimore calls 'transgressive reinscription' into mainstream culture. Such a process may indeed lack the romantic heroics of modernist subversion. But it also precisely accomplishes or puts on open display that connection between civilisation and 'perversion' which, for Dollimore, is intrinsic to the social itself. Above all, however, the process is ethical. The novels in question challenge and displace the self-intoxication that is gender identity. Narration becomes an ethical evasion or a resistance to the reductions of gender. Gender politics and postmodern ethics come together and are inseparable.

NOTES

1. The phrase in the original is 'incessant dégrisement du Même enivré de soi'. Levinas, *La Mort et le Temps* (Paris: Éditions de l'Herne, 1991), p. 25. All translations of Levinas are my own. Where comment on translation is required, I also supply the original.
2. Willa Cather, *My Ántonia* (London: Virago, 1980), p. 353.
3. Willa Cather, *A Lost Lady* (London: Virago, 1991), p. 84.
4. Levinas, *Entre Nous* (Paris: Grasset, 1991), p. 58. The last sentence runs: 'Il est en proie à des événements qui l'ont d'ores et déjà déterminé'. It is perhaps significant that the phrase 'd'ores et déjà' is everywhere in Levinas. It is somewhat difficult to translate. The literal meaning is 'from today', 'from right now', which functions almost as a direct address to the reader in his or her present time.
5. Levinas, *Entre Nous*, pp. 54–5.
6. In the original, 'Il ne peut exister que comme un Je s'intéressant à un Tu ou comme un Je saisissant un *Cela*'. Levinas, *Noms Propres* (Paris: Fata Morgana, 1976), p. 33.
7. In the original, 'L' "entre-les-deux", l'intervalle entre le Je et le Tu, le *Zwischen*, est le lieu ou s'exerce l'oeuvre même de l'être', *Noms Propres*, p. 36.
8. In the original, 'la notion d'un être-contenu, d'un être-realisé, d'un être narré', *Noms Propres*, p. 36.
9. I address this problem in my recent *Towards a Postmodern Theory of Narrative* (Edinburgh: Edinburgh University Press, 1996). In particular, in Chapter 6, I raise the question of narrative levels. I suggest that the concept of the narrative text as composed of homogenous, distinct, pure strata arranged in a downward-looking perspective discounts any possibility of osmosis or seepage between the

strata. Such a model also discounts any hint of ambivalences, irrational features, anomalies, mixtures, hybridities that might cross, break down or raise questions about the boundaries between strata.

10. Judith Butler, *Gender Trouble* (London: Routledge, 1990), p. 143.

11. Butler, *Gender Trouble*, p. 144.

12. Judith Butler, *Bodies That Matter: On the Discursive Limits of 'Sex'* (London: Routledge, 1993), p. 10. Here as elsewhere, Butler's 'radical constructivism' takes on a grimly deterministic aspect which is surely problematic. She appears to conceive of herself as stoically Foucauldian, but her world is not one in which there is any possibility of radical rupture by the historical event, as Foucault's surely is.

13. Levinas was later to claim that *De l'Evasion* – first published in 1935 – was marked by his presentiment of the Nazi horror. See Catherine Chalier, *Levinas: L'Utopie de L'Humain* (Paris: Albin Michel, 1993), p. 159. Chalier is one of the few Levinas scholars to have paid any attention to *De l'Evasion*, and I owe much, here, to the account of it she gives in her helpful, lucid book. If *De l'Evasion* is a response to Nazism, there is surely a connection between the political concerns that underlie it and the fact that it has been seen as Levinas's exodus. What the commentators mean by that is that *De l'Evasion* marks an 'exodus from being', the beginning of a long journey that will culminate much later in the major philosophical works, *Totality and Infinity* and *Otherwise than Being*.

14. Marie-Anne Lescourret, *Emmanuel Levinas* (Paris: Flammarion, 1994).

15. Levinas, *De l'Evasion* (Paris: Fata Morgana, 1982), p. 73.

16. In the original, 'Le fait d'être mal à son aise est essentiellement dynamique', *De l'Evasion*, p. 78.

17. This is to resort to a term that Levinas himself uses in *Difficult Freedom*, trans. Séan Hand (London: Athlone, 1990), pp. 226–8.

18. *Alterité et Transcendance* (Paris: Fata Morgana, 1995), p. 42. This passage is difficult to translate: 'Durée comme pure durée, comme non-intervention, comme être-comme-insistance, comme être-sur-la-pointe-des-pieds, comme être sans oser être; instance de l'instant sans l'insistance du moi et déjà laps, qui "sort en entrant"! . . . Sans nom, sans situation, sans titres. Présence qui redoute la présence, qui redoute l'insistance du moi identique, nue de tous attributs.' The phrase running from 'instance' to 'entrant', which converts so awkwardly into English, appears to be mimetic in intention. By 'laps', Levinas means an elapsing of time, with an implication of minuteness, here as elsewhere.

19. Alan Sinfield, 'Should There Be Lesbian and Gay Intellectuals?', in Joseph Bristow and Angela R. Wilson, eds, *Activating Theory: Lesbian, Gay, Bisexual Politics* (London: Lawrence and Wishart, 1993), p. 22.

20. Butler, *Bodies That Matter*, p. 228.

21. See J.K. Gibson-Graham, 'Postmodern Feminist Social Research', in Nancy Duncan, ed., *Bodyspace: Destabilizing Geographies of Gender and Sexuality* (London: Routledge, 1996). Gibson-Graham gives some helpful indications as to further reading in her account of the theoretical problem and debates, particularly with reference to feminism and the social sciences.

22. See Judith Lorber, *Paradoxes of Gender* (New Haven: Yale University Press, 1994). Lorber's case is different to the one I elaborate here. She argues that it is impossible to live socially as both woman and man, for gender is above all a social institution. But it is surely the case that, on some level, what she means

by 'woman' and 'man' has been institutionally defined from the start, so her argument is circular.

23. Clare Hemmings, 'Resituating the Bisexual Body: From Identity to Difference', in Bristow and Wilson, eds, *Activating Theory*, p. 123.

24. Jonathan Dollimore has recently produced a deconstructive account of Freud on the 'polymorphous perverse' in which he sees 'the social' as 'marked by an interconnectedness so radical [of civilization and the perversions] that it has to be disavowed in most existing forms of social organization'. Jonathan Dollimore, 'The Cultural Politics of Perversion: Augustine, Shakespeare, Freud, Foucault', in Joseph Bristow, ed., *Sexual Sameness: Textual Differences in Lesbian and Gay Writing* (London: Routledge, 1992), p. 22. If this is the case, then, in Hemmings's account of it, bisexuality marks the limits of that disavowal, an acknowledgement of homosexuality as integral to the very heterosexual culture that seeks to repress it or hold it at bay.

25. Butler, *Bodies That Matter*, pp. 233–4.

26. Butler, *Bodies That Matter*, p. 86.

27. Jacqueline Rose, *Sexuality in the Field of Vision* (London: Verso, 1986), p. 91.

28. For discussion of Rose, see Allison Weir, *Sacrificial Logics: Feminist Theory and the Critique of Identity* (London: Routledge, 1996), p. 137. Weir herself argues, however, that Rose's position on this issue – like Lacan's and Adorno's – is stoic and tragic, because she misconstrues identity as repression. Weir's difference with Rose thus moves in an opposed direction to my own. See pp. 142–4 and 200.

29. Bristow, 'Introduction', *Sexual Sameness*, p. 5.

30. Gordon Burn, *Alma Cogan* (London: Minerva, 1992). All references in text.

31. Peter Ackroyd, *Dan Leno and the Limehouse Golem* (London: Minerva, 1995). All references in text.

32. Iain Banks, *The Wasp Factory* (London: Abacus, 1990). All references in text.

33. Patricia Duncker, *Hallucinating Foucault* (London: Serpent's Tail, 1996). All references in text.

34. Martin Amis, *Other People* (London: Penguin, 1982). All references in text.

35. Jeanette Winterson, *Sexing the Cherry* (London: Vintage, 1996). All references in text.

36. Winterson, *The Passion* (London: Vintage, 1996). All references in text.

37. Winterson, *Written on the Body* (London: Vintage, 1996). All references in text.

38. Valerie Miner, 'At Her Wit's End', *The Women's Review of Books* (April 1993).

39. See Cath Stowers, 'Journeying with Jeanette: Transgressive Travels in Winterson's Fiction', in Mary Maynard and June Purvis, eds, *Heterosexual Politics* (London: Taylor and Francis, 1995), p. 150.

40. Stowers, 'Journeying with Jeanette', p. 140.

41. Stowers, 'Journeying with Jeanette', p. 140.

42. Stowers, 'Journeying with Jeanette', p. 142.

43. Jonathan Dollimore, *Sexual Dissidence: Augustine to Wilde, Freud to Foucault* (Oxford: Clarendon, 1991), pp. 313–15. For example, in Genet, 'authentic selfhood is denied and then reconstituted in a perverse, parodic form – and then denied again, transformed from other to same and then back to a (different) other'.

CHAPTER THIRTEEN

The queer spirit of the age

Mandy Merck

When do people begin to speak of a 'spirit of the age'? Writing in 1831, John Stuart Mill maintains that the expression is no more than 'fifty years in antiquity. The idea of comparing one's own age with former ages, or with our notion of those which are yet to come, had occurred to philosophers; but it never before was itself the dominant idea of any age.'[1] As Reinhart Koselleck was to argue 150 years later, '[t]he triad of Antiquity, Middle Ages and Modernity have only fully come into use . . . since the second half of the seventeenth century. Since then, one has lived in Modernity and been conscious of so doing.'[2] With this consciousness of time comes the anticipation of futurity, and an 'exulatation' (Mill's word) in progress. So much so, insists Koselleck, that temporality in the eighteenth century accelerates, robbing 'the present of the possibility of being experienced as the present'[3] to escape endlessly into the future. But if the Spirit of the Age which first claims to have such a spirit is, historiographically, *proleptic*, it is also, and in an importantly related way, *spiritual*. The German 'geist der zeit' shares etymological connections with godhead ('der heiliger Geist', the Holy Ghost, Third person of the Trinity) and other phantoms and spirits,[4] including perhaps the most heavenly of all, alcoholic spirits. Thus the Spirit of the Age is at once temporal and spectral.

This combination is clearly observable in William Duff's 1767 *Essay on Original Genius*, an English treatise on what its author describes as 'the philosophical spirit of the times'.[5] Poetic genius is Duff's interest, and his ghostly evocation of the work of the imagination (a precursor of better-known Romantic meditations on the subject) reminds us that the term 'genius' encompasses both creative power and supernatural presence (witness the Romans' 'Genius loci', or guardian spirit of the place). Arguing that the 'truly Original' poet, 'finding no objects in the visible creation sufficiently marvellous and new . . . naturally bursts into the ideal world, in quest of more surprising and wonderful scenes',[6] Duff describes the author as spirit-raiser, calling

> shadowy substances and unreal objects into existence. They are present to his view, and glide, like spectres, in silent, sullen majesty, before his astonished and intranced sight. In reading the description of such apparitions, we partake of the Author's emotion, the blood runs chill in our veins, and our hair stiffens with horror.[7]

The reader's tumescent reaction to these apparitions, like that described by Freud in his essay on the Medusa, suggests that spectres can also be sexy.[8] The shadows summoned into existence by creative genius bespeak erotic possibilities hitherto unacknowledged. Among these is the eighteenth-century phantom whose proleptic relation to our own time has been brilliantly evoked in a study I very much admire and occasionally disagree with, Terry Castle's *The Apparitional Lesbian*.[9]

The lesbian, Castle argues, enters literature as a ghost. Eighteenth-century fiction registers the spectral appearance of the female couple, but the apparitional ontology of the pair (their 'hauntology' in Derrida's pun)[10] enables the Enlightenment to consign lesbianism to a Gothic already disavowed by modernity. Invoking Freud's essay 'On Negation', Castle concludes that this strategy permits the fictions of the period both to acknowledge and to deny the phenomenon of female homosexuality as 'only' a phantom. But if the ghost is, in the French term, a 'revenant', whose first appearance is already a return from the dead,[11] Castle's ghost differs from its counterparts in coming back from the future rather than the past. The spectre of the Enlightenment is, in her account, an anticipation of her embodied sisters – the lesbians of today. The final chapter of *The Apparitional Lesbian* moves from phantom to flesh, from the eighteenth century to the twentieth, and from fictional characters to a real-life performer, mezzo soprano Brigitte Fassbaender in the operatic role of Richard Strauss's *Der Rosenkavalier*.

Significantly, Castle's hommage to Fassbaender's homoerotic rendition of the role moves altogether out of the realm of spectrality. In her avowed project of reincarnation '[t]he dead are indeed brought back to life'. 'Used imaginatively – repossessed, so to speak – the very trope that evaporates can also solidify. In the strangest turn of all, perhaps, the lesbian body itself returns.'[12] But this embodiment has its price. The staged ghostplay in the opera's final act, the device by which the hero frightens his rival and gets the girl, must necessarily disappear, and with it, a thematically crucial scene of sexual indeterminacy. This reply is about my refusal to give up those ghosts.

The homosexual haunting of heterosexuality (as the late nineteenth-century term of exclusion necessary to confer legitimacy on those enclosed within the straight and narrow) has been noted by many critics in the 1990s. Where Diana Fuss, like Terry Castle, laments the abjection of the homosexual implicit in its phantomisation,[13] Teresa de Lauretis stresses the political productivity of the apparitional in her analysis of the film, *She Must be Seeing Things*.[14] Among the fantastic sights suggested by the film's title is the central couple's butch-femme role-playing: 'exciting', declares de Lauretis, 'not because it represents heterosexual desire, but because it doesn't; that is to say, in mimicking it, it shows the uncanny distance, like an effect of ghosting, between desire (heterosexually represented as it is) and the representation'.[15]

This conflict represented by these varying views – between a desire for a recognised identity so often figured as embodiment and a desire to flout such identities by satirical mimicry or resignification – could be said to characterise contemporary lesbian and gay politics. Where Leo Bersani argues, in his insistently titled *Homos*, that 'resignification cannot destroy; it merely presents to the dominant culture spectacles of politically impotent disrespect',[16] others have taken the very temporality of the term 'queer' as evidence to the contrary. It's now common for theorists to begin their books with a position on this question, albeit one which may attempt to appropriate the best of both worlds. Readers of the queer collection on Andy Warhol, *Pop-Out*, will see detailed accounts of the artist's homosexuality repeatedly juxtaposed with descriptions of how his work problematises any such identity. Even more incorrigibly, the anti-identitarian tenure of the work is frequently adduced as evidence of the opposite in life (you can tell Warhol is queer by how indifferent he is to such labels), a low trick to which my own contribution to the volume might plead guilty.[17]

For Castle, on the contrary, lesbian identity is as real as it is physical – 'sensual', 'fleshly', 'carnal' – and therefore its retrieval from phantomisation becomes a literal matter of life and death. The first beneficiary of this attempted rescue is the author herself. Her study opens on a self-portrait of the academic with writer's block, stuck in the ambitious account of eighteenth-century spectrality which ultimately became *The Female Thermometer*.[18] She suddenly finds herself drafting something very different – a memoir of a living lesbian, a striking butch called Ed, encountered in her California childhood. 'Scandalously energised' by 'the growing realisation that is was possible to write about something other than vapor' (the very physical Ed, first met in a YWCA locker-room), Castle sets aside her 'big book' for something more personal.[19] And more polemical. *The Apparitional Lesbian* is prefaced with an unashamedly square rebuke to 'younger lesbian and gay scholars trained in Continental philosophy (including a number of the so-called queer theorists)' who question 'the very meaningfulness of terms such as *lesbian* or *gay* or *homosexual* or *coming out*'.[20]

We know who she means. Indeed, it is one of the ironies of the milieu that Castle excoriates that those of us who would insist upon the unstable, ambiguous, indeed 'phantasmatic' character of the signifier 'lesbian' would be equally certain that she is referring to Judith Butler. And so, when we turn over the page, it turns out to be – Butler at her most provocative, on the 'non-self-identical status of [the] "I" or its "being lesbian"':

> What or who is it that is 'out', made manifest and fully disclosed, when and if I reveal myself as a lesbian? . . . To claim that is what I *am* is to suggest a provisional totalisation of this 'I' . . . But if the I can so determine itself, then that which it excludes in order to make that determination remains constitutive of the determination itself.[21]

Castle disagrees. The irritating younger theorist brings to mind a (presumably still younger) graduate student, who pesters her in class with endless questions about the meaning of the term 'lesbian':

> Was a lesbian simply any woman who had sex with women? What then of the woman who had sex with women but denied that she was lesbian? What about women who had sex with women but also had sex with men? What about women who wanted to have sex with women but didn't? Or wanted to but couldn't? And so on and so on, to the bizarre hypothetical case of a physically handicapped married woman, unable to have sex with her husband (or anyone else), who considered herself heterosexual, yet unconsciously desired to have sex with women. Inevitably, I responded to such questions by saying I used the term in the 'ordinary' or 'dictionary' or 'vernacular' sense. (A lesbian, according to *Webster's Ninth*, 'is a woman characterised by a tendency to direct sexual desire toward another of the same sex'.)[22]

I want to begin with that student – not just for her questions (which seem all too familiar these days) but for her youth, or at least her junior status in comparison to her teacher's. For the apparition is a matter of time, of two times in Derrida's account, then and now, past and present ('It *begins by coming back*').[23] And this dual temporality may have some bearing on sexual, as well as spectral, signification.

Castle's literary history of lesbian identity reverses the conventional order of biography. Her lesbian starts as an eighteenth-century ghost and ends up alive and singing, from the stage of the Munich Opera House, in a 1979 production of *Der Rosenkavalier*. Unlike Defoe's Mrs Veal or Diderot's Mother Superior, unlike Anne Lister or Janet Flanner, the German singer Brigitte Fassbaender is neither fiction nor history. Instead, like the vividly remembered Ed, whose recollection frees the blocked author from her world of phantoms (and the scholarly closet), Fassbaender is 'something other than vapor'. (Given the butch style which she shares with Ed, one wonders whether a certain masculinity, as well as the admitted love of pasta which ultimately led Fassbaender to abandon trouser roles, enhances this impression of solidity.) If, despite a career of intensely realised travesty roles and controversial recordings of traditionally male parts in German lieder, Fassbaender wasn't exactly out when Castle wrote her tribute, many of her fans were. And in admitting to be among the most devoted of these, Castle outs herself as that most embarrassing of lesbian lovers, a 'diva-worshipper'. *The Apparitional Lesbian* gives way to the embodied lesbian, doubly embodied in the persons of the author and the artist she admires for performing the love of women so passionately.

Does it matter that this is performance, that Fassbaender's enthusiasm for women is (as Castle is careful to point out) revealed onstage, indeed that Castle has never seen her perform 'live', but only as an electronically produced simulacrum? Not, perhaps, to that younger theorist who regards matter as performative, nor, I think, to Castle's student inquisitor, who might smugly observe that her teacher's definition of a lesbian is elastic enough after all to extend to an actress who plays love scenes to women with apparent enthusiasm, but whose personal sexual perference remained, until recently, unstated. But if this ambiguous figure seems an interesting choice with which to rematerialise the apparitional lesbian, the opera on which Castle concludes her study is even more so. Hugo von Hofmannsthal and Richard Strauss's *Der Rosenkavalier* is undoubtedly a lesbian cult classic, in which not two but three women sing their love for one another at its heart-rending finale, but it is also an extended observation on the instability of that passion, and of time and identity itself.

Set in 'a half imaginary, half real' version of the Vienna of 1740,[24] the 1911 opera opens after a night of love between Marie-Therese, the Field Marshal's wife, known as the Marschallin, and her young cousin, Count Octavian. Their morning after is disturbed by an unexpected arrival, and, fearing the return of the Field Marshal, Octavian disappears to disguise himself as a chambermaid. The visitor is revealed to be the Baron Ochs, a rustic relation of the Marschallin, who seeks her support for a financially advantageous match with Sophie von Faninal, daughter of a newly ennobled, and very wealthy, bourgeois. While the lecherous Baron interrupts his appeal to pursue her striking young maid around the room, the amused Marschallin nominates Octavian as the bearer of the customary silver rose of betrothal. Only later, as she reflects on the unseemly union of the middle-aged Baron and his young bride, does the Marschallin come to realise that her own young lover will some day forsake her.

In Act II, Octavian presents the silver rose to Sophie and they immediately fall in love. Enraged by Ochs's oafish condescension to the Faninals, Octavian challenges the fortune-hunter to a duel, which is quickly averted by Sophie's father, furious at this threat to his ambitions for social elevation.

In the subsequent plot to deliver Sophie from her disastrous engagement, Octavian invites the Baron to an evening's rendezvous, signing the invitation as the Marschallin's maid, Mariandel. The third act sees Octavian attend the assignation in disguise and eventually expose Ochs's philandering to Sophie's father. When the Marschallin is summoned to vouch for her disgraced relation, she sees that Octavian and Sophie are in love and gracefully gives way. At the opera's end, the Baron has been dismissed and the two lovers are united in a final duet.

The anachronisms in *Der Rosenkavalier* are deliberate and thematic. The establishment of the bourgeoisie is backdated to the opera's ostensible setting in the mid-eighteenth century, while the score includes references to the later classicism of Mozart, nineteenth-century waltzes and modernist discords, 'to give the music, like the drama, a sense of the layering of history'.[25] Baroque and Beardsleyesque, the work was designed by a founding member of the Vienna Secession, Alfred Roller, who inflected its rococo sets with a Jugendstil sensibility. Moreover, the telescoping of time is a central theme in the opera, most famously in the Marschallin's moving soliloquy as she gazes into her mirror and contemplates the fate of Sophie at the end of Act I:

I too can recall a young girl,
who was ordered, fresh from the convent, into holy wedlock.
Where is she now? Yes, look for the snows of yesteryear!
I say that lightly,
But how can it really be,
that I was once little Resi
and that one day I shall be an old woman?[26]

And when Octavian comes to say goodbye, she warns the youth of 'the frailty of everything earthly' in the face of time:

At times I hear it flowing – inexorably.
At times I get up in the middle of the night
and stop all the clocks, all of them.

The passage of time preoccupied *Der Rosenkavalier*'s librettist, Hugo von Hofmannsthal, throughout his writing, from his *Tercets on Transcience*, published at the age of twenty ('my Self held back by nothing/Stole across to me from a young child')[27] to his libretto for Strauss's *Elektra* eight years before *Der Rosenkavalier*:

Where has it all gone to, where?
It is not water that runs away,
It is not a thread, that runs and runs
from the spool, it is I, I![28]

In each instance, age renders the subject a stranger to herself: no more recognisable than a 'silent dog' the *Tercets* lament, while the Marschallin wonders how the convent girl can become an old woman and still be 'the same person'? And if identity threatens to fracture under the weight of time, it is also imperilled by passion. *Der Rosenkavalier* begins with Octavian marvelling to his mistress in phrases that will seem strangely familiar to readers of queer theory:

> You, you – what does it mean, this 'you'?
> This 'you' and 'I'? Do they have any meaning?
> They are words, mere words, are they not?
> Say so! . . . this 'I' is lost in this 'you' . . .
> I am your boy, but when sight and hearing
> forsake me – Where is your boy then?

Where indeed, since the singer of this extraordinarily knowing passage is a woman, cast in pastiche of Mozart's Cherubino, another boy played by a soprano who must, in the course of this story, disguise himself as a girl. In writing 'a role for a young and graceful girl dressed up as a man',[29] Hofmannsthal could plead the sanction of convention (albeit a very dated convention) as well as the prestige of his eighteenth-century predecessors, Mozart's librettist Da Ponte and the French playwright who created the original Cherubino, Beaumarchais. And so most critics continue to do. (The Lacanian scholar Michel Poizat has recently offered an ingenious psychoanalytic reading of the sexual indeterminacy of the high voice, connoting juvenile masculinity, mature femininity and an ethereal mediation 'between the human and the divine, the angel'.)[30] But at the same time we find critics complaining, of one of the most popular works in the repertory:

> it seems distasteful that Hofmannsthal should have cast so sexually virile a figure in a female role, particularly in the opening scene which demands overt demonstration of the most passionate love – it is seldom that the two actresses involved manage to avoid suggesting a repellent sort of lesbianism as they hug and caress one another, crooning torrid endearments.[31]

Does this settle the ontological question? Is the lesbian phantom finally made flesh? It seems likely that Hofmannsthal, an extensive reader of Freud whose library included *The Interpretation of Dreams*, *Totem and Taboo*, *The Psychopathology of Everyday Life* and – most importantly for this opera – the *Three Essays on the Theory of Sexuality*,[32] was aware of the implications of what he called his 'psychological comedy'. As for his audience, they were already familiar with the Eulenberg scandal of 1907, in which the German press was filled with accusations of homosexuality in the nation's military, diplomatic corps and nobility – including Eulenberg himself, a princely favourite of the Kaiser famous for composing a suite of 'Rosenlieder'. So widespread was this scandal that it provoked complaints in the Reichstag about the 'many hundreds and thousands of people who earlier hadn't the foggiest notion of the things now being discussed in public [who] will, after having been enlightened about these things, be tempted to try them out with their own bodies'.[33] In a similar vein, one critic of the period was moved to condemn both Strauss's hugely successful opera and the erotic perspective of the young Viennese.

But if *Der Rosenkavalier* could be said to bring female homosexuality 'into focus' (to borrow Castle's phrase), that recognition nevertheless depends, however paradoxically, on ambiguity. There is no lesbian character here as such, but a young man played by a woman, a role whose sexual ambiguity is deliberately underlined by having the character disguise himself as a woman. And when Octavian becomes 'Mariandel', the ghost arrives in the twentieth century. In the opera's final act, the hero sets out to destroy the reputation of Baron Ochs, his brutish rival for the hand of Sophie, by inviting him to an assignation in a local inn. There, resuming his disguise as the Marschallin's chambermaid, he entertains the duplicitous suitor, while secretly contriving to reveal his character to Sophie's father. To do so, Octavian fills the inn with a troupe of ghostly figures enacted by hired confederates. When the Baron remarks on Mariandel's uncanny resemblance to our hero ('That face! Accursed boy! Haunts me waking and sleeping!') the first of these spectres rises, literalising the apparitional identity of the serving girl. As the terrified Ochs points to the spot where the ghost has loomed and vanished, Mariandel insists that 'There's nothing there'. 'There's nothing?' the Baron asks, and running his hand over his/her face, repeats 'And nothing there either?'

Eventually Ochs steadies himself for another pass at Mariandel, but when their eyes meet he is again startled by her resemblance to his rival. At a signal from Octavian, the room fills with apparitions, and in the ensuing uproar, the confounded Baron is finally exposed and forced to withdraw from his engagement to Sophie. With performances as enthusiastic as Fassbaender's, the young couple's final union can be read as a triumphant assertion of lesbian love, but this is not achieved at the expense of spirit. The ersatz spectres, and Ochs's belief in them, can be identified with the superstitions of a doomed aristocracy about to be succeeded by the rising bourgeoisie, but they are also representative of the sexual ambiguity which haunts this work.

As the scene indicates, the uncertain gender of Ochs's object of desire is directly related to the uncertain ontology of the ghost (indeed, a *simulated* ghost, an apparition of an apparition): something/nothing, flesh/phantasy. Perhaps the most obnoxious collation of these multiple ambiguities occurs in the turn-of-the-century epithet 'fairy', combining as it does the notion of male homosexual inversion, effeminacy, with the disdainful accusation of dimunition and disembodiment ('flitty', 'airy fairy', 'a bit light on his feet').[34] Similarly, but characteristically more positively in female to male cross-dressing, Octavian's sexual identity is also represented as ontologically ambiguous, 'angelic' in its indeterminacy. Dressed to present the ornamental rose in a silver suit of lights, this figure modelled on Mozart's cherubic page is immediately compared to an angel by Sophie's duenna. And in a pose reminiscent of Gabriel at the Annunciation,[35] the angelic emissary proffers a floral ensign – itself both phallic bough and feminine bloom – to the future bride.

Noble knight, female vocalist, angelic messenger: Octavian's triadic identity retraces the triangles which structure this opera's sexual contretemps: the Marschallin, her husband and Octavian; Ochs, Sophie and Mariandel; Octavian, Sophie and the Marschallin; Mariandel, Octavian and the woman who plays both. The refusal of the binary – of one sex, one status, or the other – is given form in the figure of the silver rose. A hybrid flower if ever there was one, its precious petals are compared by its recipient to 'roses of holy paradise'. 'It's like a greeting from Heaven', Sophie sings. 'There's Time and Eternity in this moment of bliss.' Listening to her ecstatic exclamations, Wayne Koestenbaum has observed that Sophie's instant infatuation with another woman (male though she is in character) undoes the reality of time 'to create pockets – momentary, unending – of sacred or divine duration': 'Disturb gender, and you disturb temporality; accept the androgyne, and you accept the abyss'.[36] Tracing this 'torquing' of time to the canonical figures of modernism, he cites Marcel Proust, Albert Einstein, Henri Bergson (who comments on the theory of relativity in the second edition of his *Duration and Simultaneity*) and, most centrally, Sigmund Freud.

Sexuality, Freud argues, develops in two temporalities. Our social initiation, the ordinary erotogenic exchanges between children and their carers, inevitably occurs too early, while organic maturation happens too late. The result is trauma, but a trauma which is experienced retrospectively, when the pubescent subject finally has the affective means to make sense of infantile arousal. The sense of *déjà vu* which accompanies Sophie and Octavian's first encounter expresses something of this dual temporality – but in the register of erotic ecstasy rather than pain: 'Where and when have I been so happy? I must return there, yes, even if I should die on the way.' (Note, however, that even here the shadow of death, the depredation of time which so troubles Sophie's predecessor, darkens the present moment, which both lovers promise to remember 'till I die').

In Freud's account of *nachträglichkeit*, or 'deferred action', the adolescent, newly aroused by some sexual stimulus, reacts with an intensity provoked by an unconscious memory of an unassimilated excitation in the past. As that past obtrudes into the present and the present into the past, the disturbing stimulus suddenly registers as trauma. In *Der Rosenkavalier*, temporality is even more convoluted. The young lovers identify their 'moment of bliss' with some prior state of jouissance, to which Sophie vows to return in the future. Temporalisation – past, present, future – is momentarily absorbed into timelessness, into Eternity's silver rose. Yet this message from heaven is also a message *of* heaven, of the end of bodily life which Sophie – in that ambiguous act of negation which Castle observes in lesbian ghost stories – both denies and declares: 'I must return there, yes, even if I should die on the way. But I shall not die. That is far away.' For this young lover, as for the older one who preceeded her, death is on the horizon, and with it the ghost.

How can we reconcile this spectre, anticipation of the body's end, with Castle's phantom, precursor of the embodied lesbian to come? One key point of convergence, as Act III so vividly represents, is the related indeterminacy of Mariandel's gender and the ghosts which finally unnerve Ochs. The spectral harbingers of the Baron's failure – to marry the heiress and revive his class's declining fortunes – are also the apparitions of his own exuberant eroticism, the polymorphous lusts he proudly proclaims to the Marschallin and her maid in Act I:

> Would I were as old Jupiter with a thousand forms!
> I'd have a use for every one!
>
> . . .
>
> I'd have a use for a thousand different shapes,
> to embrace a thousand girls.
> None would be too young, too sour,
> none too humble, none too rude!
> I'd be ashamed of nothing.
> If I see something I like, I must have it.

But as the Marschallin reminds the Baron, the price of such multifarious passions is the dissolution of identity, the successive metamorphoses of the divine seducer:

> What, even for the bull? Would you be so crude?
> Or would you rather play the clouds and come
> whispering along
> as a whiff of damp air?

As the true homosexual of this drama, the one character who, however unwittingly, pursues another of the same sex, the bovine Baron himself becomes nothing other than vapour. Homoeroticism, this opera endlessly suggests, confounds coherent identity, unambiguous embodiment. And thus it serves to illustrate all eroticism, the pervasive threat that passion poses to the subject's sense of self and temporality. In this very contemporary sense, *Der Rosenkavalier* must be described as a queer work.

'Repossessed', Terry Castle argues, 'the very trope that evaporates can also solidify'. Her own account of the historical transformation of the apparitional lesbian testifies to the continual metamorphosis of sexual identities, a phenonemon which *Der Rosenkavalier* takes as a theme. For all the solidity of its silver rose – ecstasy eternalised – the spirit of this work is one of constant volatility. The rapid rise of the Faninals marks the accelerated accession of the bourgeois epoch, and with it the vaporisation of all that is solid, 'all fixed, fast-frozen relations',[37] including those of love. At the opera's finale, when the young lovers are united at last, Sophie sings to Octavian:

> It is a dream, cannot be really true
> that we two are together,
> together for all time
> and for eternity!

Then, even as the couple conclude their duet with the words 'I feel only you alone!' and fall into a final embrace, the brevity of passion is signalled one last time, as Sophie's handkerchief slips unnoticed from her grasp onto the stage.

'The history of the ghost', Derrida writes, can be read two ways, as a 'history of the becoming-true of a fable' or 'the reverse, a fabulation of truth, in any case a history of ghosts'.[38] My argument here is that Castle's history of the becoming-true of the apparitional lesbian since the eighteenth-century must also account for its fabulous resignifications in our own. Like the reconfigured conventions of eighteenth-century opera, spectrality survives into the twentieth century precisely to signify those states of being which are at once liminal *and* legible. Given the proliferation of these at the fag end of the century – which has witnessed the rise of such chimerical figures as the drag king and the virtual lesbian, as well as the countless gliding spectres of the graduate student imaginary – it seems unlikely that sexual identities will settle down, solidify, any time soon. Indeed, such might be a fate worse than death, the veritable petrification of the subject and its desires. In any case, not a history of ghosts.

NOTES

1. John Stuart Mill, 'The Spirit of the Age', *Examiner* (6 Jan.–29 May 1831), reprinted in *Essays on Politics and Culture* (New York: Anchor Books, 1963), p. 1.

2. Reinhard Koselleck, *Futures Past* (Cambridge, Mass.: MIT Press, 1985), trans. Keith Tribe, p. 12.
3. Koselleck, *Futures Past*, p. 18.
4. Jacques Derrida, *Spectres of Marx: The State of the Debt, The Work of Mourning, and the New International*, trans. Peggy Kamuf (New York: Routledge, 1994), p. 125: '*Geist* can also mean spectre, as do the words "ésprit" or "spirit". The spirit is also the spirit of spirits.'
5. William Duff, *An Essay on Original Genius* [1767] (New York: Garland Publishing, 1970), p. 245.
6. Duff, *An Essay on Original Genius*, p. 179.
7. Duff, *An Essay on Original Genius*, p. 177.
8. The erectile responses described by both authors is intended to confine such visions to men, and Duff explicitly argues, in *Letters on the Intellectual and Moral Character of Women* (1807), that genius is a male attribute. This idea ultimately derives from the Latin origins of the term, which referred to the sacred pro-creative powers of the male head of the family, or *gens*. See, in reply, Christine Battersby, *Gender and Genius: Towards a Feminist Aesthetics* (London: The Women's Press, 1989).
9. Terry Castle, *The Apparitional Lesbian* (New York: Columbia University Press, 1993).
10. Derrida, *Spectres of Marx*, p. 10.
11. Derrida, *Spectres of Marx*, p. 11.
12. Castle, *The Apparitional Lesbian*, pp. 46–7.
13. Diana Fuss, Introduction, in Diana Fuss, ed., *Inside/Out* (London: Routledge, 1991).
14. Directed Sheila McLaughlin, 1987, US.
15. Teresa de Lauretis, 'Film and the Visible', in Bad Object Choices (editorial collective), *How Do I Look?* (Seattle: Bay Press, 1991), pp. 250–1.
16. Leo Bersani, *Homos* (Cambridge, Mass.: Harvard University Press, 1995), p. 51.
17. See Mandy Merck, 'Figuring Out Andy Warhol', in Jennifer Doyle, Jonathan Flatley and José Estaban Munoz, eds, *Pop Out: Queer Warhol* (Durham: Duke University Press, 1996).
18. Terry Castle, *The Female Thermometer: Eighteenth-Century Culture and the Invention of the Uncanny* (Oxford: Oxford University Press, 1995).
19. Castle, *The Apparitional Lesbian*, p. 4.
20. Castle, *The Apparitional Lesbian*, p. 13.
21. Judith Butler, 'Imitation and Gender Insubordination', in Fuss, ed., *Inside/Out*, p. 15.
22. Castle, *The Apparitional Lesbian*, pp. 14–15.
23. Derrida, *Spectres of Marx*, p. 11.
24. Hugo von Hofmannsthal, cited in Gerd Uerkermann, '"Time Is a Strange Thing . . .": Past and Present in "Der Rosenkavalier"', from the introduction to the libretto of the 1986 Decca production, conducted by George Solti, p. 23.
25. Lewis Lockwood, 'The Element of Time in *Der Rosenkavalier*', in Bryan Gilliam, ed., *Richard Strauss: New Perspectives on the Composer and his Work* (Durham: Duke University Press, 1992), p. 253.
26. Quoted by permission from Boosey and Hawkes Music Publishers and Schott and Co.

27. Cited in Uerkermann, 'Time is a Strange Thing', p. 22.
28. Cited in Uerkermann, 'Time is a Strange Thing', p. 22.
29. Hugo von Hofmannsthal, cited in Norman del Mar, *Richard Strauss*, vol. 1 (London: Barrie and Rockliff, 1962), p. 337.
30. Michel Poizat, *The Angel's Cry: Beyond the Pleasure Principle in Opera*, trans. Arthur Denner (Ithaca: Cornell University Press, 1992), p. 113.
31. William Mann, *Richard Strauss: A Critical Study of the Operas* (London: Cassell, 1964), p. 104.
32. See Bernd Urban, 'Hofmannsthal, Freud und die Psychoanalyse', in *Europaische Hochschulschriften* (Frankfurt: Peter Lang, 1978).
33. Cited by James D. Steakley, 'Iconography of a Scandal: Political Cartoons and the Eulenberg Affair in Wilhelmine Germany', in Martin B. Duberman, Martha Vicinus and George Chauncey Jr., eds, *Hidden From History: Reclaiming the Gay and Lesbian Past* (New York: Meridian, 1990), p. 256.
34. The *Oxford English Dictionary* traces this usage to 1895, and a reference in the *American Journal of Psychology* to 'The Fairies' of New York, one of 'the peculiar societies of inverts'.
35. See Poizat, *The Angel's Cry*, pp. 120–1.
36. Wayne Koestenbaum, *The Queen's Throat: Opera, Homosexuality and the Mystery of Desire* (London: Poseidon Press, 1993), p. 218.
37. See Karl Marx and Friedrich Engels, *Manifesto of the Communist Party*: 'Constant revolutionising of all production, uninterrupted disturbance of all social conditions, everlasting uncertainty and agitation distinguish the bourgeois epoch from all earlier ones'. *Selected Works* (London: Lawrence and Wishart, 1968), p. 38.
38. Derrida, *Spectres of Marx*, p. 123.

Index